Mythologies of Nothing

Mythologies of Nothing

MYSTICAL DEATH
IN AMERICAN POETRY
1940-70

Anthony Libby

University of Illinois Press

URBANA AND CHICAGO

Publication of this work was supported in part by grants from The Ohio State University and the Andrew W. Mellon Foundation.

The following poems are quoted by permission of the publishers: "Those Being Eaten by America" from *The Light around the Body: Poems* by Robert Bly. Copyright © 1966 by Robert Bly. "Shack Poem" from *Sleepers Joining Hands* by Robert Bly. Copyright © 1971 by Robert Bly. "Ariel" from *Ariel* by Sylvia Plath. Copyright © 1965 by Ted Hughes. All reprinted by permission of Harper & Row, Publishers, Inc. "Obit" from *Notebook* by Robert Lowell. Copyright © 1967, 1968, 1969, 1970 by Robert Lowell. "Mermaid, #5" from *The Dolphin* by Robert Lowell. Copyright © 1973 by Robert Lowell. Both reprinted by permission of Farrar, Straus and Giroux, Inc. W. S. Merwin, "The Saint of the Uplands," in *The Moving Target*. Copyright © 1963 by W. S. Merwin. Reprinted with the permission of Atheneum Publishers. "The Red Wheelbarrow," in *Collected Earlier Poems of William Carlos Williams*. Copyright © 1938 by New Directions Publishing Corporation. Reprinted by permission of New Directions.

This book is printed on acid-free paper.

Library of Congress Cataloging in Publication Data

Libby, Anthony, 1942-
  Mythologies of nothing.

  Includes bibliographical references.
  1. American poetry — 20th century — History and criticism.   2. Nothingness in literature.   3. Death in literature.   4. Mysticism in literature.   5. Negativity (Philosophy) in literature.   I. Title.
PS310.N66L5   1984   811'.54'09354   83-3460
ISBN 0-252-01049-3

For Shannon and Quentin

Contents

Acknowledgments

I wish I could thank everyone, starting with my parents, or with those childhood teachers who (intentionally or not) started me thinking about the limitations of orthodoxy. But my most immediate debt is to present friends, colleagues, and students — especially those students who helped me teach myself to deal with *An Ordinary Evening in New Haven*. And to the College of Humanities of Ohio State, which gave me two quarters of free time to get away from those students and brood.

Among friends and colleagues: thanks to Gordon Grigsby, for telling me to read Robert Bly in the first place, and to Julian Markels and John Muste for general support. Suzanne Ferguson, Marlene Longenecker, John Muste, and Chris Zacher read part or all of my manuscript and told me how good and/or bad it was; Cary Nelson and (especially) Ed Folsom made helpful suggestions from afar; Mari Vlastos read this book many times, in almost all of its various forms, by her commentary teaching me how to write it.

Practical assistance came from Wendy Yaross, who ploughed through every imaginable critic for me, and from Mary Raines, who typed and silently edited the manuscript. At the University of Illinois Press, Ann Lowry Weir has been a nearly ideal editor, thorough and consistently responsive, and Patricia Hollahan has shown an admirably light touch in preparing the manuscript for publication. Very practical aid came from Master Choon Mo Yang, who helped me to take my mind off the whole business, and from Judy Fairly, an inconstant source of encouragement when everything got tiresome. Maybe I could have done it all by myself but it would have been lonely.

Introduction

This is a book about hymns to negation. To say that it is also a study of the central American poetry of our time may seem like overstatement. But oddly enough the poetry of this post-Christian age is often mystical poetry, negative in two parallel ways: it reveals an inordinate preoccupation with death, as metaphor and as actuality, and it tends to define what it seeks as nothing: in Wallace Stevens's words, "the nothing that is." The scope of my investigation of the poetry of death is narrow, including the years from about 1940 to about 1970, with brief excursions before and after: one human generation. But in the history of American poetry, those years cover three "generations" of poets, from the final flowering of Stevens, Eliot, and Williams in long meditative poems that now seem among their best, through the entire careers of Lowell and Roethke, to the new surrealist dreams of Plath, Bly, and Merwin. Necessarily a selective list, especially at its contemporary end, this still includes many of our essential modern poets. They share not only a preoccupation with death and often apocalypse, but a tendency to formulate the essential poetic and ontological questions in a variety of mystical terms. By this I mean not the vague "mystical susceptibility" that William James finds evoked by lyric poetry generally,[1] but a deliberate negative mysticism which is often the subject as well as the mode of modern poetry. It often reflects — in some cases distantly, in others directly — the medieval *via negativa;* it tends to imagine figural or literal death as the ground of revelation; and as the century progresses it tends to depict that revelation as terrifying or apocalyptic. Often it comes from and leads to nothing, as these poets offer serious responses (years before the wish is voiced) to A. R. Ammons's "How I wish great poems could be written about nothing."[2]

Nothing is the center, and the presence of death is somehow the key, but does that really add up to a variety of mysticism? The few critics who have accepted a mythic vision of American neo-romantic poetry over the past two decades have carefully avoided the word "mystical." It reminds everyone of old-fashioned theologies; it evokes the scorn of rationalist critics. So J. Hillis Miller wrote in 1965 that modern poetry sought "a visionary or apocalyptic union of subject and object,"[3] and Harold Bloom began in the early seventies to describe what he called "the new tran- scendentalism," "the Orphic strain" which Emerson made "the revealed religion of American poetry."[4] By the end of the seventies, Charles Altieri, whose understanding of two of the poets in this study (Bly and Merwin) comes very close to mine, was describing post-modern poetry as a poetry of "presence," "immanence," "numinous moments."[5] Now it seems possible to suggest that all of this terminology evokes the word "mysticism" by its evasions; now it is possible to accept Stevens's "fiction" that poetry involves a "mystic marriage," "ecstatic identities" between self and world.

But the term is large and spreading. As James suggests, all post-romantic poetry has some element of the mystical about it, now that poet is priest. What makes this (probably dominant) strain of American poetry special, strange, and hard to penetrate, is its preoccupation with negation, dark- ness, and death. When Altieri sees this in what he calls the poetry of "plenitude" it worries him; is there something "pathological" in Robert Bly's search for nourishment in death?[6] Admittedly this is a difficult ques- tion, complicated by the specter of Sylvia Plath, but the voice in Bly's poems hardly suggests self-destructiveness. If the central importance of the negative way in our poetry can be properly understood, it will be clear that the preoccupation with nothingness and death shared by all of these poets — even the old optimist Williams — is not inconsistent with ecstatic identities, apocalyptic union, Orphic ecstasy, numinous moments: in short, mystical union with the other world understood as this world.

The *via negativa* is only the most distant analogue for such paradoxical ecstasy, though it remains the most exact. Closer to these American poets in space and time is the Whitman "of the lilacs and the mocking-bird,"[7] the poet of "heavenly death" and cosmic merging. Not — in D. H. Law- rence's terms — the Whitman of the open road, but the stranger and more compulsively mystical poet whom Lawrence stridently mocks in *Studies in Classic American Literature*. A tempting target, Whitman may deserve some of this attack, but Lawrence mocks on, with little subtlety or wit. Of course he is attacking that part of himself drawn to a more destructive vision of death than Whitman's, and before long he makes his peace: "Whitman would not have been the great poet he is if he had not taken the last steps and looked over into death."[8] This side of Whitman is described by Harold Bloom as the essential one, "the real me" (opposed to "my self," the open-road Whitman, "one of the roughs, an American") ; Bloom partly explains, "The real me or me myself is night, death, the mother, and the sea."[9] This constellation of images irradiates the poetry of American secular mysticism, from Stevens, whom Bloom claims as Whitman's son, through Roethke and Bly, who have announced their own debts to Whitman, to Merwin, who seems north to Whitman's south but who clearly encompasses the same landscape, as both Charles Altieri and L. Edwin Folsom have independently argued.[10]

If the dark and cool Merwin seems the temperamental opposite of the open and expansive Whitman who provided mystical paternity and visionary inspiration to Allen Ginsberg, he frequently comes close to the Whitman of night, death, and the mother. And even closer is Merwin's contemporary, Bly, whose celebrations of mystical death often directly echo Whitman, especially the Whitman of "Out of the Cradle Endlessly Rocking," and "When Lilacs Last in the Dooryard Bloomed." In "Lilacs," the sorrowful lament for the fallen Lincoln is almost totally swamped by the rhapsodic chant celebrating "the flood of thy bliss O death."[11] Death is "lovely and soothing," "delicate," the "Dark Mother," "cool-enfolding," as it is elsewhere "mystical," "heavenly," "O my mother." No simple death wish appears here, but almost the opposite: a capacity to find an abiding vitality in the contemplation of death, all the more mysterious because not fully transcendent but rooted in the ordinariness of this world. Bloom looks back to Whitman when he describes the basic characteristic of his great descendant; "the alliance in Stevens between naturalism and a visionary faculty"[12] is also evident in Whitman.

Contemporary negative visionary poetry seems as fixed on the idea of nothingness as on the idea of death; it sparks an equally paradoxical ecstasy. As Nathan Scott reminds us in his book on poetry and the sacred,[13] some definition of this idea can be had from Heidegger, the primary philosophical exponent of the way of negation in this century. He began his career with examination of the medieval thinker Duns Scotus, and ended with extended contemplation of the visionary romantic Holderlin, an important influence on Bly and an archetype of the mad seer. (As Heidegger sweetly puts it, he was finally "received into the protection of the night of lunacy.")[14] For this philosopher, for whom "the writing of

poetry is the fundamental naming of the gods,"[15] the only way to a perception of the essence of Being involves "that latent and nonsensical idea
of a Nothing that 'is.' "[16] Later he goes so far as to quote Hegel's revelation
that "pure Being and pure Nothing are thus one and the same,"[17] and to
argue that the perilous way to the essential vision of Nothing comes
through Dread, and "the horrors of the abyss." Such ideas, too often oversimplified into "existentialism," recall Heidegger's original study of Duns
Scotus, and the essentially medieval idea of the dark night of the soul
that must precede revelation. Heidegger develops this line of thinking with
a beautifully inventive and paradoxical logic in "What Is Metaphysics?,"
but its end lies somewhere beyond logic, in a vision of immanent being
much like that vision once focused lovingly on the one transcendent divine
Being.

One of the most precise models for contemporary mystical immanence
comes, ironically, from a time when that Being was an immediate simple
reality throughout Christendom. The medieval connection — most conspicuous in the early poetry of Robert Lowell — provides one clear way
to distinguish this death-oriented mystical writing from the California
zen visions of poets like Rexroth, Ginsberg, and Snyder. Not only is
eschatological poetry a more substantial and continuous strain in American
writing, most of it is also a more organic product of Western culture. The
work of Pound and later of Snyder opened American poetry to a beneficial
but perhaps excessively celebrated current from the East. But most of our
modern mystical poetry is rooted in the tradition of Western dualistic
thinking, touched only lightly by Eastern monism. Though few of the
poets to be considered are Christian, or even believers in a personal God,
the roots of their secular mysticism can often be found in medieval
England and sixteenth-century Spain. Some (Bly and Roethke directly)
have also been influenced by one of Emerson's Western masters, the German Jacob Boehme. William James quotes his explanation in *The
Varieties of Religious Experience* to clarify the significance of the essential
nothing: "Primal love . . . 'may fitly be compared to Nothing, for it is
deeper than any Thing, and is as nothing with respect to all things, foras-
much as it is not comprehensible by any of them.' "[18]

More general influences include such participants in the fourteenth-
century flowering of mysticism as Meister Eckhart, Juliana of Norwich,
and the author of *The Cloud of Unknowing*. Almost all of the poets under
consideration show some specific awareness of the two later Spanish
mystics, St. Theresa and St. John of the Cross, the great exponent of the

via negativa. (The more common positive way of prayer consists not of concentration on the Nothing that may reveal mystery, but of meditation on the attributes of God, the suffering of Christ, etc. Its secular equivalent appears in many of Ginsberg's all-embracing meditative poems, especially "Wales Visitation.")

Greater difficulty attends even a primary definition of the negative way, especially the secular negative way to mystical union. Like the experience of sexual love that sometimes serves as catalyst or metaphor for mysticism, the mystical experience fits a single universal pattern. But as James insists it takes radically different forms; as in the case of love, the nature of the interaction is determined not only by its subject but by its object. The traditional mystic like St. John sought transcendent union with a God perceived as pure love. Such union would elevate the mystic above the limitations of time, space, and the body, but it would usually be preceded by a period of spiritual agony, the dark night of the soul, caused by the painful consciousness of human limitations. Most of the modern poets also describe (in some cases experience) some sort of cosmic union which brings revelation, an impression of timelessness, and frequently something like a dark night, but each poet embodies the general experience in his own distinct particulars. Some emphasize the receiving of sudden revelation over the achievement of union, though for many true vision, even of simple realities, depends on union. Others imagine union not with any anthropomorphic deity, Christian or post-Christian, but with nature, or the flow of existence, or something even more abstract or ineffable.

The major difference between the medieval mystics and nearly all of these poets, even the Christian ones, is evident in their habitual imagery. Where St. Theresa speaks of rising (sometimes of physical levitation), transcendence, the modern mystics tend to imagine descent, immersion, frequently immersion in dark water, as the sign of union. Even when their theology (like Eliot's) or their terminology (like Stevens's) implies transcendence, their imagery tends to dramatize immanence, participation in the flow of this world. Frequently transcendence struggles with immanence in a particular poet's vision; often immanence wins. The struggle has always been one focus of theological debate; the decline of Christianity (at least among poets) in this century has intensified it. What replaces the transcendent God can be nature romantically considered,[19] or sheer undifferentiated flow, but in some cases there emerges another type of deity, the spirit of nature given shape as a savage god. Especially when this deity of the dark roots appears, the strangeness of contemporary mystical vision startles and sometimes terrifies. Not only has the experience become kinetic, rather than the traditional "standing beyond" implied by "ecstasy," it has become violent; even as early as in Lowell's "Quaker Graveyard," the imagery of descent, of the dark night of the soul, blurs into the imagery of ecstatic vision. The mystic, or the poet trying to reproduce the impression of mystical vision, finds himself open to a world of stormy flow, and dark night and illumination become not sequential but simultaneous, as images of clear light give way to imagery of flickering illumination, or luminous darkness. For some of those poets, especially Roethke and Plath, for whom the mystical way of seeing became an actual way of being, such vision either causes or accompanies psychic disintegration.

So the truths of immanent mysticism do not necessarily redeem, or make glad. Sometimes they fit the patterns of religions more ancient and less cheerful than Christianity, patterns embodied in the duality (or sometimes trinity) of the Great Mother, on the one hand muse and fecund protectress, on the other the Teeth Mother naked at last. Yeats correctly foresaw that the deity who followed Christ in the imagination of the race would be Christ's antithesis. But he could not foresee that the opposition would come to involve divine gender, that for poets like Bly and Plath the savage god would turn out to be the Great Mother, and mystical contact a terrifying as well as fulfilling experience. Signs of her appear throughout the century, even in Lowell's Mary or in the mysterious mother who inhabits Stevens's poetry.

So another semi-anthropomorphic divinity has emerged, but for the poets of immanence she is more a psychic or ecological reality than a heavenly one. Their movement remains downward, into the unconscious as well as into the flow of physical being through death. At times the terminology of Jung is more appropriate for Great Mother mysticism than that of John of the Cross. As science was the medieval handmaiden of theology, now the secular theology of poets draws science into the service of its own high visions. Not only is the spiritual materialist Jung a predictable influence, so also is Darwin, or at least the general concept of evolution. For many of these poets, emphasis on the single mystical experience, whether simply epiphany or descent to timeless union, gives way to prophecies linking evolution and apocalypse, frequently a subject of mystical revelation.

In fact revelation is the primary meaning of "apocalypse," but in common usage the word more often means doom; this meaning was certainly dominant during the political and cultural turmoil of the late sixties when, as in the late fourteenth century, doom seemed imminent. For contemporary poets, the word now suggests something analogous to the Second Coming, the End but also a new world. It implies a period of evolutionary turmoil, destructive for our culture, perhaps for our stage of humanity, but it also involves some mysterious evolution, rebirth for the few or the many. Some of the more recent death-oriented writers, especially Lowell and W. S. Merwin, who tend to depict the failure of mystical contact as much as its desperate necessity, are finally more oracles of apocalypse as doom than apocalypse in the sense of revelation. For others, like Bly, the coming destruction looms like a collective dark night of the soul; possibly a collective revelation follows. Again the revelation is bound up with death, often paradoxically imagined as a new birth.

Paradox also forms a primary poetic tool for the *via negativa;* logic is used to transcend the limits of logic. This seems inevitable in a poetic undertaking that begins with the dualistic ontology implicit in our language and logic but attempts that reconciliation of opposites James sees as basic to all mysticism. Such reconciliation, if only of self and other, is so difficult to dramatize in lines of words, even with the anti-linear tools of paradox and metaphor, that a certain type of critic argues that mysticism is not a fit subject for poetry, simply indescribable. No response to this dictum is really possible, though the obvious temptation is to suggest that the indescribable is the only fit subject for poetry (and to bring up again the analogy of sexual love). But admittedly the subjects of death and revelation create problems which frequently obstruct poems, especially when the poems concern the failure of that revelation which provides the basis of poetry. For Stevens, the poet who fails to achieve some sort of oneness with that other which he describes inevitably falsifies that other, but such union tends to be sporadic. By the time of Merwin, the problem has become serious to the point of impossibility, since the poet's very identity seems to depend on such union, which almost never occurs. Naturally Merwin continues to exist and to write, but he ends up the most pessimistic poet of negative mysticism, piling negation on negation until he becomes a poet not of revelation but of apocalyptic doom.

With revelation intermittent as well as ineffable, poets as well as critics wonder whether such poetry can logically be written; Stevens seems to wonder nothing else. Their poetry becomes a record of such doubts, as well as the struggle to penetrate ultimate mysteries; often it records as much struggle as achievement, with aesthetic results that can be either obscure or very uneven. The struggle can mar the poem that it energizes, so often the most important poems by Stevens, Roethke, or Lowell are the least polished, their conflicts unresolved, final unities elusive (or, in the case of Williams, rejected). Not only does Stevens argue that the imperfect is our paradise, he makes imperfection the condition and the subject of his work. But this poetry of struggle into mystery asks larger questions and offers a deeper excitement than the poetry of tranquil recollection.

The mixture of success and failure essential to the poetry of deep exploration complicates not only the problem of ultimate evaluation but the more elementary problem of initial critical choices. The preoccupation with death and union is so central to American poetry that a study like this must begin by excluding: not only the California poets of positive mysticism (or a poet like A. R. Ammons, with his traditionally romantic landscape meditations) but several of the dark poets as well. Specifically, the choice of Sylvia Plath inevitably raises the possibility of Anne Sexton, as Robert Bly brings up James Wright and James Dickey. Partly my choice involves numerous responses to individual poems, but I was also guided by the expectation that a poet's world should develop and expand. Sexton undeniably demonstrated an involvement with death and God, but her desperate religiosity seemed before long more melodramatic than mystical. Dickey and Wright were more impressive to begin with, but less exploratory than Bly, finally falling into predictable and fairly shallow patterns. When possible I have chosen poets, from Eliot to Merwin, whose work demonstrated real growth and radical changes. Bly, for a long time more a force among other poets than a favorite of academic critics, is, despite the ups and down of his development, perhaps the most interesting of the more recent poets I consider, if only for the large visions he has pursued. Like Eliot, Bly may too enthusiastically don the prophetic role of the poet, but that role affords him a type of fundamental energy too often lacking in more restrained poetry.

And some of my choices are not purely aesthetic. The intention of this study is to demonstrate how much of the same vital energy flows through poets too often perceived as opposite, like Williams and Eliot, or the moderns and post-moderns. These are very disparate poets; their approaches to death and vision often come to radically different conclusions. But given the variety of their spiritual visions and of their stylistic idiosyncrasies, reading them becomes a surprisingly constant experience of discovering correspondences, convergences. Not only do they share the same concerns, they share patterns of imagery, even the same sounds, rhythms, duplicated lines. Now it seems clear that all of them, even Eliot, think out of one dominant strain of the romantic tradition, begin with romantic distress over the split between human consciousness and the alien reality of the universe. For many of them the gap has grown so wide that only death or mysticism can close it. But fortunately for us as well as the poets themselves, the leap into vision great or small is not only recorded but sometimes caused by the poem, the vehicle of secular grace in this imperfect paradise. Not that the poem approximates mystical experience exactly, any more than it necessarily depends on actual mysticism: it would take spiritual as well as critical arrogance to declare that, say, T. S. Eliot was or was not an actual mystic. But the poem can evoke a clear perception of radical otherness within the ordinary world. Such perception, and the permanent alteration of ordinary awareness it creates, form the primary pleasure, the central affirmation, of the poetry of negative vision.

This changed awareness can lead, as mystical vision has always done, almost outside the human. It draws some of these poets, especially the more recent ones writing out of the turbulence of the sixties, to distinctly anti-human conclusions. So the furthest reach of vision becomes an ultimate limitation. For many of these poets, at the end of the poetry of visionary negation there comes a turn to a simpler affirmative poetry of the things of this world, and the people. Often they end by writing love poetry, as does Williams, or Lowell, or Merwin, poetry which retains some visionary sense but little of the impersonal or even misanthropic quality of their mystical writing. The poetry of death and negative prophecy is one of the dominant modes of our century, but it represents — like earlier orthodox mystical poetry — only a phase in the developing vision of the culture. No poetic mode is ultimate; our poetry lives through constant revision of that final reality which constantly eludes us.

NOTES

1. William James, "Mysticism," in *The Varieties of Religious Experience* (1902; rpt., New York: Longman's, Greene, 1923), p. 417.

2. A. R. Ammons, "The Make," in *Diversifications* (New York: Norton, 1975), p. 32.

3. J. Hillis Miller, *Poets of Reality* (Cambridge: Harvard Univ. Press, 1965), p. 2.

4. Harold Bloom, *Figures of Capable Imagination* (New York: Seabury Press, 1976), p. 75.

5. Charles Altieri, *Enlarging the Temple* (Lewisburg, Pa.: Bucknell Univ.

Press, 1979), p. 42. Much of Altieri's understanding of the poetry of the sixties, his primary subject, seems to complement Miller's seminal work on the early moderns. But like too many good critics Altieri chooses to stress opposition between modern and post-modern rather than their myriad continuities.

6. Altieri, *Enlarging the Temple*, p. 92.

7. T. S. Eliot uses this phrase in "Whitman and Tennyson," rpt. in *Walt Whitman*, ed. Francis Murphy (Harmondsworth, Middlesex: Penguin, 1969), p. 207.

8. D. H. Lawrence, *Studies in Classic American Literature* (New York: Boni, 1930), p. 252. Altieri gravitates to one pole of Lawrence's ambivalence, echoing his praise of the Whitman of the open road, presenting Whitman's fascination with merging and death as a limitation to be transcended. Altieri's account of Whitman is reasonable, but it somewhat simplifies Lawrence's commentary and ignores the evidence of Whitman's strongest poetry, often poetry of death and merging. Despite Altieri's sensitivity to the work of the heirs of Whitman, he will remain reluctant to admit the vitality of their preoccupation with death.

9. Harold Bloom, *Wallace Stevens: The Poems of Our Climate* (Ithaca: Cornell Univ. Press, 1977), p. 12.

10. L. Edwin Folsom describes their contact largely in terms of precise opposition. *The Lice*, for instance, is "an anti-song of the self." "Approaches and Removals: W. S. Merwin's Encounter with Whitman's America," *Shenandoah*, 39 (Spring 1978), 60. Altieri uses similar terminology, describing Merwin's "For Now" as a "negative 'Song of Myself' " (*Enlarging the Temple*, p. 205).

11. Walt Whitman, *Complete Poetry and Selected Prose*, ed. James Miller (Boston: Houghton Mifflin, 1959), p. 237.

12. Bloom also refers to Wordsworth's similar blend of natural and visionary (*Wallace Stevens*, p. 23). But elsewhere he has dismissed the influence of Wordsworth with the cryptic but somehow convincing remark that, in creating the vision of American Orphism, Emerson committed subsequent American poets "to the enterprise that British High Romanticism was either too commonsensical or too repressed to attempt" (*Figures*, p. 75).

13. Nathan Scott, *The Wild Prayer of Longing* (New Haven: Yale Univ. Press, 1971), pp. 64ff.

14. Martin Heidegger, *Existence and Being* (London: Vision Press, 1949), p. 305.

15. Heidegger, *Existence and Being*, p. 311.

16. Heidegger, *Existence and Being*, p. 363.

17. Heidegger, *Existence and Being*, p. 377.

18. James, *Religious Experience*, p. 417.

19. A rather different perspective on nineteenth-century treatments of many of the concerns discussed in my study is offered by M. H. Abrams in *Natural Supernaturalism* (New York: Norton, 1971). Abrams surveys "visionary" and "apocalyptic" romantic poetry and philosophy, but he is primarily concerned with "the secularization of inherited theological ideas," especially the secular use of biblical terms and images, an area of investigation that offers more precise and limited definition than my own broadly defined "mysticism."

1

"The Delineaments of the Giants"

> Death is the mother of beauty; hence from her,
> Alone, shall come fulfillment to our dreams
> And our desires. Although she strews the leaves
> Of sure obliteration on our paths,
> The path sick sorrow took, the many paths
> Where triumph rang its brassy phrase, or love
> Whispered a little out of tenderness,
> She makes the willow shiver in the sun
> For maidens who were wont to sit and gaze
> Upon the grass, relinquished to their feet.
> She causes boys to pile new plums and pears
> On disregarded plate. The maidens taste
> And stray impassioned in the littering leaves.[1]

Wallace Stevens wrote those thirteen lines in 1915; they embody and anticipate a central preoccupation of the American poetry of the entire century, certainly of the two dying generations (Lowell's and Plath's) of "contemporary" poets. As the century has slouched through the disasters of history toward this present, our poets have been increasingly fascinated by death and the strange passions and illuminations attendant on thoughts of death. Contemporary poets extend the engagement with death characteristic of the poets of 1915. But the pattern of poetic inheritance is far from neat. Lives last, and the boundaries of generations are confused by a longevity that seems almost as characteristic of the early modern poets as it has been unusual among the later ones. Sylvia Plath had written her first poetry about death before Wallace Stevens had written his last. Stevens, T. S. Eliot, and William Carlos Williams, the three ancestors who were most important in shaping the world of modern poetry for the death-oriented and mystical poets of the forties, fifties, and sixties, were still alive and writing their most significant and visionary poetry during two of those decades. Eliot, though he wrote no nondramatic poetry during his last twenty years, managed to outlive not only Roethke, the second-generation poet whom he had influenced, but also Plath, the third-generation poet whom Roethke had influenced. (Plath and Roethke, along with William Carlos Williams, died in 1963, a generally bad year; Eliot survived until 1965.)

So we may consider the three giants from the past not simply as fore-runners, but as the contemporaries of Plath and Lowell, as Wordsworth was Shelley's elder contemporary and survivor. If they are shaping influences they also participate in the continuing exploration. Each one wrote, in the forties and early fifties, a long sequence-poem which is central in the continuing development of American oracular poetry, and which in each case has been called the poet's masterpiece. (In each case also, such praise has generated intense critical controversy.) The three poems provide the focus for my attention to these poets as contemporaries: *Four Quartets* (which actually began in 1935, though not as the *Quartets*), *Paterson*, and *An Ordinary Evening in New Haven,* all loose extended meditations on specific places moving through eternity, poems of external geography become internal in oddly similar ways.

Though the three early masters began with radical differences, they meet, eventually, on paths subterranean or transcendent. They meet in celebration of death, surely, and more mysteriously in celebration of death as the mother of more than beauty. The mystery appears conspicuously in "Sunday Morning"; one of the poem's fascinations is that at certain points it "resists the intelligence" not "almost successfully," as Stevens said poetry must,[2] but altogether successfully. We can explain why death should be described as the mother of beauty in that instantly memorable fifth stanza. For instance: death is the necessary concomitant of change, of that flow from immaturity to ripeness to dessication that Stevens considers so essential to the beauty of this imperfect world. Without change till death, life would be less. But then why not call change the mother of beauty? The line as it is forms almost too sharp a paradox in a poem that rebukes its protagonist for the religious nostalgia that tempts her to "give her bounty to the dead." Stevens in stanza V is of course considering a more final sort of death, but he gives it bounteous praise. And when the stanza goes on to describe the "fulfillment" that death brings, it seems for a moment questionable whether Stevens will really hold fast to his attack on the idea of paradise. He does, he will in the following stanza, but first he describes the "maidens" who are related to death the mother, and to the death-oriented woman who speaks in the poem, because they turn away from the bounty of earth, the ripeness which death makes possible, to "stray impassioned in the littering leaves." As much as the boys or the barely tasted fruit, it is the pervasive sense of death in the willow, the leaves, that causes their passion, not death as something that makes us appreciate life by contrast, but death as death. Stevens seems to feel their passion not as false or unhealthy but as valid and elevated; their straying is a motion uncertain but powerful, "impassioned," that will be echoed in the pigeons' "ambiguous undulations" into darkness at the end of the poem. But why should death create such vital passion that Stevens claims, "from her / Alone, shall come fulfillment to our dreams / And our desires?" Whitman is similarly absolute and mysterious in "Out of the Cradle Endlessly Rocking," in which the word out of the sea, "the low and delicious word death" causes him to become impassioned also. "The messenger there arous'd, the fire, the sweet hell within, / The unknown want, the destiny of me."[3] Here is neither simple death wish nor excited meditation on life made more precious by opposition to death, but something more true and more strange.

The truth of Stevens's stanza seems as inexplicable as it is undeniable. He would come to successively clearer visions of this passion about death as he came closer to his own death. As critics frequently remark, death is an "obsession"[4] throughout Stevens's poetry, perhaps more than it is for Eliot or Williams. But in their late work the three confront death in similar terms; they seem to draw closer together. Though their philosophical differences remain extreme, it is finally possible to see how they form a unified poetic heritage, instead of a triangle of opposed voices (with Pound lurking somewhere on the long hypotenuse between Eliot and Williams). Of course, they generally saw themselves as opposed, especially Stevens and Williams against the more prominent Eliot. Williams's irritation with *The Waste Land* is famous,[5] and Stevens wrote in a 1950 letter, "After all, Eliot and I are dead opposites and I have been doing about everything that he would not be likely to do."[6] Stevens is largely correct, but 1950 was the year after the composition of *Ordinary Evening* and the dead opposition no longer seemed so complete.

By that time, similarities of theme and preoccupation had emerged, but perhaps more surprisingly the three poets had begun to *sound* alike at times. In their late poetry all three had developed a long meditative line (sometimes fragmented, "triadic," in Williams) often without images, abstract; it was well designed for the extended examination of states of consciousness, acts of the mind, and the ultimate human questions. Sometimes the similarities in these lines are fully intentional; like Roethke's later responses, Williams's borrowings and parodies from *Four Quartets* are obvious, though they offer no essential conflict with Williams's own voice. But Stevens was probably not trying to sound like "Burnt Norton" when he wrote this Eliot-like stanza from *The Auroras of Autumn:*

> There may be always a time of innocence.
> There is never a place. Or if there is no time,
> If it is not a thing of time, nor of place. . . .
>
> (*Palm,* 314)

Here the point is not influence, but convergence. Though Eliot, the midcentury high priest of poetry, was probably less aware of Stevens and Williams than they were of him, he wanders at times into the territory of their characteristic tones, for instance in such straight Stevens phrases as "the unimaginable / Zero summer" in "Little Gidding."[7] In the *Quartets* Eliot never sounds like the early imagist Williams, but by the forties neither did Williams. Their voices converge in more abstract passages, such as the following backward glances at the relation between memory and experience: Eliot's relaxed tone and parallel structure in this section from "The Dry Salvages" suggest the sound of that most characteristic late Williams poem, "The Descent," from *Paterson II.* Compare Eliot:

> We had the experience but missed the meaning,
> And approach to the meaning restores the experience
> In a different form, beyond any meaning
> We can assign to happiness.
>
> (*CPP,* 133)

to Williams:

> The descent beckons
>   as the ascent beckoned
>   Memory is a kind
> of accomplishment
>   a sort of renewal
>   even
> an initiation, since the spaces it opens are new
> places.[8]

By no coincidence time is the shared preoccupation of all of these meditative passages, time which obscures or reveals past experiences, time which flows toward death. Perhaps, along with love and God, roses and rivers, death is a central subject of all poetry, especially since the romantic period. But American poets since Whitman and Dickinson have been unusually drawn to the subject, almost as much as the poets of "the only country where death is the national spectacle, where death blows long fanfares at the coming of each Spring."[9] The country is Spain, the description Lorca's, from an essay on death and poetry which describes more than Spanish poetry. His essay on "the *Duende*" argues that whether or not death is the subject of the poem, struggle with it must accompany the highest poetic utterance. *Duende,* which simply means "sprite" or "hobgoblin" throughout most of Spain, becomes in Andalusia a way of describing the basic emotional power behind flamenco music and dance. "Soul" might be an American equivalent for the *duende* that great Spanish music has, but Lorca wants to expand the term to include other forms of art, especially poetry. His definition develops slowly. *Duende* involves "black sounds," is "the earth-force," is a principle of artistic struggle. But finally Lorca defines *duende* in terms of death. "The *Duende* . . . will not approach at all if he does not see the possibility of death, if he is not convinced he will circle death's house, if there is not every assurance he can rustle the branches borne aloft by us all." As the definition develops, the experience of *duende* poetry begins to sound specifically mystical; the poetry is "magical, miraculous," provides an "almost religious transport." Two famous possessors of the *Duende* whom Lorca uses as exemplars are St. John of the Cross and "that paragon of the flamenco and daemonic way Saint Theresa — flamenca not for her prowess in stopping an angry bull with three magnificent passes — though she did so . . . but rather for the simple circumstance that she was one of the rare ones whose *Duende* . . . pierced her with an arrow, hoping thereby to destroy her for having deprived him of his ultimate secret: the subtle bridge that links the five senses with the very center, the living flesh, living cloud, living sea, of Love emancipated from Time."[10]

Lorca makes explicit a basic connection between mysticism and death that occurs in Eliot, who was also interested in John of the Cross and "Love emancipated from Time," and occurs as well in Stevens and Williams and their younger contemporaries. At least until Plath, death in American poetry is seldom the violent experience at the end of a knife central to Lorca's drama. But the *sense* of death is fundamental to our poetry; death is the mother of poetry as well as other forms of beauty. And the idea of death is often connected with the ideas of mysticism, whether the mysticism of John of the Cross, as in Eliot, or the mysticism of a new and different mythology, as in Stevens. So the sense of death as well as the mystical experience becomes not only the subject but also the condition of poetic creation for a surprising number of central poets in this place and century which are not particularly characterized by religious devotion. When Stevens repeats his memorable line in the sixth stanza of "Sunday Morning," he adds a word: "Death is the mother of beauty, mystical."

What Stevens means by "mystical" is not always clear, but he offers some elaboration in a discussion of the theory of poetry which is more specific than Lorca's in defining the connection between mysticism and the vitality of poetry:

> The theory of poetry, that is to say, the total of the theories of poetry, often seems to become in time a mystical theology or, more simply, a mystique. The reason for this must by now be clear. The reason is the same reason why the pictures in a museum of modern art often seem to become in time a mystical aesthetic, a prodigious search of appearance, as if to find a way of saying and of establishing that all things, whether below or above appearance, are one and that it is only through reality, in which they are reflected or, it may be, joined together, that we can reach them. Under such stress, reality changes from substance to subtlety. . . . It was from the point of view of another subtlety that Klee could write: "But he is one chosen that today comes near to the secret places where original law fosters all evolution. And what artist would not establish himself there where the organic center of all movement in time and space — which he calls the mind or heart of creation — determines every function."[11]

Though characteristically somewhat evasive — how are we to take the shift from "mystical theology" to "mystique"? — this passage does claim for poetry several of the qualities of the traditional mystical experience: a sense of seeing beyond ordinary appearance, a conviction of cosmic unity, and immediate personal participation in the godlike "heart of creation." The difference between this and the mysticism of St. Theresa or Eliot's St. John is that it avoids transcendence. The heart of creation is "an *organic* center," and the unity of all things is to be experienced "only through reality," not beyond it.

A similar vision is implied, though far more vaguely, in *Spring and*

All, when Williams, also using painters as examples, says the poet's imagination must help "the individual rise to some appropriate co-extension with the universe."[12] This definition of the roots of poetry may be read to suggest the mystical identification and unity Stevens describes; but obscurely closer to his actual terminology is a remark by Williams about *Paterson,* which does attempt to create a consciousness coextensive at least with the surrounding landscape. The chapter about *Paterson* in Williams's *Autobiography* begins "Even though the greatest boon a poet grants the world is to reveal that secret and sacred presence, they will not know what he is talking about."[13] There is no antecedent to "that," to answer the question *which* "secret and sacred presence" he means, but *Paterson,* with some earlier poems, suggests an answer.

Eliot also accepts as probable the overlap between poetry and mystical exploration, but the discovery tends to worry him. Since he is still a believer in religion of the traditional sort, poetry is perhaps not such a necessary component of his spiritual experience; in fact, after the *Quartets* he managed to get along without writing poetry (nondramatic poetry, at least) for his last twenty years. And he remained suspicious of poetry, especially poetry based on unorthodox belief, that aspired to replace religion. He expresses in particularly post-modern terms the danger of looking "in poetry for religious satisfactions. . . . No one can read Mr. Yeats' *Autobiographies* and his earlier poetry without feeling that the author was trying to get as a poet something like the exaltation to be obtained, I believe, from hashish or nitrous oxide."[14] There is no record of what Eliot might have thought of Mr. Stevens, high on invisible giants, supreme fictions with mythic aspirations, and extraordinary New Haven. If the three poets might agree that something based or patterned on mystical experience happens in some poetry, it remains doubtful that they would agree on what. Certainly there are radical differences in their particular mystical visions.

If actual geography is not too crude a symbol, let it suggest the landscape of these poetic distances. Cape Ann, site of "The Dry Salvages," is at least 150 miles by crow from Paterson, and New Haven lies about halfway between the two. The remaining three quartets take place across an ocean. The *Quartets* become clearly and explicitly mystical in an orthodox mode, finally reaching beyond the world into transcendent realms. Stevens's mysticism is more hesitant and vague, and opposed to orthodoxy or transcendence; *Ordinary Evening* is characterized by flashes of cosmic imagery, by mythic creatures peering over the edge of the universe, but finally it locates its visions "In the metaphysical streets of the physical town" (*Palm,* 337). At the furthest extreme from Eliot lies *Paterson,* so resolutely a poem of the physical world that no matter what Williams says about it it is not consistently a mystical poem at all, except in its Whitmanesque sense of authorial identification with humanity. Though it is recognizably mystical only in occasional flashes, it points a direction, especially in its emphasis on physical immersion, and indicates a way of visualizing the world that was already — as *Paterson* was being written — evident in the work of younger mystical poets.

But such stress on their obvious differences overemphasizes the separations among poets who have been understood too separately for too long. In each poet, the two mysticisms, transcendent and immanent, combine and often struggle with each other. Especially in the *Quartets* the tensions are evident, as imagery that seems appropriate to immanence is used in the service of a transcendent vision. Such tension energizes *Paterson* and *Ordinary Evening,* as well as the *Quartets,* but it can weaken them too, in ways that will have to be admitted when we consider them individually. Certainly it is not just the fluctuations of reputation that explain the extreme varieties of critical response to these poems, each obviously intended as some sort of culmination of its author's life and vision.

The three poems can only be evaluated section by section; especially the *Quartets* and *Paterson* vary considerably in quality. But it seems in general that each achieves something unique in American poetry, something that had to be taken into account by a wide variety of writers. Eliot especially has had a considerable impact on poets (like Roethke) who claimed to dislike his work. Part of the impact of these three poems came from the poet's very willingness to accept some failure in the exploration of new poetic areas. Exploration became more important than pure poetic success, and this in itself was something that influenced later poets. Each poem announces or enacts its own "failure." After recording a lament for "the pure poem of the first part" (*P,* 171) *Paterson IV* deliberately refuses to resolve the tensions established by the first three books, and describes, in conclusion, instead of the symbolically satisfying "Run to the Sea" promised by its title, a quick dip in the water then a turn back inland. The poem stops rather than ends, which gave Williams freedom to add *Paterson V* several years later. The *Quartets* are full of complaints about the general inadequacy of language (or of the previous stanza). "East Coker" goes so far as to say "The poetry does not matter" and later grumbles about the wasted decades the poet has spent

> Trying to learn to use words, and every attempt
> Is a wholly new start, and a different kind of failure.
>
> (*CPP*, 128)

Failure too is implied by the way poetry proceeds, never quite reaching the final definition, in *Ordinary Evening:* "an and yet, and yet, and yet—" (*Palm*, 331) or "a philosopher practicing scales on his piano, / A woman writing a note and tearing it up" (*Palm*, 351). As with Eliot, the poem is never more than a temporary answer to an unanswerable question.

Inevitably the question is large. Post-romantic poets feel the need, as always, to define man's relation to that which is not man, but they must do so in a world increasingly characterized by discontinuity, separation of all sorts, what Williams laments as "divorce." Eliot must confront the absence of God in such a world, and Stevens, who can do without God, broods over the absence of any complete sense of external reality, a divorce between man and the world that must somehow be resolved by a new poetic vision. Ordinary vision, like ordinary language, is no longer enough; only the leap of mystical vision can bridge the gap. But for Stevens the mysticism must be mysticism of this world, or the gap will only widen. Eliot's search in the *Quartets*, which I will examine first, involves more than one world, and his poetry reflects the conflict between perspectives generated by heaven and earth. To understand that conflict between the mysticism of immersion and the transcendent mysticism, it will be necessary to think for a moment about that continuing critical problem, Eliot's religion.

T. S. Eliot

For Eliot the path to God, and to a new vision of the world in God, is theoretically less hazardous because it has already been explored by his mystical masters. But actually Eliot's connection with the whole tradition of Christian mysticism and the quality of his descriptions of moments of revelation are characterized by an ambivalence not unlike Stevens's ambivalence over poetic definitions of "reality." Eliot begins as a poet of death and darkness; in the blasted landscape of *The Waste Land* "We who are living are now dying" (*CPP*, 47) even after Christ has sacrificed himself for us in the previous lines; the Resurrection remains questionable. Eliot will move toward the risen Christ in later poems, but the movement will afford him little unadulterated comfort. The few affirmative passages in *The Waste Land* establish a pattern of ambivalence about the nature of illumination that will persist even in Eliot's most ecstatic later poems. For instance there appears a certain confusion in the passage about the hyacinth girl, who seems to bring to the speaker not only love among the ruins but a vision like the rose garden vision of "Burnt Norton."

> Your arms full and your hair wet, I could not
> Speak, and my eyes failed, I was neither
> Living nor dead, and I knew nothing,
> Looking into the heart of light, the silence.
>
>   (*CPP*, 38)

Between life and death, the speaker seems to experience the dark night of the soul as simultaneous with luminous vision, not something transformed by vision; in the line that follows, this dark sense is reinforced by a reference to the dying Tristan waiting for Isolde, staring over the empty sea. A similar ambiguity has led to basic critical disagreement over the Phoenician sailor sequence. In a poem about spiritual drought, water is presumably baptismal; the death by water leads to resurrection. But the passage may as easily be read for its focus on death as dissolution, not necessarily any more redemptive than Prufrock's imagined immersions. Drowning would become a major symbol in later American poetry, but only Lowell, while himself a Catholic, would handle it so bleakly.

As Eliot moved toward Anglo-Catholicism, perhaps marking the path for Lowell, he found something of a nostrum for his melancholy, his habitual aversion to this decadent world. But though the tone of his poetry changed, so that for instance he could offer more resonant prayers than the rather arbitrary "Shantih shantih shantih" of *The Waste Land*, much of his essential vision remained constant. Conversion can only cut so deep, especially a conversion of this sort. Eliot obviously needed a structure of belief, one not improvised like Yeats's, but a traditional and impersonal Truth, a basis for the sort of poetry he wanted to write, as well as for the sort of life he wanted to live. But to give himself to Anglo-Catholicism seems to have been, like his romantic decision to be a royalist, a consciously archaic act.

The problem of Eliot's religion has disturbed critics of his poetry, even the resolutely Christian ones; there are indications in the late poetry that it may have troubled him as well, that being a Catholic was especially in the forties no longer quite so simple a choice as conversion in earlier times. John Lynen, among others, makes the argument that "Eliot's readers, who

habitually concede that in some contexts — the Bible, Dante, or Milton, to cite some obvious examples — the language of faith is validly used, ought to adopt a like tolerance here, judging the dogma Eliot's poems contain according to its consistency with the kind of experience the poems record."[15] Such tolerance sounds admirable but — wholly aside from the question of consistency — the analogies are false. As Eliot has pointed out, Dante's faith was the faith of his culture; Eliot's faith deliberately opposes the lack of faith of his very different time. Amid the gradual collapse of Christianity that both Eliot and Stevens had been recording from different perspectives, being a Christian poet was a complicated business. Surely it was a violation of Eliot's famous dictum that it was the poet's "business to express the greatest emotional intensity of his time, based on whatever his time happened to think. Poetry is not a substitute for philosophy or theology or religion."[16] For all Eliot's warnings against philosopher-poets, he was in danger of becoming one, especially by the time of "Burnt Norton," even if his philosophy was based on a traditional religion. The point is that it was a waning tradition, progressively further away from "whatever his time happened to think." The effort to revive it in all its vitality would create basic tensions which would sometimes energize, sometimes break, the poetry.

The breakage occurs primarily when the dogma becomes too explicit. If *Four Quartets* is conceivably Eliot's greatest poem, it also contains some of his worst poetry (though there is strong competition from some of the ultimately specious obscurities of *The Waste Land*). Eliot's problem in the *Quartets* is to make a mystical experience of this world intelligible in terms of a faith oriented toward another world, a problem complicated by the possibility that his poetic perception of spiritual reality has more to do with this organic world than his theology dreams of. So at times in the *Quartets* immanence wars with transcendence. In an essay on Eliot's unacknowledged romanticism, George Bornstein argues that Eliot believes in ascent to heaven but dramatizes immersion in the world. " 'Four Quartets' spatializes reality in terms of movements and forces downward and within. . . . Most important among inner places is 'the still point of the turning world.' . . . To the extent that the poem's spatializations clash with its overt allegiances, Eliot's poetic drives subvert his own orthodoxy."[17] But the clash is not so simply described. J. Hillis Miller, using the same evidence to make a different case, describes Eliot's later work as "one more example of that recovery of immanence which has been the inner drama of twentieth-century literature."[18] Instead of a clash, Miller's

Eliot — after the revulsion against the flesh that characterized *The Waste Land* — enacts a wedding between transcendent longings and the materialities of immanence, a wedding made logically possible by the (transcendent) doctrine of Incarnation.

Given the complexity of the terminology, this critical disagreement is not surprising. As Eliot himself put it, such terms "slip, slide, perish, / Decay with imprecision, will not stay in place" (*CPP*, 121). Especially in the land of paradox created by mystical belief, "immanent" and "transcendent" are far from true opposites. So we call Emerson's and Whitman's (immanent) belief that holy spirit resides within matter Transcendentalism. So a transcendent religion like Christianity — that is, one that worships a primary deity above and independent of the universe — celebrates in its central ritual the miraculous coming of that deity into matter, into man, into immanence. Miracle and mysticism frequently involve the wedding of contraries, and always seem to establish a linguistic context in which words can become their opposites.

And yet, and yet, some distinctions can be made. The Christian Eliot reveals his transcendent convictions in habitual imagery as well as statements of belief. He offers the clearest example of the *via negativa* to appear in modern poetry, sets the pattern by which the more secular poets may be measured, because he revives medieval dogma along with medieval approaches to revelation. More often than not his imagery remains consistent with that dogma. Not the poet of water and immersion, he is drawn to desert imagery, the ascetic purity of sandy places, dry, burnt Norton. When he needs water to suggest the flow of spiritual vitality in "Burnt Norton," it is imagined water, "water out of sunlight," dryly rising "even while the dust moves" (*CPP*, 118, 122). Fire and light and a rising away from the flesh to the purity of spirit make Eliot finally a transcendent dreamer; the downward images cannot ultimately change that. But his preoccupation with death and revelation (sometimes violent revelation) would persist in the minds of the poets of immersion, his imagery having undergone a sea change.

Not that Eliot achieves complete poetic solutions to the problems of his theology; if Bornstein overemphasizes his ambivalence, Miller overstates his success in creating a new vision. Much of that vision was old, and inadequately imagined into poetry. Eliot's orthodoxy does offer a perfect solution to the mystical tension between immanence and transcendence, Christ's Incarnation. In Christ there is no up or down; if a transcendent god becomes earthly man, then the heavenly center becomes an organic

center, immanent, and Eliot's conceptual problems are solved, miraculously. But especially in "Little Gidding" Christ seems too simply a deus ex machina introduced for automatic resolution of tension; there theology most conspicuously obstructs poetry. "Burnt Norton" is theologically more subtle, apparently aimed at a less than fully Christian body of readers; the often dogmatic Eliot here seems careful to evoke the essential mystical experience in comparatively naturalistic terms, unbounded by dogma. But by the end of "East Coker" poetry as dogma has begun at times to replace poetry as the record of spiritual exploration, as the focus of the poem begins to shift from the mystic's immediate personal experience to a set of beliefs abstracted from the experience of someone distant from him in time and space, Christ. The poetry conspicuously suffers in such notoriously bad passages as the "wounded surgeon" section of "East Coker," with its labored allegory of the Fall and Redemption. Here everything seems wrong, from the description of Adam as a "ruined millionaire," which reflects that embarrassing biblical tendency to describe spiritual capacity in terms of economic capital, right down to those silly *Old Possum's* rhymes: "nurse/curse/worse," "knees/freeze," etc.

The poetry goes most badly flat in the last half of "The Dry Salvages." After all Eliot's complex speculation on time and redemption, the climax of the poem offers this moral promise: "And right action is freedom / From past and future also." "Whatever "right action" is, it hardly seems probable that it offers the type of freedom from time imagined in "Burnt Norton." But by the time we reach "The Dry Salvages" the whole context of spiritual discussion has changed. The focus is no longer on mystical illuminations possible in any life, but on the experience of "the saint," who is distinguished from "the rest of us" humans, who can at best manage an occasional flash of radiance. And even the saint should not be as intent on his own experience as on Christ's; the only genuine "point of intersection of the timeless / with time" is "Incarnation." The ultimate spiritual value is not expansion of one's own mystic consciousness, but "self-surrender," humility, submission to Christ. Not the moment in the rose garden but "right action." The orthodox Church has always nursed a strong suspicion of mystics and mysticism, worrying quite correctly that the mystical perspective might outreach accepted dogma. Here Eliot does what he can to tame mysticism in the service of dogma, nearly ruining his poem in the process. No wonder Donald Davie, defending the general greatness of the *Quartets*, felt compelled to argue, heroically but unconvincingly, that the whole of "The Dry Salvages" was a clever parody, so

that Eliot's "incompetence turns out to be the dazzling virtuosity," and the inhumanity of the conclusion reached turns out to be only a parody of the true conclusion reached in "Little Gidding."[19]

If some of Eliot's Christian dogma seems arbitrarily forced into the poetry, he found certain aspects of the Christian tradition that were so close to his habitual poetic and psychological tendencies that his use of them is completely natural. His early poetry, especially "Prufrock," and *The Waste Land,* is characterized by states of internal passivity, blankness, nothingness. It seems inevitable, then, that he should be drawn to that type of mysticism, traditional though not exactly orthodox, that depends on a psychic leap from nothing to everything. The *via negativa* described by St. John of the Cross makes a virtue of that complete mental emptiness which in other poems amounts to a state of psychological desperation. The repetitions of "nothing" in section II of *The Waste Land* reveal dead souls: " "Do / You know nothing? Do you see nothing? Do you remember / Nothing?" " (CPP, 41). In the *Quartets* such internal poverty is "the way of ignorance" (CPP, 127) which ends in the white light of divine communion.

But often, in the *Quartets,* the old despair is not really vanquished by ecstasy; ecstasy takes on the lineaments of despair; as the negative way becomes more genuinely negative than St. John imagined. Eliot's orthodoxy is often diluted by a characteristically modern ambivalence of response, for he fails to make the traditional sharp separation between the dark night of the soul and the timeless moment of illumination. Or if the two are separated, the dark night tends to follow, as well as precede, the illumination, casting a final shadow where St. John would have allowed only the memory of light. Partly because of Eliot's irrepressible tendencies toward immersion in an unevenly dark world, the sign of mystical contact is not necessarily the steady light of tradition, but a shimmering or flickering, as it will be in the terrible mysticism of Roethke or Plath, a rapid alternation of light and darkness. Eliot sounds like those later poets (or like Plath's husband Ted Hughes) in phrases like "The bone's prayer to Death its God" from "The Dry Salvages," but it is in "Little Gidding" that his vision is both most contemporary and most suggestive of the dark side of orthodoxy. There, as it will later be in Lowell, World War II becomes apocalyptic as Eliot meditates on death at "the world's end," and ordinary values are swallowed up in a grim transcendence. Eliot's purgatorial mood and his aversion to physical existence allow him to wrench a German bomber into a symbol of the Holy Ghost bearing the fire of

purgation and illumination; appropriately "the dark dove" has a "flickering tongue" (*CPP,* 140).

The sense of death is constantly the condition of illumination in the *Quartets,* not only in "Little Gidding," where death is literally close and spirits pass "Between two worlds become much like each other" (*CPP,* 141), but in "East Coker," where the darkness of the dark night is identified with the darkness of death. In both realms "the darkness shall be light" and "the agony / Of death and birth" (*CPP,* 127) is one agony. For the orthodox Eliot, the light the dying are born to is of course the light of heaven, where an afterlife of perfection is infinitely superior to this fleshly existence. Immediately after the "dark dove" passage in "Little Gidding" Eliot's familiar spirit comes to voice a bitterness about old age and life in general that is even more than Yeatsian. In extent and even in some of its phrasing — Eliot also has Dante's voice in mind here — this is a medieval disgust at the horrors of this vale of tears. As Stephen Spender suggests, Eliot's way of dealing with the horrors has medieval overtones as well: "The rituals of living which he yearned for come with the medieval Catholic tradition."[20]

The *via negativa,* with its denial of human reason as well as human sensation, is perhaps the ultimate ritual for transcending this evil world, dying to the world before actual death; one of its most complete formulations comes in the somewhat opaque fourteenth-century *Cloud of Unknowing,* which Eliot quotes in "Little Gidding." The negative way is naturally difficult to describe verbally; the paradoxes implicit in the experience itself are sharpened by the attempt to write poetry about it. Eliot makes a virtue of this problem in "Burnt Norton," in order to write logically about something not logically describable. A series of prosaic logical statements is used to break through the boundaries of logic, using paradox or flat contradiction — the quartet's epigraph translates "The way up and the way down is one and the same" — to push language into an ultralogical evocation of the ineffable. The indelible opening lines of "Burnt Norton"

> Time present and time past
> Are both perhaps present in time future.
> And time future contained in time past.
> If all time is eternally present
> All time is unredeemable.
>
> (*CPP,* 117)

exist not so much to prove anything about time — Eliot is not quite so
fatalistic as the lines suggest — as to begin the play with logic that will
lead to the destruction of logic, that system for ordering reality in terms of
time, progression, cause and effect. Logic cannot of course be completely
vanquished, especially in a poem which presents such a logical surface
of abstract statement, a poem to be understood more than experienced.
But probably the poetry of logic can go further in transcending logic than
the poetry of sensation can rise beyond sensation to convey the mystical
experience. The way of paradox, rooted in the negative way, is one of
the sources of unresolvable tension that usually energizes "Burnt Norton."

Northrop Frye calls "Burnt Norton" "an apocalyptic poem [which] gives
us a bird's-eye view of the whole range of experience covered in its
successors."[21] For this reason and because the power of the *Quartets* is
most consistently evident here, "Burnt Norton" is the quartet that most
rewards careful examination. It may also be the most mysterious quartet,
partly because of the rose garden sequence that follows its initial paradoxes
and describes a visionary experience without dark night or any other of
the usual theological terms. The sequence involves an odd and compelling
mixture of vivid immediacy and distance of various sorts. The distance is
established partly by the use of past tense; here is vision recollected in
tranquility, unlike the present-tense action and speculation of most of the
Quartets. A different distance is established by the blunt but ambiguous
statement that the rose garden experience never happened, though paradoxically it is remembered:

> Footfalls echo in the memory
> Down the passage which we did not take
> Towards the door we never opened
> Into the rose-garden.
>
> (*CPP,* 177)

And the beings confronted in the garden are, even in the scene constructed
not from memory but by a free imagination, invisible, possible selves dis-
tanced from the other possible selves who explore the garden.

Despite this distance, and considerable confusion about who these
imagined beings might be supposed to be, the sense of mystic fullness is
conveyed with a sensual immediacy unusual in any poem, and stylistically
atypical in this one. The sense of revelation is natural, not forced into
theological signification. With the possible exception of the "lotos," the
symbolism of the passage remains understated, implicit. If the presence

of death is suggested by "autumn heat," the suggestion is a delicate one, and the roses remain primarily roses, their symbolic resonance permitted but not stressed. There appears the "glitter," the shimmer of "vibrant air," the interaction of light and shadow that happens in our poetry when the other world touches this world, and out of this shimmer Eliot organically evokes the way transcendence becomes immanent, joining his worlds convincingly.

> Dry the pool, dry concrete, brown edged,
> And the pool was filled with water out of sunlight,
> And the lotos rose, quietly, quietly,
> The surface glittered out of heart of light.
>
> (*CPP,* 118)

Light and air assume the density of water, as they actually seem to do in the most common sort of mirage, and Eliot conveys a visionary sense of spiritual flow become immanent in the things of this world, without seriously violating verisimilitude. Questions of dogma aside, this natural incarnation of the heart of light is rendered with far more immediacy and apparent conviction than the later passages about the Incarnation.

Following the pattern of the rose garden section, each quartet's initial section is marked by an unusual sensual vividness and specificity. These sections take the shape of ritual; like the beings in the garden they move "in a formal pattern" in anticipation of the more abstract rituals of the second or third sections of each quartet. But they describe a series of comparatively natural and earthbound experiences of revelation. As well as sudden falls into vision (of the denizens of the garden, or the dancers out of time past in "East Coker") these involve various experiences of timelessness: in "The Dry Salvages" the night sea intimation that "time stops and time is never ending," or in "Little Gidding" the evocation of "Midwinter spring . . . Suspended in time" (*CPP,* 131, 138). The heightened precision of observation in these passages of natural description establishes and periodically renews a sense of physical context for Eliot's highly theoretical descriptions of the techniques of unknowing, used in a calculated rather than instinctive way to induce revelation.

Again in section IV of "Burnt Norton" natural imagery creates a sense of mystic immersion, but the imagery has become less specific, less descriptive of a particular scene and more evocative of the dominant mystical theory of the poem. The *via negativa* appropriately evokes a movement from daylight to a darkness like death and then to light again "at the still point of the turning world" (*CPP,* 121). If it were not for the sunlight, the still point here might seem to be in deep earth rather than air. The stanza describes movement always downward, and the speaker's viewpoint seems beneath the movement, as if in the grave. The sense of death implicit in the negative way (or in the orthodox way through actual death to heaven) is especially felt when the stanza pauses for a sudden moment on "Chill."

> The black cloud carries the sun away.
> Will the sunflower turn to us, will the clematis
> Stray down, bend to us; tendril and spray
> Clutch and cling?
> Chill
> Fingers of yew be curled
> Down on us?
>
> (*CPP,* 121)

Then peacefully, with the naturalness of death, the setting sunlight comes to the seer immersed in the flow of vegetable existence.

Here more than in the garden passage, Eliot attempts to wed images of the natural, immanent, organic vision to his more otherworldly and abstract orthodoxy. He achieves a unity of tone, and the sense of revelation, but the substance of revelation remains elusive. It is somewhat less elusive in the catalogue of negations which describes mysticism (in section II in this quartet); where Eliot suggests a more transcendent mystical vision, more explicitly dependent on "dessication of the world of sense" (*CPP,* 120).

> At the still point of the turning world. Neither flesh nor
>   fleshless;
> Neither from nor towards; at the still point, there the dance is,
> But neither arrest nor movement. And do not call it fixity,
> Where past and future are gathered. Neither movement from
>   nor towards,
> Neither ascent nor decline. Except for the point, the still point,
> There would be no dance, and there is only the dance.
> I can only say, *there* we have been: but I cannot say where.
> And I cannot say, how long, for that is to place it in time.
>
> (*CPP,* 119)

Even this comparative transcendence allows, through some of the paradoxes that beat down logic to make way for the sense of vision, something of a balance between mysticism of this world and elevation into another.

At the still point we are "neither flesh nor fleshless," not in the body, but not rejecting the body either. The paradoxes all seem to war against dualistic logic, either by wedding opposites (like "still point" and "dance") or by denying both terms of a linguistically all-inclusive set of possibilities (like "neither arrest nor movement"). But dualism persists in the repetition of the pairs, in the constantly parallel structures of this poem about liberation from "time past and time future." The "Neither . . ." clauses chant beyond time and logic, without leaving their realm, not actually transcendent, though too full of ancient negations to be in the usual sense immanent.

Perhaps the way out of time is even more difficult to describe in poetry, so inevitably sequential, than Stevens's and Williams's ways of struggle against the divisions in space that frustrate the mystic unions they imagine. The actual description of the mystical experience that follows the chant of negations offers little in the ways of positive definition of the *"there"* where "we have been." Beyond mention of the sense of release from limitation and the experience of "white light," Eliot avoids concrete description, as he does in all the *via negativa* sections. He takes the negative way of describing too, especially in the teaching from John of the Cross at the center (in section III this time) of "East Coker."

> To arrive where you are, to get from where you are not,
>   You must go by a way wherein there is no ecstasy.
> In order to arrive at what you do not know
>   You must go by a way which is the way of ignorance.
> In order to possess what you do not possess
>   You must go by the way of dispossession.
> In order to arrive at what you are not
>   You must go through the way in which you are not.
> And what you do not know is the only thing you know
> And what you own is what you do not own
> And where you are is where you are not.
>
> (*CPP,* 127)

For linguistic rather than theological reasons, John's insistent negation and abstraction are perhaps not so effective as Eliot's own in achieving the near description of something indescribable. But he makes the final end of this seeking darkly clear: "To arrive where you are." Mystical reality is ordinary reality, ordinarily masked because "where you are is where you are not." The visionary experience provides the only true clarity, and this turns out to be the clarity of the illuminated quotidian, as in the rose garden, or "in the electric heat," hypnotic, of the visionary summer at the start of "East Coker."

As there exists a definite tension in the later *Quartets* between mysticism and that variety of orthodoxy which somewhat distrusts mystical experience, there emerges at least an apparent conflict between the comparatively simple visionary experience of the rose garden and the achieved mystical integration at the end of the negative way. In commenting on the final vision that emerges from "Little Gidding" David Ward refers to "the *visionary* excitement which makes the episode in 'Burnt Norton' finally a deception."[22] But in fact the rose garden experience only begins with "the deception of the thrush"; what is final in it is apprehension of what Eliot calls "reality" (*CPP*, 118), the visionary experience of the ordinary. And in the last section of "Little Gidding," at the end of the *Quartets*, the imagery of the Edenic rose garden, "the unknown, remembered gate," "the children in the apple-tree" (*CPP*, 145), and the rose itself are conspicuous in Eliot's final summation of what lies at "the end of all our exploring." The rose garden experience is not rejected as deception but elevated, though its peaceful mysticism is blended with the fiery mysticism of the dark dove from the London blitz passage. For Eliot, postlapsarian mysticism must involve the fire as well as the rose; the final ecstasy cannot in this world be separated from the painfully purifying flame.

> All manner of things shall be well
> When the tongues of flame are in-folded
> Into the crowned knot of fire
> And the fire and the rose are one.
>   (*CPP*, 145)

The various circularities of *Four Quartets* result inevitably from its central intention, to restore experience of the ordinary real to its true deepest resonance, a resonance that finally comes to involve, in Eliot's mind, the center of Christian supernaturalism, the fact of Christ. But initially the point is the type of understanding of experience that makes experience new. "We had the experience but missed the meaning / And approach to the meaning restores the experience" (*CPP*, 133). So the vision hidden in the rose garden is to be restored, or made fully real for the first time, by the analytic thrust of the poetry as well as the carefully calculated logical disciplines of the negative way. The fundamental paradox of the way of unknowing is that we find it here surrounded by the most intense and studious knowing, the knowledge of tradition as well as the analytic knowledge of personal experience. At times Eliot seems engaged in a vaguely Wordsworthian recapturing of "innocent" or "natural" mystical experience through a means highly sophisticated and artificial. Since it is the knowing "of many generations" that Eliot brings to the experience, tradition threatens to submerge the individual mystic. And finally, for Eliot, it is more the knowing than the individual experience that matters. Christ's experience forms the end of meditation: the experience of the visionary present, though not rejected, becomes secondary to knowledge of the miraculous past, the Incarnation, and the apocalyptic future.

So the apotheosis described in "And the fire and the rose are one" is not really of this world but of the next; Eliot's ultimate concerns transcend all the versions of mystical experience in "Burnt Norton." He comes out thoroughly orthodox in the end, though here his orthodoxy is understated enough not to get in the way of the poetry. These lines about fire, which look forward to "a condition of complete simplicity / (Costing not less than everything)," have a literally apocalyptic resonance. They seem to refer to the Second Coming, medieval history's anticipated final complement to the Incarnation, when the world will be purified by a variety of fires. Then the sense of death which accompanies immanent mysticism will be swallowed up in that general human dying which will lead to heaven and eternity; the mysticism of this world will be irrelevant in all of its manifestations at the end of the world as Eliot's faith imagines it. The descent through unknowing to the still point, as well as the more mundane moment of immersion in the rose garden, will fade in significance. For Eliot, by the time of "Little Gidding," the mystical experience immanent or transcendent has become not an end but a means, and possibly a way of anticipating the common experience of the faithful when through time time is conquered.

William Carlos Williams

Whatever his irritation with Eliot's poetic inclinations, Williams like everyone else in the forties and early fifties had to work in his shadow. *Four Quartets* had been published, to great acclaim, before Williams really began *Paterson*. Further, in the year that *Paterson I* appeared, Robert Lowell published *Lord Weary's Castle*. Its dark Catholic obsessions and its densely referential poetry seemed to demonstrate Eliot's dominance over still another generation of the American poetic imagination. (Lowell would not publish *Life Studies*, the book that effectively ended the reign of obscure "impersonal" poetry, until thirteen years later, one year after *Paterson V.*) In a 1947 introduction to Williams's *Selected Poems,* Randall Jarrell, who had just written the review that canonized *Lord Weary's Castle,* found it necessary to defend the loose "musical" organization of *Paterson I* by comparing it with *Four Quartets,* which he called "probably the best poem of our time."[23] Now few would claim that peak for the *Quartets,* though some might for *Paterson.* But Williams's star was not to rise fully until after his death.

In 1947 he felt opposed to Eliot as well as overshadowed. Though in retrospect "no ideas but in things" hardly seems alien to Eliot's "direct sensuous apprehension of thought," at the time Williams seemed the poet of things and Eliot the poet of thoughts, abstractions. Both of them turned from mystical experience at the end of their long poems, but they turned in opposite directions, following tendencies implicit from the start. In the final *Quartets* Eliot leaves the individual mystic's immediate experience for the more abstract harmonies of heaven and the risen Christ; Paterson in *Paterson IV* leaves the mystic sea for the more concrete realities of inland geography and history. Throughout *Paterson* Williams has amused himself with the opposition between the two poets. As Joseph Bennett complained in a 1952 attack on *Paterson* (an attack based on the common critical values of the time, values inspired if not created by Eliot), "Eliot is alternately attacked, parodied, and imitated — almost every style of Eliot's long career is copied in parts of Williams's verse."[24] Though this outmoded partisan description now seems excessive, Williams's sometimes playful, sometimes irritated consciousness of Eliot forms a definite minor strain in *Paterson.*

In the area of visionary utterance, though, the verbal resemblances suggest something deeper than either imitation or parody; here the similarity seems natural, not dependent on Williams's awareness of Eliot. When Williams begins a section of *Paterson I* with the slightly archaic "Whither" the old traditionalist Eliot comes immediately to mind, and in fact the echo comes from "Burnt Norton," though the particular word does not.

> There is no direction. Whither? I
> cannot say. I cannot say
> more than how.
>
> (*P,* 18)

> I can only say, *there* we have been: but I cannot say where
> And I cannot say, how long, for that is to place it in time.
>
> (*CPP,* 119)

The two passages describe opposite ends of one sequence of experiences. Williams evokes a dark night sense of psychological and spiritual confusion and Eliot is describing the visionary plenitude that — for him, perhaps not for Williams — follows the confusion. The two poets draw closer in their development of another aspect of the dark night vision, purgative fire. Like Eliot's "Little Gidding," much of *Paterson III* ("The Library") involves something like a descent into the underworld, here "Hell, New Jersey" (*P,* 97). Both poems contain evocations of various forms of elemental destruction, especially "the death of water and fire" (*CPP,* 140), but fire is depicted in both not as punishment but purgation, the instrument of transformation. The transformation Williams imagines is more specifically aesthetic, less spiritually resonant than Eliot's. Williams's fire is the fire of "decreation," the term Stevens takes from Simone Weil to define the way we perceive "modern reality." The definition immediately follows the passage about mysticism in *The Necessary Angel;* there is a dramatization of the same idea in "Credences of Summer":

> Let's see the very thing and nothing else.
> Let's see it with the hottest fire of sight.
> Burn everything not part of it to ash.
> (Palm, 288)

Williams goes a step further. His fire of the imagination burns the very thing as well; the fire transforms, vivifying an old bottle as it warps "to a new distinction." Williams assents to this burning, "the whole city doomed," as Eliot accepts the "dove descending . . . / With flame of incandescent terror" (*CPP,* 143) during the London blitz.

> Calling the fire good
> So be it. The beauty of fire-blasted sand
> that was glass, that was a bottle: unbottled.
> Unabashed. So be it.
> (P, 117)

The terms of William's aesthetic acceptance are at least superficially religious, as the repeated "So be it" (one translation of "Amen") suggests. Williams even connects the flame with his own version of Eliot's dove, though this turns out to be a woman, not a Spirit: "Beautiful thing, / my dove, unable and all who are windblown, touched by the fire" (*P,* 96). Despite the very different contexts operating here, the similar images suggest a basic connection. Williams is certainly not mystical in any orthodox sense, but for him the act of perception itself can be mystical, at least in the sense of establishing identity between the perceiver and the world. In fact ordinary perception is not enough; some extraordinary new vision must occur if Paterson is to emerge, in the "Library" section, from what Joel Conarroe calls "the dark night of his soul."[25] For Williams the dark night reaches its nadir in the experience of meaningless plenitude, the parody of immersion/revelation enacted by the flood. Water flows like words from the library, words to carry that knowledge which causes divorce ("Divorce is / the sign of knowledge in our time" (*P*, 18)), which buries genuine knowing in the muddy final "detritus" left by the flood.

> — to the teeth, to the very eyes
> uh, uh
>   FULL STOP
> — and leave the world
>   to darkness
>   and to
>   me.
>   (*P*, 140)

But after each descent, as Williams has assured us, comes "a new awakening: / which is a reversal / of despair" (*P*, 78). As the destructive fire (described as upward water, *P*, 120) became the fire of decreation/revelation, so the destructive water causes not only the submerging of visionary consciousness, but the subsequent elevation of vision beyond language. Again Paterson achieves "Knowledge / by way of despair" (*P*, 98); again Williams echoes the mystical phrasing of *Four Quartets*.

> Neither the past nor the future
> Neither to stare, amnesiac — forgetting.
> The language cascades into the
> invisible, beyond and above: the falls
> of which it is the visible part —
>   (*P*, 145)

Here the critic of Williams needs to resist the temptation to fit this poet wedded to ordinary particulars too neatly into any mystical pattern. Despite its use of most of the varied arsenal of mystical paradoxes and ways of thinking — its contemplation of the dark night, of immersion, of unknowing, its conviction that ignorance and descent lead to visionary knowledge as the way down suddenly becomes the way up — *Paterson* dramatizes isolation, "divorce," not fusion or union. But, to add one more paradox, it contemplates the subject of separation from the perspective of union, between poet and city, if not poet and cosmos. So the terminology of mysticism — though seldom the dangerous word itself — flows with some regularity from the pens of Williams's critics. Conarroe refers to the dark night of the soul, Nathan Scott calls *Paterson* (along with the *Quartets* and Stevens's "The Auroras of Autumn") one of the few American products of the "sacramental imagination," which captures "the tremendous mystery of the Holy."[26] Ekbert Faas wonders about "the ultimately mystical orientation of Williams's poetic aims."[27] And of course J. Hillis Miller, arguing that modern poets in general achieve "a visionary or apocalyptic union of subject and object, earth and heaven," makes Williams a secular dark night mystic: "Williams gives himself up in despair and establishes a self beyond personality, a self coextensive with the universe."[28]

As Miller indicates, one basis for such bold statements is Williams's own account of himself in a 1934 letter to Marianne Moore. He thanks her for recognizing the "inner security" of his work — "you looked at what I have done through my own eyes" — and goes on to explain the source of that security in terms precisely reminiscent of the active passivity of dark night mysticism. "It is something which occurred once when I was about twenty, a sudden resignation to existence, a despair — if you wish to call it that, but a despair which made everything a unit and at the same time a part of myself. I suppose it might be called a sort of nameless religious experience."[29] The pattern sounds familiar; despair leads to resignation leads to cosmic union. But mystical experience does not necessarily create mystical poetry, any more than mystical poetry proves actual mystical experience. *Paterson* constantly approaches union, crystalization; the dominant imagery of the poem suggests a mysticism of immersion in the physical flow of existence. But Williams feels a deep and shifting ambivalence about the connections between immersion and death. Before examining that connection, and looking at a type of minor mysticism more evident in the visionary moments of his earlier poetry, I want to pause for a moment on what is less debatable, more obvious: the sexual component in *Paterson*'s visionary pattern.

When the "beautiful thing" associated with the fire becomes clearly a person, her description at first suggests a very elevated Christian vision of ecstatic death.

> Rising, with a whirling motion, the person
> passed into the flame, becomes the flame —
> the flame taking over the person.
>
> (*P,* 121)

This person is not saint or Holy Spirit, despite the Pentecostal flame and the term "dove"; she is, in Williams's somewhat sentimental reversal, a lower-class black woman with a broken nose, "Persephone / gone to hell," "black plush, a dark flame" (*P*, 125, 128). Her constant association with fire emphasizes that she is the incarnation of imaginative beauty. She carries the mystical overtones that Eliot attaches to Mary, though perhaps she is more precisely similar to Stevens's "inamorata" (*Palm*, 348), the symbol of the unimaginative reality of earth he evokes in *Ordinary Evening* and elsewhere. Even closer to Stevens's vision is the essential spiritual force to which Williams prays shortly before the "Library" section. She is first compared to a bride, then to nature described as a force in which all are one.

> You are the eternal bride and
> father — quid pro quo,
> a simple miracle that knows
> the branching sea, to which the oak
> is coral, the coral oak.
> The Himalayas and prairies
> of your features amaze and delight —
>   (*P*, 75)

She is the life force, mother earth, the mother of beauty, of union. Generally her manifestations in Williams are, like the "beautiful thing," less androgynous, more specifically sexual, as Williams creates a mythic context based, like the cabala and other mystical systems, on metaphors involving sexual opposition and union. The stated intention of *Paterson* is a paradoxical unity through immersion in particulars, *"by multiplication a reduction to one"* (*P*, 2), not only the unity involved in "the city / the man, an identity" (*P*, 3), but a unity between man and other men, man and nature, man and his imagination. The two last pairs, especially, are often described in implicitly or explicitly sexual images, when Paterson and the female Garrett Mountain are depicted as giants lying together, or when Williams conflates various relationships in "a man like a city and a woman like a flower / who are in love" (*P*, 7). But Paterson is the city of "divorce," fracture of all connections, so the various unions can only be achieved through extraordinary efforts, efforts usually doomed to failure in the naturalistic world of this poem.

The Falls immediately become a general symbol of such effort, whether they represent language that will leap the gap (*P*, 7), the fire of decreation that makes new vision and language possible (*P*, 96), the supernatural

flow of sexual connection (*P,* 24), or the physical flow that provides
eternal immersion for those desperate enough to leap beyond the possible
and drown. A life force like "the eternal bride and father," the Falls are
also a place of death, initially for Sarah Cumming and for Sam Patch,
with whom the poet Paterson is identified. For these two, as for Eliot's
Phlebas the Phoenician who "passed the stages of his age and youth /
Entering the whirlpool" (*CPP,* 46), watery immersion means not vision
but a blind reduction to origins, rolling down into chaos. They are no
more mystical than the drowned sailor with blank staring eyes who surfaces in Lowell's "Quaker Graveyard." But no less, perhaps, though they
serve to introduce the poems' overwhelming, and for Williams unusual,
preoccupation with death and violence. Edward Dahlberg's accusation
that Williams "takes up violence in his arms as a bride"[30] may not be
entirely fair but it suggests some of the darkness of the Mother glimpsed
in *Paterson* and more fully revealed in mystic accounts of descent into the
violent storms of matter described by such grim visionaries as Lowell and
Plath (for whom contemplation of death does turn to wish for oblivion).
The Falls into which Sarah and Sam plummet power the river for the
run to the sea, which is described by one of the voices in *Paterson IV* as:

> Thalassa
> immaculata; our home, our nostalgic
> mother in whom the dead, enwombed again
> cry out to us to return.
> the blood dark sea!
> (*P,* 202)

Williams will resist this cry, but will not deny its power, or the river's
"roar / of eternal sleep . . . challenging / our waking —" (*P,* 18). Again
death is the mother of beauty.

Much of *Paterson* revolves around this struggle with and toward
death. Not sex but death provides the focus for Williams's most complex
mystical speculations. In a passage from Book III reminiscent of the
negations of the *via negativa* Williams associates death with an emptiness
at the heart of being.

> Look for the nul
> defeats it all
>
> the N of all
> equations

        that rock, the blank
        that holds them up

           . . .
        that's past all
        seeing

        the death of all
        that's past

        all being.
               (*P,* 77)

In a 1948 review of *Paterson II,* Robert Lowell connects this rock with an earlier lithic image in the poem to emphasize the linkage between death and imagination. "The rock is death, negation, the *nul;* carved and given form it stands for the imagination 'like a red basalt grasshopper, boot-long with window-eyes.' The symbols are not allegorical but loose, intuitive, and Protean."[31] Lowell refers to a stone grasshopper that comes to Paterson's mind when real ones in the park burst out at him like a vision, "aflame only in flight." In a moment with the quality of revelation his mind becomes what he envisions:

        He is led forward by their announcing wings.

           . . .
        — his mind a red stone carved to be
        endless flight.

           . . .
        The stone lives, the flesh dies
        — we know nothing of death.
              (*P,* 49)

This articulation of a conventional belief in the immortality of imagined beauty, of art (reminiscent of Stevens's "The body dies; the body's beauty lives" (*Palm,* 10)) suggests one of *Paterson*'s fundamental complexities. Death may be the mother of beauty, but death is also the enemy, and visionary beauty is valued partly as an escape from time and death. Williams is still mulling over this in his long afterthought, *Paterson V,* where he attempts to formulate it in a rather confusing image: "death is a hole / in which we are all buried." But there is a hole in death's hole (which becomes "the cavern of death") and through the hole's hole "the imagination / escapes intact" (*P,* 212).

    Williams's ambivalence about the poetic value of death is most clearly enacted in *Paterson IV,* "The Run to the Sea," which ends with a walk out of the sea. The title suggests a proper poetic climax to a poem that began with destructive immersion, the two drownings; final images of a Whitman-like transcendent immersion in the flow of life and death would have provided a neat closure. But Williams obviously came to see such unity as artificial, imposed, and though one of his voices argues for an eternal return to the sea and the Mother ("Seed / of Venus, you will return"), another deeper voice resists: "The sea is not our home" (*P*, 202, 201). Conceptual flow is sacrificed for a more mundane vision of the world: "Waken from a dream, this dream of / the whole poem" (*P*, 200). Death becomes not a mystical but a physical reality, as Williams comes finally to resist mysticism immanent or transcendent for a more practical and arguably more ethical response to death. The luminous sense of mystical death recedes in the face of actual deaths, and Williams turns at the end of *Paterson IV* from the Whitman of merging and death to the Whitman of the open road, the one that Lawrence finally celebrated. Williams had probably read Lawrence by 1951; certainly he was aware of someone's mocking criticism of Whitman. He writes, describing Paterson's turn away from the mystic sea of death and merging: "In the end man rises from the sea where the river appears to have lost its identity and ... turns inland toward Camden where Walt Whitman, much traduced, lived the latter years of his life and died" (*P*, headnote). Like Whitman's own actual death, the multiple deaths that end *Paterson IV* are not symbolic and not at all romantic, as Paterson contemplates wars (including the impending Korean war), executions, and the ordinary domestic butchery that makes of human history "a sea of blood." Death is the mother of ugliness, too, as in the prose account of the factory worker who fractures his baby's skull with her high chair tray "when her crying annoyed him as he was feeding her" (*P*, 196).

The same refusal to allow death — especially death by water — to be quite so alluring as it can be in Eliot or Stevens (or, later, Lowell) characterizes Williams's earlier treatments of death. The drownings of Sam Patch and Mrs. Cummings in the Falls are spectacular enough to invite symbolism, but the symbolism tends to be realistically negative. The two are perhaps heroic, because they try to transcend ordinary life, but Williams suggests that they die because of basic failures, "divorce" from others, from a real sense of place, or from a meaningful language. They enact immersion, but without the overtones of mystical fulfillment that will accompany images of immersion in the poets who are to follow Williams.

Yet the sense of revelation, when it does come in *Paterson,* is often linked to water, to the deadly Falls and the Passaic River. The revelation anticipated in the preface comes "rolling up" out of the river, as the man "a nine months' wonder" (*P*, 3) emerges from water to which he must return. Various other passages go beyond immersion to enact the union hinted here between the river and the poet dreaming his poem. From Book III:

> The ears are water. The feet
> listen. Boney fish bearing lights
> stalk the eyes — which float about,
> indifferent.
>
> (*P*, 129)

Like Eliot in "East Coker" ("The dahlias sleep in the empty silence. / Wait for the early owl," *CPP*, 123) Williams here sounds more like his poetic descendant Roethke (who had published *The Lost Son* the year before *Paterson II* came out) than himself.

No matter how often Williams insists on plain visions of plain things — "NOT prophecy! / but the thing itself" (*P*, 208) — he will return to these images and formulations that make his plain visions seem prophetic. This unresolved tension in basic attitude is one of the reasons for *Paterson*'s uneven quality, especially in Book IV, where Williams somewhat clumsily externalizes his ambivalence about death as prophetic symbol and as plain reality, and decides not to unify or really end his poem. As Joel Conarroe says, "*Paterson* has even less poetic consistency than *Four Quartets*, itself a very unequable work."[32] The later books especially are marked by an unevenness due to poor judgments as well as unresolved tensions. There are passages of abstraction where Williams forgets about "things" (once he changes the line to "No ideas but / in the facts") and out-theorizes Eliot. The political sensitivity to the human aspects of social problems evident in Book II becomes in Book IV apparent political commitment to the theory of "social credit" extensively and crankily put forth, without any real economic sense. It gets in the way of the poetry more than Eliot's theology obstructs his. Then *Paterson V*, though often interesting in itself (partly for Williams's plain style excursions into Eliot's medieval territory) has nothing to do with the first four books, and contradicts their insistence on particular place.

Despite these clear failures *Paterson* remains a heroic poem, for qualities it shares with Williams's earliest poetry as well as for the far greater scope of its ambitions. Like the early "pure" poetry, *Paterson* tries to reveal the radiance in ordinary existence, tries to heal the gaps in daily lives. Though

Williams deliberately resists large mystical statements or conclusions he implies a hidden magic, for instance in the "beautiful thing" section where he anticipates the story of Madame Curie told in *Paterson IV*. Using religious terminology for both, he compares the difficulties of the poet of the commonplace with her difficulties in discovering radium.

> Give it up. Quit it. Stop writing.
> "Saintlike" you will never
> separate that stain of sense.
>
> . . .
>
> — never separate that stain
> of sense from the inert mass. Never.
> Never that radiance.
>
> (*P*, 108)

Whether "saintlike" refers to the nobility of the poet's effort or the inevitability of his failure is not immediately clear. But the radiance he seeks is further defined on the next page by association, not surprisingly, with death:

> Death lies in wait,
> a kindly brother —
> full of the missing words,
>
> . . .
>
> The radiant gist that
> resists the final crystallization.
>
> (*P*, 109)

Though the poet cannot separate the strain of sense from things, Williams describes what happens when he manages to get the things themselves into a poem. His images for such moments of revelation involve, like Eliot's, light still or flowing. Very early he describes trees in terms suggestive of his *Autobiography* reference to "that secret and sacred presence."

> split, furrowed, creased, mottled, stained —
> secret — into the body of the light!
>
> (*P*, 6)

Later the poet, contemplating the most ordinary aspects of his personal environment — his ear, melting snow, linoleum, his thumb — hopefully imagines his own flowering, visionary and perhaps sexual:

> : And his thoughts soared
> to the magnificence of imagined delights
> where he would probe

as into the pupil of an eye
as through a hoople of fire, and emerge
sheathed in a robe

streaming with light.

(*P*, 31)

The only explicit statement of mystical union, containment of and
immersion in the flow, accompanied by the obliteration of time, comes
both before and after *Paterson* proper. In Book V Williams quotes a
germinal poem he wrote about the "filthy Passaic" three decades before
Paterson, the first of the *Collected Earlier Poems,* "The Wanderer."

"the river has returned to its beginnings"
and backward
(and forward)
it tortures itself within me
until time has been washed finally under:
and "I knew all (or enough)
it became me."

(*P*, 233)

Perhaps "The Wanderer" can be understood as an attempt to give a
name to the "nameless religious experience" he described in a letter to
Marianne Moore. The poem enacts a ritual immersion in the Passaic and
the world, and announces the poet's dedication to the mother of beauty,
who appears as crow and seagull, a goddess in the river, an ugly old
woman, and finally the bride of the Passaic. Like the "beautiful thing" of
Paterson III, she is "the beauty of all the world," but here she is also the
force which "recreat[es] the whole world" in the imagination;[33] in her
the world and the poet, perceived and perceiver, are one. As opposed to
the "divorce" that dominated *Paterson,* marriage wins here; to the
"marvellous old queen" Williams prays for "always / A new marriage," a
union with her and the world that will lift him "Up from before the death
living around me" (*CEP,* 6). But if the initial route toward this muse is
ecstatic transcendence, flight above life and death, the final movement
toward her is downward to watery immersion. At the end of his "novitiate"
— Williams's use of the term suggests that other sacred marriage between
the nun and Christ — the poet describes his ritual flow into the river in
the lines he would repeat three decades later. Now he is not the husband
but the son the Mother brings to the river in a "clear marriage" (*CEP,*
12).

"The Wanderer" directly anticipates *Paterson* when it dramatizes the calling of the poet. Williams's verse form changed, but his preoccupations, like Stevens's and to a lesser extent Eliot's, remained the same. To extend the final definition of *Paterson*'s quest for radiance, it helps to look momentarily at one or two of Williams's early poems, poems bare enough so that radiance is almost all there is. The intimation of revelation in the ordinary is more the point of this poetry than any traditional sense of mystic unity or transcendence. Unlike "The Wanderer," most of the early poems enact not a leap into cosmic union but a carefully logical process of internalization of particulars. It is Williams's logical description, like Eliot's logic of paradox, that leads to the radiance.

Often critics argue that Williams rejects the dualistic and analytic logic of Western thought and that his early poetry, like the implicitly monistic Eastern haiku which centrally influenced the imagists, evokes transcendent visions which are not only not paraphrasable but also not ultimately susceptible to logical analysis. Even J. Hillis Miller, who argues convincingly that Williams the post-romantic creates a world without "depth or transcendence," frequently discusses Williams in implicitly transcendent terms. In Williams's poetry, Miller says, "anywhere is everywhere, and all times are one time."[34] Here Miller quotes Williams, but "Anywhere is everywhere" only represents one Williams mood; earlier he wrote "Here / is not there / and never will be" (*P,* 235, 211). Miller's emphasis involves misinterpretation of Williams's avowed intention to discover the universal in the particular; by overemphasizing the universal Miller pays insufficient attention to Williams's constant sense of the particularity of individual things. Even in the most impressionistic early poetry, Williams is seldom quite so far from traditional dualistic logic as Miller suggests. If his poetry early and late achieves the effect of revelation it usually does so not through the transcendent evocations of the haiku, not through breaking down the barriers between things, but through a rather surprisingly rigorous process of logical analysis.

Much of this poetry fits a characteristically modern aesthetic pattern, but a pattern that develops out of traditional Western aesthetics rather than out of the rejection of that tradition. Many of the early short poems focused on simple scenes come very close to matching James Joyce's definition of the epiphany. The idea of epiphany is perhaps overused in discussion of modern poetry, used very loosely, for instance, in discussions of Eliot's rose garden, but given Joyce's precise definition it does much to clarify the effect of Williams. The epiphany involves a rather unusual and generally logical approach to revelation, an anti-transcendent mysticism of particular place, a vision of the spirituality of individual things which can unite subject and object without necessarily implying any escape from ordinary reality. There occurs a perception of the ultimate significance of the ordinary, a sense of heightened reality which need not suggest underlying spiritual forces, need not, like the haiku, even imply the basic unity of all things. Joyce's, or rather Stephen Dedalus's, most explicit definition of the epiphany appears in *Stephen Hero*. Stephen means by epiphany "a sudden spiritual manifestation," but he describes that manifestation in the rigorously logical terms of Aquinas's requirements for beauty. The first two are integrity and symmetry; the third is radiance, *claritas*.

> *Claritas* is *quidditas*. After the analysis which discovers the second quality the mind makes the only logically possible synthesis and discovers the third quality. This is the moment which I call epiphany. First we recognize that the object is *one* integral thing, then we recognize that it is an organized composite structure, a *thing* in fact: finally, when the relation of parts is exquisite, when the parts are adjusted to the special point, we recognize that it is *that* thing which it is. Its soul, its whatness, leaps to us from the vestment of its appearance. The soul of the commonest object, the structure of which is so adjusted, seems to us radiant. The object achieves its epiphany.[35]

Indicatively, it achieves this epiphany not in cosmic unity but in separation — Stephen's first step in perceiving is to isolate the object from what it is not — and as a result not of meditation but of structured analysis. Ideally, the epiphany reveals things simply as they are, but as they are in their particular essences. Revealed is the ideal form of the thing in the thing itself, its *"quidditas,"* its "soul." The epiphany suggests a mysticism of this world, without recourse to any sort of transcendence; this is the heart of much of Williams's early poetry.

Without transcendence, and within the terms of dualistic logic, there is nonetheless the perception of radiance. What Stephen describes as *claritas,* Williams in *Paterson* frequently describes in images of brightness, or flame, or the radiance of precious metals, an essence hidden in things. In discovering this essence, the poem "focuses the world,"[36] but this does not mean, as Miller claims, that in the poem "the particular is the universal," that is, "all existence." It is only itself, though it may be *a* universal of sorts, almost a Platonic form, but embedded in things.

> so much depends
> upon

```
          a red wheel
          barrow

          glazed with rain
          water

          beside the white
          chickens.
              (CEP, 277)
```

This scene remains particular, with its own individual radiance, though it is not particularly realistic in any superficial sense. Williams seeks a deep reality of essences, not surfaces, and he creates it through visible analysis and deliberate artificiality. The primary analytic force in the poem comes from the line divisions, which fragment the image, forcing apprehension of one quality, almost one essence, at a time. As Miller points out (about another poem), "Williams' metrical effects have an extraordinary power to bring each word out in its 'thingness.' "[37] The separation between "red wheel" and "barrow" fractures the original word in a way that could be interpreted in terms of the medieval scholastic separation between substance and accidents, between redness or wheeledness and barrowness. In the last four lines of the poem, the substance-accident distinction is suggested even more literally by the separations between "rain" and "water" and between "white" and "chickens." Having separated the scene from the rest of reality, having defined its integrity, Williams proceeds to reduce it artificially to idealized essences. Particularly the red (not rust) and the white (not mud-speckled) give the sense of the stark simplicity of abstract forms perceived in things.

In the curiously vital tradition of medieval philosophy that influenced Eliot and gave Joyce terms for his definition of the epiphany, the poet becomes almost a logician, applying to experience a consciously artificial and abstract logic but recording or creating an individual essential reality with the superlogical clarity of a visionary absolute. He conveys a mystical exultation, but grounded in immediate fact, in a mysticism of particulars appropriate to the imagination of immanence that resists universals as it resists other routes to transcendence. From such radiant particulars ("To make a start / out of particulars" (*P,* 3)) *Paterson* constructs its visionary world of sporadic and partial union, never losing sight of the parts in the sum. Williams's visions remain subject to Williams's questions, especially in *Paterson,* and if the question of mystical union is answered at all, the answer is negative. The question will be sharpened by Stevens, who moved beyond the seductions of the image more quickly than Williams, and whose final approach to the problem of union between visionary poet and native ground is directly reflected in a Williams poem of magic from the decade of *Paterson,* "The Sound of Waves."

> Past that, past the image:
> a voice!
> out of the mist
> above the waves and
>
> the sound of waves, a
> voice, speaking.[38]

More explicitly than the voice of the Passaic, this voice speaks revelation of the type Stevens will hear in the many words of his many earthly mothers; he will often write of the mysterious "voices" of the natural world.

Wallace Stevens

Somewhere between Eliot's finally otherworldly theology and Williams's final refusal to transform the world of matter even through a vision of immanent spirit lies Stevens's territory of mystical immanence. He is the one, the most perfect model and the most freely acknowledged influence on the poets who followed him in dreaming the holy dream of matter. But he starts out far more the rigid realist than Williams. In "Nuances of a Theme by Williams" (1918), Stevens states his theme by quoting the whole of Williams's "El Hombre," in which the poet takes "a strange courage" from the apparent independence of a star shining despite the sunrise. Stevens chastizes Williams for the anthropomorphic implications of his vision, taking a very high tone as he admonishes the star not to symbolize, not to reflect human feeling, to "mirror nothing."

> Lend no part to any humanity that suffuses
> you in its own light.
> Be not chimera of morning,
> Half-man, half-star.
>
> *(Palm,* 39)

At this time, the difference between the two poets seems radical. Not only do they speak differently, Williams instinctively assumes a spiritual interpenetration between man and nature that Stevens will spend his postromantic life questioning, denying, and finally laboriously reconstructing on his own terms. But by the time of *Paterson* Williams has lost some of that instinctive and near-mystical sense of contact with the world that informs his early poems. In the time of "divorce," visionary immanence becomes something that must be struggled for, a question of faith because no longer surely known. And as Williams moved toward doubt about the basic connection, the older Stevens moved away from his early cynicism, toward acceptance of the supreme fiction as a valid bridge, sometimes mystical, between poet and world: a thing itself, a being, part of being. In *Ordinary Evening,* Stevens calls the poem "part of the res itself and not about it" (*Palm,* 338), reflecting over the years Williams's comment in *Spring and All* that poetry should be a "new form dealt with as a reality in itself" (*SA,* 67). This form has "power TO ESCAPE ILLUSION and stand between man and nature as saints once stood between man and the sky" (*SA,* 38). The creator poet is correspondingly elevated, as he is when Stevens uses similarly theological language in the *Adagia* to echo the mystical assurance of the young Williams. Stevens writes "The poet is a god," though he cannot resist continuing, "or, the young poet is a god. The old poet is a tramp" (*OP,* 173).

Gods tramping through increasingly similar landscapes, the philosopher-poets and dreamers in reality's flux that both poets create combine incongruously comical names (Canon Aspirin, Noah Faitoute Paterson, etc.) and ambitions of a giant seriousness. Stevens's Professor Eucalyptus says it for all of them when he claims, " 'The search / For reality is as momentous as / The search for god' " (*Palm,* 345). Only the mystic can find god in this life; only the mystic really searches. For Stevens more than Williams, the true vision of the real is possible only in something like mystical experience. The comparison between the openings of these two central poems shows the similarities in the ways they frame the visionary question; both move toward Eliot's *via negativa* in imagining the answer, though as we will see *Ordinary Evening* finally goes beyond the shared vision of nothing.

Stevens begins *Ordinary Evening* as Williams begins *Paterson,* by arguing the extreme difficulty of the search. In meditating on "the eye's plain version" the poet must confront

> the question that is a giant himself:
> Of what is this house composed of if not of the sun,
>
> These houses, these difficult objects, dilapidate
> Appearances of what appearances,
> Words, lines, not meanings, not communications,

> Dark things without a double, after all,
> Unless a second giant kills the first —
> A recent imagining of reality,
>
> Much like a new resemblance of the sun,
> Down-pouring, up-springing and inevitable,
> A larger poem for a larger audience.
>
> (*Palm*, 331)

In this description of the decreation of worn visions, the giant is not the perceiver, but that myth through which the perceiver apprehends the perceived. The vision comes not from on high to a deliberately passive recipient, as it would in Eliot, but is "up-springing" as well as "down-pouring." Like Paterson the man and the city, the giant includes both the activity of the dreamer and the manifestation of the dream.

Before "The Delineaments of the Giants" in his "Preface" to *Paterson*, Williams describes his poetic ambitions in terms reminiscent of Stevens in general and the opening of *Ordinary Evening* in particular. Williams's "how will you find beauty when it is locked in the mind past all remonstrance?" (*P*, 3) suggests a desire to return to "the first idea" of Stevens's *Supreme Fiction* (*Palm*, 208). Williams depicts revelation "rolling up" out of the water, not "down-pouring, up-springing," but after it emerges from the river it is "rained down and / regathered," so the duality of motion is similar. Also there occurs the human interaction with revelation implied by Stevens's "up-springing," as Williams constructs an identification between the poet and the vision. The vision is not "a resemblance of the sun," but the equally pure "ignorant sun / rising in the slot of / hollow suns risen" (*P*, 4). This "ignorant sun" also suggests, as Glauco Cambon writes, "What Stevens would call 'first idea,' the sun to be perceived only at the price of becoming an ignorant man again."[39] Both poets describe the clear imagining of reality as the result of "interpenetration," though Williams imagines a more literal, physical, type of union than Stevens. Williams's images combine two natural cycles, the human cycle of birth and death and the river-cloud-rain cycle of water's changes; the poetry makes man and nature flow as one.

Both poets imagine such contact with the real as violent, though unlike Williams Stevens seldom depicts the violence as deadly. Not so much death as a more abstract sort of negation shapes Stevens's most explicit evocations of earthly revelation. When he defines the desire for the first idea in *Notes* — "It knows that what it has is what is not" (*Palm*, 208) — Stevens could almost be quoting from one of Eliot's evocations of the *via negativa* of John of the Cross. The late Stevens constantly defines perception by negation. In "A Primitive like an Orb," written the year before *Ordinary Evening,* "the central poem," which becomes "the world," is described as "the giant of nothingness." This poem is celebrated by "clairvoyant men . . . / The lover, the believer, and the poet" (*Palm,* 318). These visionaries, one of them religious, perceive and become part of the giant of nothingness, as Stevens enacts a traditional mystical paradox, and nothing becomes all. As *The Cloud of Unknowing* exhorts all clairvoyant men, "Lat be þis eueriwhere & þis ouȝt, in comparison of þis noȝwhere & þis nouȝt. Reche þee neuer ȝif þi wittys kon no skyl of þis nouȝt; for whi I loue it moche þe betir. It is so worþi a þing in it-self at þei kon so skyle þer-apon. . . . Our inner man clepiþ it Al; for of it he is wel lernid to kon skyle of alle þinges, bodely or goostly, wiþ-outen any specyal beholdying to any o þing by it-self."⁴⁰ (Leave alone this everywhere and this anything, and follow this nowhere and this nothing. Never worry if your mind has no knowledge of this nothing; for that reason I love it much better. . . . Our inner man calls it All; for it teaches him to know all things, physical or spiritual, without any special attention to any particular thing.)

Williams's "nul," "that rock, the blank / that holds them up" in *Paterson II* is connected with this way of thinking, which is almost a mystical commonplace, Oriental as well as Christian. The sense of death in this "blank" echoes when Stevens introduces it into *Ordinary Evening.* In the canto that follows Canto XVI's evocation of "death's poverty" and "total leaflessness," Stevens discusses the blank and the richness of images that flow from it like Old Testament revelation.

> A blank underlies the trials of device,
>
> The dominant blank, the unapproachable.
> This is the mirror of the high serious:
> Blue verdured into a damask's lofty symbol,
>
> Gold easings and ouncings and fluctuations of thread
> And beetling of belts and lights of general stones,
> Like blessed beams from out a blessed bush
>
> Or the wasted figurations of the wastes
> Of night, time and the imagination.
>
> (*Palm,* 341-42)

This prophetic cloth suggests the garb of peace after death in "The Owl in the Sarcophagus." Peace at our "Holy doom" is "Damasked in the originals of green," is

> vested in a foreign absolute,

> Adorned with cryptic stones and sliding shines,
> An immaculate personage in nothingness.
> (*Palm*, 305)

A less death-bound nothingness appears early in Stevens, and a brief glimpse of the earlier Stevens does much to prepare us for the austere complexities of *Ordinary Evening*. Perhaps "The Snow Man" most directly anticipates what Stevens will become; its resounding last lines create a play on negative meanings that makes Eliot's similar "distracted from distraction by distraction" (*CPP*, 120) sound comparatively tricky and shallow. The mythic man who has "a mind of winter" becomes

> the listener, who listens in the snow,
> And, nothing himself, beholds
> Nothing that is not there and the nothing that is.
> (*Palm*, 54)

The first "nothing" involves escape from human subjectivity, the target of the dark night's purgation. The second "nothing" is the word used in its common sense. The third nothing is everything, being, simply and impossibly what is, seen in superhuman vision at the end of the way of negation.

In the last phrase of "The Snow Man," Stevens creates the magic words that will be echoed (doubtless unwittingly) in a few years by Heidegger, whose own fascinated contemplation of "a Nothing that 'is' " will lead him beyond logic to the vision of the blank, the unreasoning he imagines at the heart of reasoning. As he suggests in calling the whole idea of extant Nothing "nonsensical," in pointing out that the question "What is Nothing?" "deprives itself of its own object," his essay rings enough paradoxical changes to undercut logic severely. " 'Logic' is only *one* exposition of the nature of thinking"; perhaps more basic is "the experience of the truth of Being." He continues, "Being is not a product of thinking. It is more likely that essential thinking is an occurrence of Being."[41]

Such statements are both highly logical and grounded in mystical assumptions that subvert ordinary logic, contradicting the principle of contradiction. Especially when Heidegger quotes the Hegel line that Being and Nothing (like Eliot's way up and way down) are "one and the same," he subverts the basic axiom that a thing cannot be and not be at the same time. As J. Hillis Miller points out, in Stevens's late poetry "the theme of nothingness gradually becomes more dominant . . . underlies everything as its present reality."[42] So, though Stevens has a more analytic habit of mind than either Williams or Eliot, he is at the same time more impelled to burst the limits of analytic logic.

As the ultimate abstraction Nothing becomes more and more Stevens's subject, not only does his style like Eliot's become more abstract, less imagistic, but his mode of thinking changes in tune with his dominant thought. In *Notes,* where "The nothingness was a nakedness, a point / Beyond which thought could not progress as thought," Stevens frequently opposes the rational to the visionary, as in this passage evocative of epiphany:

> But the difficultest rigor is forthwith,
> On the image of what we see, to catch from that
>
> Irrational moment its unreasoning,
> As when the sun comes rising, when the sea
> Clears deeply, when the moon hangs on the wall
>
> Of heaven-haven. These are not things transformed.
> Yet we are shaken by them as if they were.
> We reason about them with a later reason.
>
> (*Palm,* 225)

In the depiction of revelation without transformation, those last lines suggest the essence of the mysticism of immanence, as well as the essence of Stevens's poetry, the same essence of the same "Mystical theology." "Unreasoning" forms the way to both, but reasoning both precedes and follows it.

But the earthly ordinariness of the vision must also be stressed. What is first obvious about Stevens's mysticism, in "Sunday Morning," is what it is not: Christian. But problems of terminology abound, because of the almost automatic Christian referents of such traditional words as "mystical" or "transcendent." Critical problems with the terms are constant, as are Stevens's own imprecisions. Ralph Mills, for instance, is forced into oxymoron (and italics) to describe Stevens in terms of "the *immanent transcendence* in the writing of Joyce or Yeats, a transcendence achieved within the natural world yet raising the participants above the range of time and space."[43] This somewhat blurred definition of epiphany works better than many critical attempts to describe Stevens's "transcedence."

Edward Kessler uses the terms without immediate (and probably necessary) qualification, but then argues that Stevens's "transcendence is not
mystical" for "he seeks no divine union."[44] Obviously not, but why not
then say his mysticism is not transcendent? Still, "divine union" may be
the sense of "mystical" Stevens has in mind when, in the early essay in
The Necessary Angel, he distinguishes between "the adherents of the
imagination," who "pass from one mysticism to another," and "the adherents of the central" who believe that "the central problem is always
the problem of reality." "The adherents of the central are also mystics to
begin with. But all their desire and all their ambition is to press away from
mysticism toward that ultimate good sense which we term civilization"
(*Angel,* 116). This may seem contradictory, coming from a book which
will ultimately define "the theory of poetry" as "a mystical theology."
Stevens's use of terms shifts. But the description of mysticism as a stage
through which the adherents of the central must pass may be understood
in terms of a final vision — in some of his last poems — of a reality beyond
the mystical.

That final reality is deeper in, not further out, the triumph of immanence, not a shift either to simple materialism or to transcendence.
Probably Stevens's ambivalence about the word "mysticism" comes from
its association with plain old Christianity, from which he wants to be dissociated. Even now, naive critics still refuse to accept Stevens's secular use
of traditional religious terms as completely secular; they try to imagine
for him a religion made in the literal image of Christianity. It may be
proper to sense the Holy Spirit in any dove that appears in Eliot's poetry,
but surely not in the pigeons of "Sunday Morning," as Adelaide Kirby
Morris does, in line with her program for reconverting Stevens to the
context of faith: "God becomes one with the imagination, Christ becomes the poet-hero or incarnation of the imagination, and the Holy
Ghost becomes the active though diffused presence of imagination in
human life."[45] Here dogma swallows mystical resonance, as the Christian
scheme obscures not only the variety of Stevens's poetry but the real thrust
of his spiritual thinking from "Sunday Morning" on.

Though marked by a frank nostalgia for belief in transcendence, "Sunday Morning" shows little ambivalence in its attack on those modes of
vision which rigidify spiritual experience into dead assertions about gods
and heaven and holy spirits. When Stevens eventually experiences something of a conversion, with mythic overtones, the conversion remains true
to the negation of "Sunday Morning" as well as its affirmations. It involves

a developing faith not in divine but in human creative power, in the imagination's power to create reality, to see the world without obscuring it. As "Nuances of a Theme by Williams" implies, Stevens begins with considerable suspicion of the basic act of the poet, and such other early poems as "Anecdote of the Jar" suggest that the ordering imagination will not only distort but devitalize what is perceived and captured for poetry. Even "The Snow Man," read without recourse to the rather special mystical interpretation of "nothing" the *via negativa* allows, suggests that such reductively clear vision is impossible, that no man really has "a mind of winter." This cynicism about the possibility of perception continues to be a strain in Stevens, strongly stated, for instance, in "The Motive for Metaphor" of 1943. But there develops a counterbalanced faith in the ability of the imagination to overcome the problem of perception, first fully, though confusingly, stated in "The Idea of Order at Key West," more completely described in *Notes,* and most dramatically enacted in *Ordinary Evening.*

"Key West" begins to give a sense of what, besides nothing, Stevens's mysticism involves. The poem develops an odd combination, though not an unusual one in Stevens's visionary poetry, of unreasoning and careful reasoning. Especially in a poem which is the record of a struggle to force a visionary intuition into philosophical shape, this allows confusion. As the reckless but perceptive explicator Harold Bloom has finally been bold enough to say, "the *Key West* poem has its desperate equivocations and its unresolvable difficulties, more perhaps than even so strong a poem can sustain. In some respects, it is an impossible text to interpret, and its rhetoric may be at variance with its deepest intentionalities."[46] Bloom goes on to argue that the poem fails to locate the source of the dominant voice it describes, leaving the relation between human and natural voices ambiguous. This problem, resolved in various and sometimes conflicting ways, lies at the center of much of Stevens's poetry about oppositions and unities between man and the world. Often the most fundamental connection is described as the human ability to hear a clear, natural voice or "sound," most often "cry." In "The Snow Man" the wind blows for the man of nothing, "the listener," so that he may understand "the sound of the land" (*Palm,* 54). At the end of Stevens's time of writing, the problem remains. "The Course of a Particular" asks whether in "the nothingness of winter" the "cry of the leaves" speaks to us at all. That it may not violates a sense of union: "though one says that one is part of everything, / There is a conflict, there is a resistance involved" (*Palm,* 367).

In the "Key West" version of the same transaction, conflict is all there is at first; the woman sings, the sea "caused constantly a cry . . . inhuman" (*Palm,* 97), and their two sounds will not blend or interact. The woman seems arrogant, making her world beside the disregarded sea, imposing an order as sterile as that of the jar in "Anecdote": "it was she and not the sea we heard." The internal rhyme stresses the opposition. But suddenly what is heard is described differently; in the woman's voice the voice of the sea is included, and more. What the speaker hears is more than "the dark voice of the sea" and "the outer voice of sky"; it is "more even than her voice, and ours" because it contains all these voices. In apparently direct contradiction of the earlier "The water never formed to mind or voice," the sea is shaped by her sound: "the sea / Whatever self it had, became the self / That was her song, for she was the maker" (*Palm,* 98). There exist various possible ways of resolving this contradiction, given the number of subjectivities at play in the poem, none of them fixed or static (except possibly Ramon Fernandez's). But attempts to iron out the contradiction with logic do more than the poem does, for "Key West" is one of the first of Stevens's later poems that for all its logical surface remains more intent on capturing than explaining visionary experience.

As in Williams, union is the ultimate aim, unity at the level of perception become union at the level of being, something more important than understanding. The final phrases used to evoke such a connection suggest a context of magic and religious experience more than rational analysis (the analysis that, it is implied, the thinker Ramon Fernandez cannot offer). The lights on the water are described:

> Fixing emblazoned zones and fiery poles,
> Arranging, deepening, enchanting night.

> Oh! Blessed rage for order, pale Ramon,
> The maker's rage to order words of the sea,
> Words of the fragrant portals, dimly-starred,
> And of ourselves and of our origins,
> In ghostlier demarcations, keener sounds.

Our instinctive assent to these richly romantic lines does not particularly depend on logic. We remain unsure of the relation between the singer's rage for order and the achieved order of the lights; they may complement each other or oppose each other as different types of artificiality. We may also quibble, logically, about the clear contradiction between Williams-like "words of the sea" and the early lines asserting that the sea has no words, that the singer cannot sing what she hears in the sea "Since what she sang was uttered word by word."

But the business of the poet is always to convince on other than logical grounds, and Stevens does, raising logical questions to pass beyond logic. The idea of order is not an idea of comprehensibility but a sense of ultimate pattern, in which everything is connected. As in many of Stevens's later visionary poems, the interaction between "voices," sometimes theatrical, of man and the world suddenly gives way to the overwhelming impression of hidden unity, more easily evoked than described by the poet. In the end of "Key West" we see a reference to our beginnings that suggests a familial unity; the sea is our mother, "our origins" her "fragrant portals." But again explanation falls short of the sense of connection. Those portals are also the doors of perception; "dimly starred," like "ghostlier demarcations," suggests the pale radiance of a vision deep and far, that will not yet come quite clear.

In the next year "Like Decorations in a Nigger Cemetery" (Does its unfortunate title reduce the critical attention it receives?) would attempt another preliminary sketch of that vision, inviting Walt Whitman to preside over its meditations. For Stevens, Whitman plays the role of biblical prophet, enacting the identity with the world that is the end of mystic vision and — Stevens seems more and more convinced — the only beginning of the deepest poems. Appropriately Whitman chants a union with flow and change and death; like the singer of "Key West" he chants by a southern sunset shore; like the "savage source" in the ring of men in "Sunday Morning" he is the sun, but he is passing, dying, as the dew upon his feet shall manifest:

> In the far South the sun of autumn is passing,
> Like Walt Whitman walking along a ruddy shore.
> He is singing and chanting the things that are part of him,
> The worlds that were and will be, death and day.
> Nothing is final, he chants. No man shall see the end.
> His beard is of fire and his staff is a leaping flame.
>
> (*Palm,* 102)

Like the singer's at Key West, Whitman's relation to his landscape is not entirely clear; perhaps, singing, he can only see the world he makes. But he is luminous, mysteriously aflame, apparently more sure of the ultimate order than Stevens will ever be. Even in *Notes toward a Supreme Fiction,* he can never fully explain the faith in connection between man and landscape which makes belief in the validity of the supreme fiction possible.

And though the later Stevens will feel a definite connection, a unity, he will always describe it cautiously, in terms that carefully preserve the honest sense of mystery and doubt associated with any deep spiritual truth.

> We feel the obscurity of an order, a whole,
> A knowledge, that which arranged the rendezvous,
> Within its vital boundary, in the mind.
> We say God and the imagination are one . . .
> How high that highest candle lights the dark.
>
> (*Palm,* 368)

Increasingly as Stevens nears the end of his poetry there emerges a basic opposition between the rage to explain and the desire to envision that which can never be explained, which is conceptually nothing, for "Poetry is a search for the inexplicable" (*OP,* 173). *Notes* remains largely a poem of explanation, "Owl" and *Ordinary Evening* largely poems of vision; "Key West" is torn and almost broken between the two. For all Stevens's apparently logical ambitions as a philosophical poet, his real desire is to write "pure poetry," which he finally defines (in 1951) as "both mystical and irrational" (*OP,* 222). His poetry reveals a basic disinclination to think consistently on a logical plane that Joseph Riddel finds evinced in his prose: "Reading Stevens' prose, one is struck by how much philosophy he has read and how little he has tried to understand."[47] In his increasingly obscure late long poems, Stevens accepts his own fundamental tendency to leave the philosophical for the visionary.

The two modes are not really distinct, but ultimately the poem that partakes more of the visionary becomes a fuller reality, lights far more of the sky. The critics who have so far been drawn to the late Stevens seem, perhaps like those attracted by the obscurities of Eliot in the forties, attracted more by the prospect of rational complexity than by the hope of vision. So the developed arguments of *Notes* have been thoroughly explicated and celebrated, and *Ordinary Evening* has been looked upon with less favor. Its form is rational investigation, but it constantly leaps from reasoning into difficult vision, with an abrupt sureness that Stevens developed only after *Notes.* Now Bloom, one critic never completely fettered by the rational, asserts that *Notes, Ordinary Evening,* and *The Auroras of Autumn* are "Stevens' three finest poems" and makes an interesting distinction between the first two, one that implies evaluation: "*Notes* is a discovery that is also a confirmation . . . *An Ordinary Evening* is a majestic *performance;* the instrument has been perfected, realities have been accepted and tolerated, and the master for a last time shows the full range of what he is capable of doing."[48]

At times this extraordinary poem seems to do everything that Stevens has done in the past, touch on all his preoccupations, but the upper ends of his range are more emphasized than ever. It becomes clear from the start that the poem's basic paradox — its vision of the most mysterious realities in the most ordinary things — is to be resolved in visionary terms. To begin with, the usual visionary suspicion of "appearances" is articulated, radically new vision is demanded, and Stevens goes on to imagine a drawing of distant visions into the immediacy of the self. It is the mystical experience of plenitude, not emptiness, that is evoked as in Canto II vision breaks the limits of time and space. The result is "perpetual meditation," which leads not to knowledge, since obscurity shadows the experience, but to the love traditionally associated with religious meditation. In a line reminiscent of Eliot, the next canto (III) claims that "The point of vision and desire are the same"; II describes a loving union between visionary and vision. This can be understood primarily in terms of perception, but the terminology requires a mystical interpretation; the particular details suggest the timeless experience of the white light found in "Burnt Norton." Here the experience of illumination is presented only as a supposition, as the poet imagines:

> The far-fire flowing and the dim-coned bells
> Coming together in a sense in which we are poised,
> Without regard to time or where we are,
>
> In the perpetual reference, object
> Of the perpetual meditation, point
> Of the enduring, visionary love,
>
> Obscure, in colors whether of the sun
> Or mind, uncertain in the clearest bells,
> The spirit's speeches, the indefinite,
>
> Confused illuminations and sonorities,
> So much ourselves, we cannot tell apart
> The idea and the bearer-being of the idea.
>
> (*Palm,* 331-32)

Throughout *Ordinary Evening* Stevens's terminology remains religious, frequently biblical. The first canto announces that the subject is "meditation," though the announced form of the meditation ("an and yet, and yet, and yet") involves a constant questioning far from the passive surrender to spiritual experience involved in Eliot's Christian meditation. As the significance of Eliot's meditation can only be described in paradoxes, Stevens's thought functions and develops through revision and a particular form of contradiction: "Disillusion as the last illusion," "a permanence composed of impermanence," or "the metaphysical streets of the physical town." The search described in *Ordinary Evening* is not Eliot's search for God, but for "God in the object itself." For Stevens, no gods but in things, though the mystic creatures he creates to mediate between the human seeker-perceiver and the divine object have a definitely biblical tonality. Reality, for instance, is imagined as "naked Alpha" and opposed to "the hierophant Omega" (*Palm,* 334); put them together in the Bible and they spell God. Or, later, and more specifically biblical, there appears:

> A figure like Ecclesiast,
> Rugged and luminous, chants in the dark
> A text that is an answer, although obscure.
> (*Palm,* 343)

Like all holy writ, *Ordinary Evening* retains its own obscurities, intending as it does to convey more the experience than the theory of vision, more the image than the abstraction. But the locus of vision is clear; immanence is the point; "the physical town" is the place to look for "the metaphysical streets." Even more suggestive of the essence of the mysticism of immanence is "The brilliancy at the central of the earth" (*Palm,* 338), a phrase reminiscent of Williams's "radiant gist" and of what Eliot's "still point of the turning world" means before he introduces the idea of incarnation. As he does in many of the late poems Stevens often, in *Ordinary Evening,* imagines the union of man and landscape in terms of centers and circles (now not reductive or sterile ones as in "Anecdote of the Jar").

There also appears the familiar image of winter emptiness, but never has Stevens presented the nothing that is with a more affirmative sense of nothing as a stage, on the negative way, in the perception of everything. In the end, without any sacrifice of his own questioning perspective, Stevens approximates something like Williams's early clarity and innocence of vision.

> The bareness that appears is an exposing
>
> · · ·
>
> It is a coming on and a coming forth,
> The pines that were fans and fragrances emerge,
> Staked solidly in a gusty grappling with rocks.

> The glass of air becomes an element —
> It was something imagined that has been washed away.
> A clearness has returned. It stands restored.
>
> > (*Palm,* 350)

What Helen Vendler, no proponent of the mystical, finds in this passage is enough to move her to multiple biblical reference: "The poem becomes not only resurrection but beatific vision, as Stevens continues with a variation on St. Paul: no longer are we making rubbings on a glass through which we peer; the whole glass is suddenly transparent."[49]

Vendler's emphasis on "resurrection" here relates to her general conception of *Ordinary Evening* as an old man's sad poem about the impoverishment of age and the imminence of death, a poem that "cannot hope ... to overcome entirely the exhaustion and despair that motivate it."[50] This interpretation humanizes the poem, but rather seriously limits it, and it depends on a misreading of Stevens's fundamental attitude, which is hardly so grim or despairing. In fact the sense of the presence of death in the poem differs comparatively little from the younger Stevens's sense of death in "Sunday Morning." Even in the cantos of "total leaflessness," like the "littering leaves" stanza of "Sunday Morning," there emerges oddly ecstatic feeling. Stevens again reveals a strong emotional pull toward stark and barren vistas, great emptinesses which suggest death as well as the revelation that comes after "The last leaf that is going to fall has fallen" (*Palm,* 350). Death and revelation are linked in Canto XXI, which connects the "Romanza out of the black shepherd's isle" with the "romanza" of "another isle" which lies "close to the senses" and is described in terms Stevens habitually uses for the visions discoverable in ordinary things. He calls it "an isolation / At the center," and he calls it

> The clear. A celestial mode is paramount,
>
> If only in the branches sweeping in the rain:
> The two romanzas, the distant and the near,
> Are a single voice in the boo-ha of the wind.
>
> > (*Palm,* 345)

The world's voice speaks in obscure terms, though "boo-ha" implies, through its nonsense, that those terms somehow involve the usual paradoxical blending of opposites. In an earlier, related passage, Stevens describes "Professor Eucalyptus" in search of his own terms to complete the visionary equation. Here the "reverberation" deep in the real will not become revelation, the word it suggests, until it is properly described.

But the revelation that depends on the words of the poet also depends on
the words of the world, the "essence" outside. Professor Eucalyptus seeks
"the commodious adjective" for the object:

> The description that makes it divinity, still speech
> As it touches the point of reverberation — not grim
> Reality but reality grimly seen
>
> And spoken in paradisal parlance new
> And in any case never grim, the human grim
> That is part of the indifference of the eye
>
> Indifferent to what it sees. The tink-tonk
> Of the rain in the spout is not a substitute.
> It is of the essence not yet well perceived.
>
> (*Palm,* 340)

As *Ordinary Evening* progresses, Stevens's belief that there is an essence
beyond us and that it is perceivable by us emerges more clearly than, say,
in *Notes,* where he can only theorize, in a rather desperate tone, "It is
possible, possible, possible. It must / Be possible." There he is expressing
the hope that he may "discover," not "impose." Again, all emerges from
nothing: "Out of nothing to have come on major weather" (*Palm,* 230).
In *Ordinary Evening* the presence of major weather is certain, for instance in Canto IX where the poet returns with some assurance "To the
real: to the hotel instead of the hymns / That fall upon it out of the wind."
What is desired here is not a supreme fiction, but "the poem of pure
reality." But in that reality there are such depths and such distances that
only a visionary poem will do. Reality includes "the spirit,"

> not merely the visible,
>
> The solid, but the moveable, the moment,
> The coming on of feasts and the habits of saints,
> The pattern of the heavens and high, night air.
>
> (*Palm,* 336-37)

This is "the spirit that we sought" (*Palm,* 97) in "Key West," but in
Ordinary Evening the means of finding its voice is more surely articulated.
The centrally important Canto VIII describes a metaphysical union between the lover of the real and the world with an appropriately physical
metaphor. The visionary love that leads to union is green and "blue, as of
a secret place," as Stevens joins the colors of imagination and reality of
"The Man with the Blue Guitar," and refers to Klee's statement about

"the secret places where original law fosters all evolution . . . the organic center." The metaphor of union involves the most ordinary human action, breathing.

> Our breath is like a desperate element
> That we must calm, the origin of a mother tongue
>
> With which to speak to her, the capable
> In the midst of foreignness, the syllable
> Of recognition, avowal, impassioned cry,
>
> The cry that contains its converse in itself,
> In which looks and feelings mingle and are part
> As a quick answer modifies a question.
>
> *(Palm,* 336)

This union with the mother brings the distances of the real into the intimacy of the physical self; now there is no separation between the "cry" of the world and the cry of the poet, as Stevens imagines a type of union composed of constant interaction, not the simple reception of the traditional visionary. The poet's words are no longer a fiction because they contain the world's words.

Such assurance about the ultimate connections is not constant throughout *Ordinary Evening;* the poem argues with itself, and is occasionally weakened by a drift in its convictions as disturbing as its occasionally too obscure or clumsy passages. But Stevens no more wanted to avoid the former disturbance than Williams wanted to make *Paterson* a neat unit. *Ordinary Evening* is a poem of sometimes discrete meditations, including cantos (like **XXV**) which very much stress the "and yet" structure of the whole, basically questioning affirmations beautifully achieved in earlier cantos. The tension between Stevens's mystic convictions and his constant doubts energizes the poem, drives it onwards, and is consistent with the poem's assertions about "constant change . . . a permanence composed of impermanence" *(Palm,* 337). If, as the poem suggests "the theory / Of poetry is the theory of life / As it is, in the intricate evasions of as" *(Palm,* 349), vision must replace vision in an endless flow of revision.

But the calmly beautiful final stanzas of the poem demonstrate Stevens's conviction that the changes of the poet's vision make a progression toward a goal never reached but increasingly clearer; expression of the inexpressible, the visionary unity that can only be evoked, not fully explained. To suggest this progession, Stevens not only describes increasing subtlety in capturing the voice of the world — "the less legible meanings of sounds"

— but also transforms the "colors of the mind" of the explicitly mystical Canto II into colors never naturally seen by mind or eye, colors ordinarily nothing to us. The infrareds and ultraviolets are suggested by "the little reds / Not often realized" and "the spectrum of violet." Further, the "far-fire flowing" of Canto II reappears as a visionary fire flowing in water: "fire-foams in the motions of the sea."

> These are the edgings and inchings of final form,
> The swarming activities of the formulae
> Of statement, directly and indirectly getting at,
>
> Like an evening evoking the spectrum of violet,
> A philosopher practicing scales on his piano,
> A woman writing a note and tearing it up.
>
> It is not in the premise that reality
> Is a solid. It may be a shade that traverses
> A dust, a force that traverses a shade.
>
> (*Palm*, 351)

Stevens retains his indefiniteness to the end, but the end is still resounding. As in the passage about breath he grounded a conception of mystical union in a metaphor of physical interaction, here he links a visionary insight to the theoretical leaps of contemporary physics. Reality now seems less and less a solid, more a dust of increasingly smaller particles traversed and unified by forces we are only beginning to see clearly. In that sense physical interaction between discrete bodies, human or not, becomes as mysterious a reality as the metaphysical union between the seer and his world, exchanging voices in increasing intimacy. So it is simply reasonable for Stevens, in his "mystical theology" passage, to imagine reality changing "from substance to subtlety" under the stress of the aesthetic and scientific scrutiny that has newly perceived and shaped the world. No poetry has captured that subtlety better than the poetry of Stevens's last few years, its visions still beyond our understandings.

Three Mythologies

Three poems, three poets, three mythologies; not always have poets felt compelled to articulate so explicitly their theories of the physical and spiritual world, but most of the central poets since Eliot, Williams, and Stevens have followed them in doing so. If it was Eliot who first in this century popularized the idea that the poet must be a philosopher of

sorts, it was Stevens who explained, in "Of Modern Poetry," why. The
poet must be "a metaphysician in the dark" (*Palm,* 174) because the time
of a common belief that every poet could instinctively use is past: "the
theatre was changed / To something else." Or, as *Ordinary Evening* puts
it, "after the neurosis of winter . . . / . . . they blew up / The statue of Jove
among the boomy clouds" (*Palm,* 346), so now the poet must define "a
fresh spiritual" (*Palm,* 339). Even Eliot, temperamentally suited to "the
neurosis of winter," had to engage in a rather calculated act of the mind
to piece together his internal statue of Jove. Restoration can raise more
internal questions than creation, so it should not surprise us that the strain
of his belief shows more than the strain of Stevens's mythology in *Ordinary
Evening,* or Williams's in *Paterson.*

Actually the three fit a single fairly common archetype, involving some
sort of general human purity lost and rediscoverable again only in mystic
flashes. Eliot's Catholicism, with its cycle of Eden, sin, and redemptive
Incarnation leading to private moments of special grace, is the oldest restatement of the pattern. Original sin in Genesis consisted of eating of the
tree of knowledge of good and evil; for Stevens and Williams the Fall
is a fall into knowing of a different sort. For Stevens it involves the loss of
the purity of the first idea in the multiplicity of second ideas dulled by use.
Williams mourns the fall out of something like the Paterson-giant's union
with landscape and place into a state of divorce caused again by dimin-
ished sorts of knowing, as the "Library" section indicates. As Eliot imagines
grace as a return to beginnings more clearly perceived, Stevens and Williams see decreation and the sudden occasional grace of new vision as the
way to radiance. For them, clarity of vision becomes clarity of being.

For all of them, the way to vision is, as Williams writes, "to refine, to
clarify, to intensify that eternal moment in which we alone live" (*SA,* 3).
In the definition of the vital moment great differences appear, to balance
the somewhat reductive sense of similarity among the three created by their
sharing the archetype of the Fall. For Williams the moment expands with
the discovery of the "radiant gist," for Eliot at "the still point" the moment disappears in the white light of eternity, and Stevens's "brilliancy at
the central," though it combines their terms, remains more time-bound
than either. In fact the strongest opposition occurs between Eliot and
Stevens; their extreme philosophical difference appears in evocations of
how the moment is experienced, focused in one conspicuous instance in
their opposed use of the key word "flickering." Eliot's meditation moves
constantly toward the stasis of eternity; because his mysticism finally in-

volves freedom from movement, he tends to imagine movement (and desire the mother of movement) as a negative state of being, though from that negation the higher stasis sometimes comes. His images for human consciousness in a sort of lower vacuum, so clouded it lies outside the constructive darkness of the *via negativa,* tend to involve those particularly twentieth-century ways of moving, trains. The nightmare vision in "Burnt Norton" occurs in a subway station where people experience neither the way up nor the way down:

> Neither plenitude nor vacancy. Only a flicker
> Over the strained time-ridden faces
> Distracted from distraction by distraction.
>
> *(CPP,* 120)

In Canto XII of *Ordinary Evening,* Stevens also seeks the plenitude of the absolute present, "the poem as it is, / Not as it was: part of the reverberation / Of a windy night as it is." The canto enacts a union between the poem and the "words of the world," the poem is "part of the res," and things become thoughts. But the noun Stevens uses to describe the vital, magically present present is "flickering," the word Eliot used to evoke the sterile passage of time:

> The mobile and immobile flickering
> In the area between is and was are leaves,
> Leaves burnished in autumnal burnished trees
>
> And leaves in whirlings in the gutters, whirlings
> Around and away, resembling the presence of thought,
> Resembling the presences of thoughts, as if,
>
> In the end, in the whole psychology, the self,
> The town, the weather, in a casual litter,
> Together, said words of the world are the life of the world.
>
> *(Palm,* 338-39)

Stevens's vision of complete integration, in his usual dying autumnal scene, would bother Eliot not only because of its litter — his subway too is cluttered, by "Men and bits of paper, whirled by the cold wind" — but by its ecstatic acceptance of whirl and flicker. Eliot's mysticism ultimately moves out of time into a perfect realm where the passive soul submits to a still vision; Stevens's mysticism remains in time as it remains on earth. In the realm of "death and day / Nothing is final." Stevens evokes a union characterized by action on both sides, interaction and constant modification of vision as the words of the poet and the words of the world shape and reshape each other in an endless flow of vital energy. Eliot's vision is fulfilled by death and static heaven; Stevens's, though energized by death, remains on the side of life's constant changes.

Williams, with his visions of immersion in the moving flow of the river, naturally shares Stevens's acceptance of time, but he ends by seeing death as destruction more than inspiration, and sexual union provides a more powerful metaphor for him than the metaphors of mystical immersion. As was suggested by *Paterson I*'s depiction of the giants, and by its persistent identification of the Falls with divorce, Williams tends to imagine the union between poet and world in sexual terms. Eliot and Stevens tend to avoid any explicit linkage between sex and mystical union, but they both evolve a general impression of a female principle considered not only as muse but as earth mother, mother of vision, death mother, mother of beauty. For Eliot, naturally, the mother becomes Mary. To her he addresses the prayer for the living and especially the dead that forms the penultimate section of "The Dry Salvages." But she is more strikingly herself, and she inspires more striking poetry, as the oddly dark "Blessed sister, holy mother" of "Ash Wednesday." There she is the "veiled sister" associated with yew trees, the one who presides over the "time of tension between dying and birth," who teaches acceptance, who offers the final static union in death's immersion:

> Teach us to care and not to care
> Teach us to sit still
> Even among these rocks
> Our peace in His will
> And even among these rocks
> Sister, mother
> And spirit of the river, spirit of the sea,
> Suffer me not to be separated.
> (*CPP,* 67)

For Stevens, she is not Mary but one also connected with death, the one of fictive music: "Sister and mother of diviner love, / And of the sisterhood of the living dead" (*Palm,* 82). As Lucy Beckett puts it, "this image, associated for both poets with love and with possible rescue from the sea of desolate reality, suggests again that Eliot and Stevens are closer together in their quest and in their achievements than the division between Christian and non-Christian in most people's minds would lead them to suppose."[51] But for Stevens the reality is not always so desolate. The female force can be a spirit of poetry, or a center of exploratory perception, as she is in "Sunday Morning" or "Key West," but she can also be the object of perception, the earth "Seen as inamorata, of loving fame" in *Ordinary Evening* (*Palm,* 348). In the *Adagia,* Stevens writes, "A poet looks at the world as a man looks at a woman" (*CP,* 165). Or she can be the Great Mother in multiple roles, subjective and objective, like Williams's "Marvellous old queen" in "The Wanderer." It is she who is the eponymous heroine of "The Woman That Had More Babies than That," a poem, like "Key West," about the words of the sea:

> She is not the mother of landscapes but of those
> That question the repetition on the shore
> Listening to the whole sea for a sound.
>
> (*OP,* 82)

Like "Key West" this poem about an ultimate voice cannot tell the source of that voice, cannot explain exactly what combination of human and natural it might be, but the voice, whatever voice it is, is hers. She, more than the "central man," is the bridge between man and world, the supreme fiction, the principle of mystic union.

> She has a supernatural head.
> On her lips familiar words become the words
> Of an elevation, an elixir of the whole.
>
> (*OP,* 83)

But the most elevated mother in all of Stevens forms the vital center of his most exalted poem "The Owl in the Sarcophagus." This ultimate poem of death presents an obscure vision that remains obscure, irreducible to reasoned paraphrase. Stevens's intent is to capture some of the mind's deepest and most distant images, not to attempt explanation, so that much of the poem does not clearly speak to us, though it fully exists for us. Finally the poet imagines death from the other side, abandoning the plain sense of things and "the heaviness of time" for death's eternity, where mysterious creatures "live without our light" (*Palm,* 303). They exist in a realm of mystic circling unity, its distant perfections again evoked by the spectrum of violet:

> Where luminous agitations come to rest,
>
> In an ever-changing, calmest unity,
> The unique composure, harshest streakings joined
> In a vanishing-vanished violet that wraps round.
>
> (*Palm,* 304)

This place is filled with the perfection associated with death thirty-four years earlier in "Sunday Morning" but here perfection involves no violation of nature. The "fulfilling air" of this realm amplifies the earlier poem's line about the "fulfillment" that comes only with death. In both poems the movement of wind across water signals the stasis of death, and in both there appears a female figure "impassioned" by oblivion. By the time of "Owl" she has grown into a rich and apparently supernatural figure of mystery. She inhabits the realms of death along with the more predictable figures of sleep and peace.

> There sleep the brother is the father, too,
> And peace is cousin by a hundred names
> And she that in the syllable between life
>
> And death cries quickly, in a flash of voice,
> Keep you, keep you. I am gone, oh keep you as
> My memory, is the mother of us all,
>
> The earthly mother and the mother of
> The dead.
>
> *(Palm,* 303)

At first Stevens seems to imagine a literal afterlife, if only the eternity of a moment, doing what he warned against in "Sunday Morning," devising in death's bosom "Our earthly mothers waiting, sleeplessly." But this apparently transcendent vision reveals the deepest immanence as it becomes clear that the characters of "Owl" exist in the mind's depths, "less place than thought of place." Peace, for instance, is "an immaculate personage in nothingness":

> formed
> Out of our lives to keep us in our death,
>
> To watch us in the summer of Cyclops
> Underground, a king as candle by our beds
> In a robe that is our glory as he guards.
>
> *(Palm,* 305)

The elegant sonorities of these lines — the uniquely complex alternation between anapestic and iambic lines, the alliteration that further stresses the final stressed syllables — create a rolling rhythm suggestive of the chants of ritual. The poem celebrates more than it explains.

But its mysteries remain in the human realm of immanence, its holy guardians not the denizens of paradise, but creatures "formed / Out of our lives." The conception of the human, not supernatural, origin of the figure of peace is deepened by the imagery of immersion, which suggests the unconscious as well as the realms of classical myth. Even more clearly does the sister and mother become an archetypal being, finally closer to Jung's anima than to Eliot's heavenly Mary. Jung defines the archetype not as a symbol hidden in the mind but as a center of numinous power only reflected in external symbols, like this creature who stands "tall in self not symbol, quick / And potent, an influence felt instead of seen." Also the anima is a principle of discovery, a door into the unconscious and unknown; "both [anima and animus] represent *functions* which filter the contents of the collective unconscious through to the conscious mind. . . . They themselves are factors transcending consciousness and beyond the reach of perception and volition."[52] What Stevens imagines has something of the same quality, though she is not so far beyond reach, and remains mother as well as anima, "inner thing."

> She held men closely with discovery
>
>   · · ·
>
> It was not her look but a knowledge that she had.
> She was a self that knew, an inner thing,
> Subtler than look's declaiming, although she moved
>
> With a sad spendor, beyond artifice,
> Impassioned by the knowledge that she had,
> There on the edges of oblivion.
>
>   (*Palm*, 306)

Too literally Jungian a reading of this passage would blur it, since of course the edge Stevens imagines here is the edge of death, not that other unknown, the unconscious. But Stevens's deliberately archetypal tone interestingly anticipates the more specifically psychological modes of other poets like Roethke who were, even before "Owl" was written in 1947, carrying Stevens's mystical explorations into new and more viscerally inner arenas, areas often ruled by an archetypal female touched by death, combining qualities of anima and Great Mother.

Stevens ends "Owl" with a brief meditation on the mind's creation of such archetypes as these "monsters" of "the mythology of modern death":

> The children of a desire that is the will,
> Even of death, the beings of the mind
> In the light-bound space of the mind, the floreate flare . . .
> It is a child that sings itself to sleep,

> The mind, among the creatures that it makes,
> The people, those by which it lives and dies.
>
> (*Palm,* 306)

In its insistence on the solipsism of this particular vision this passage seems to represent the side of Stevens habitually suspicious of his own hopes for ultimate penetration to the real. But the imagery of sleep suggests the possibility of a new awakening, something the elder Stevens would touch on more than once in his few years after *Ordinary Evening.* Another late anima poem, "The Sail of Ulysses," uses a similar image to describe another mythic creature discovered within the self, "the sibyl of the self / The self as sibyl" (*Palm,* 392). She is created by "need," which she finds "At the exactest central of the earth." Ulysses describes this central being in words that suggest imminent awakening; she is "A woman looking down the road / A child asleep in its own life." The awakening will create an ultimate connection, the connection of "Key West" somewhat clarified, as the sibyl within attains "By right of knowing, another plane," and reaches the "englistered woman," the sibyl without:

> "A part of the inhuman more,
> The still inhuman more, and yet
> An inhuman of our features, known
> And unknown, inhuman for a little while,
> Inhuman for a little, lesser time."
>
> (*Palm,* 393)

As they are less poets of the Mother than Stevens, Eliot and Williams seem finally less poets of mystical vision, though they search intensely for mystical union. Eliot's apocalypse involves not so much vision as a welcome and purifying destruction by fire, fulfilling ancient prophecy but carrying no new revelation; Williams's fire of decreation leads only sporadically and uncertainly to new creation. Stevens's apocalyptic vision becomes more definite, though never quite specific, and his sense of imminent revelation increases in the poets who will follow him, from Roethke to Merwin. By the time Stevens wrote "Sail" in 1954, Eliot's long dominance over American poetic consciousness was diminishing, and poets like Roethke and Bly, consciously though not always successfully working against Eliot, were discovering new mythologies of their own, involving death, mysticism, and the Mother. These visions, often surrealist, further out but also deeper in, rooted in exploration of the unconscious, would finally derive from Stevens more than the two other ancestors. Roethke, who often *sounds* more like Eliot or Williams, ultimately says of Stevens, "Brother, he's our Father."[53] Though his sense of the possibility of the mystical apprehension of plain things still lies beyond us, Stevens was the poet who most clearly anticipated the direction and predicted the nature of the new American surrealism and the new myths, "the mythology of modern death." In "Sail" he suggests an ultimate though perhaps unachievable vision, "A life beyond this present knowing," which he also describes as "A freedom at last from the mystical, / The beginning of a final order." Near the end Stevens redreams the spiritual utopia of "Sunday Morning" where the chant of nature and men made whole comes "Out of their blood, returning to the sky." In "Sail" this vision involves "future man / And future place," when man is one with his world's reality, "And Eden conceived on Morningside." The magic real, beyond the brief temporal limits of mystical experience, will be the dream and aim of many poets to follow, as they strive not only to mysticism but through mysticism to a condition of final simplicity beyond the turmoil of enlightenment. The mysterious simplicities of the very late Stevens will influence their oracular style as his myth of a visionary real will touch their imagery.

> The ancient symbols will be nothing then.
> We shall have gone beyond the symbols
> To that which they symbolized, away
> From the rumors of the speech-full domes,
> To the chatter that is then the true legend,
> Like glitter ascended into fire.

NOTES

1. Wallace Stevens, "Sunday Morning," in *The Palm at the End of the Mind* (New York: Knopf, 1971), p. 7. Subsequent quotations will be identified in the text, by *Palm*.

2. Wallace Stevens, "Adagia," in *Opus Posthumous* (New York: Knopf, 1966), p. 17. Hereafter, *OP*.

3. Walt Whitman, *Complete Poetry and Selected Prose,* ed. James Miller (Boston: Houghton Mifflin, 1959), p. 184.

4. The term is used, for instance, by Michael Benamou, in "Wallace Stevens and the Symbolist Imagination," in *The Act of the Mind,* ed. J. Hillis Miller and Roy Harvey Pearce (Baltimore: Johns Hopkins Univ. Press, 1965), p. 94. And by Joseph Riddel in his "Walt Whitman and Wallace Stevens," *Wallace Stevens,* ed. Marie Boroff (Englewood Cliffs, N.J.: Prentice Hall, 1963), p. 33.

5. In William Carlos Williams, *Autobiography* (New York: Random House, 1951), he opposes it to poetry based on "the local conditions" (p. 141) and claims, unconvincingly, "it had set me back twenty years" (p. 174). When these

remarks are discussed by critics, his reference to Eliot's "genius" (p. 146) is too often ignored. His respect for Eliot may be ambivalent, but it is also conspicuous.

6. To William Van O'Connor, Apr. 1950, in *The Letters of Wallace Stevens,* ed. Holly Stevens (New York: Knopf, 1966), p. 677.

7. T. S. Eliot, *The Complete Poems and Plays 1909-1950* (New York: Harcourt, Brace, 1952), p. 138. Hereafter *CPP.*

8. William Carlos Williams, *Paterson* (New York: New Directions, 1958), p. 77. Hereafter *P.*

9. Federico Garcia Lorca, "The Duende: Theory and Divertissement," *Poet in New York,* trans. Ben Belitt (New York: Grove, 1955), p. 164.

10. Lorca, "Duende," pp. 162, 163.

11. Wallace Stevens, "The Relations between Poetry and Painting," in *The Necessary Angel* (New York: Random House, 1951), pp. 173-74.

12. William Carlos Williams, *Spring and All* (Dijon: Contact, 123), p. 26. Hereafter, *SA.*

13. Williams, *Autobiography,* p. 390.

14. T. S. Eliot, *The Use of Poetry and the Use of Criticism* (Cambridge: Harvard Univ. Press, 1933), p. 133.

15. John Lynen, *The Design of the Present* (New Haven: Yale Univ. Press, 1969), p. 434.

16. T. S. Eliot, "Shakespeare and the Stoicism of Seneca," in *Selected Essays* (New York: Harcourt, Brace, 1950). pp. 117-18.

17. George Bornstein, *Transformations of Romanticism in Yeats, Eliot and Stevens* (Chicago: Univ. of Chicago Press, 1976), pp. 155-56.

18. J. Hillis Miller, *Poets of Reality* (Cambridge: Harvard Univ. Press, 1965), p. 180.

19. David Davie, "T. S. Eliot: The End of an Era," in *T. S. Eliot: Four Quartets,* ed. Bernard Bergonzi (London: Aurora, 1970), p. 162.

20. Stephen Spender, *Eliot* (Glasgow: Fontana, 1975), p. 18.

21. Northrup Frye, *T. S. Eliot* (New York: Capricorn, 1972), p. 78.

22. David Ward, *T. S. Eliot between Two Worlds* (London: Routledge and Kegan Paul, 1973), p. 267.

23. Randall Jarrell, Introduction to *Selected Poems* (New York: New Directions, 1969), pp. xii, xvi.

24. Joseph Bennett, "The Lyre and the Sledgehammer," in *William Carlos Williams,* ed. Charles Tomlinson (Hammondsworth, Middlesex: Penguin, 1972), p. 181.

25. Joel Conarroe, *William Carlos Williams' Paterson* (Philadelphia: Univ. of Pennsylvania Press, 1970), p. 91.

26. Nathan Scott, *The Wild Prayer of Longing* (New Haven: Yale Univ. Press, 1971), pp. 78-79.

27. Ekbert Faas, "Robert Bly," *Boundary 2,* 4 (Spring 1976), 721. Faas goes on to spend some time worrying about whether Williams achieved these aims (Bly says not), whether any Western poet can, and — always an underlying question — whether "mystical" is the right word after all.

28. Miller, *Poets of Reality,* pp. 2, 291.

29. William Carlos Williams, *Selected Letters,* ed. John C. Thirlwall (New York: McDowell, Obolensky, 1957), p. 147.

30. Tomlinson, *Williams,* p. 204.

31. Robert Lowell, *"Paterson,* Book II," in Tomlinson, *Williams,* p. 165.

32. Conarroe, *Williams' Paterson,* p. 4.

33. William Carlos Williams, *Collected Earlier Poems* (Norfolk, Conn.: New Directions, 1951), p. 4. Hereafter, *CEP.*

34. Miller, *Poets of Reality,* pp. 291, 288.

35. James Joyce, *Stephen Hero* (Norfolk, Conn.: New Directions, 1944), p. 213.

36. William Carlos Williams, "Midas: A Proposal for a Magazine," in *Selected Essays of William Carlos Williams* (New York: Random House, 1954), p. 242.

37. Miller, *Poets of Reality,* p. 311.

38. William Carlos Williams, *Collected Later Poems* (Norfolk, Conn.: New Directions, 1950), p. 172.

39. Glauco Cambon, *The Inclusive Flame* (Bloomington: Indiana Univ. Press, 1963), p. 201.

40. *The Cloud of Unknowing,* ed. Phyllis Hodgson, Early English Text Society, No. 218 (London: Oxford Univ. Press, 1944), p. 122.

41. Martin Heidegger, "What Is Metaphysics?" in *Existence and Being* (London: Vision Press, 1949), pp. 363, 377.

42. Miller, *Poets of Reality,* p. 277.

43. Ralph Mills, "Wallace Stevens: The Image of the Rock," in Boroff, *Wallace Stevens,* p. 99.

44. Edward Kessler, *Images of Wallace Stevens* (New Brunswick, N.J.: Rutgers Univ. Press, 1972), p. 35.

45. Adelaide Kirby Morris, *Wallace Stevens, Imagination and Faith* (Princeton: Princeton Univ. Press, 1974), p. 5. The "pigeon" = "indwelling dove" equation appears on p. 87.

46. Harold Bloom, *Wallace Stevens: The Poems of Our Climate* (Ithaca: Cornell Univ. Press, 1977), p. 93.

47. Joseph Riddel, *The Clairvoyant Eye* (Baton Rouge: Louisiana State Univ. Press, 1965), p. 270.

48. Bloom, *Wallace Stevens,* pp. 253-54. Though he refuses to "judge among them" he makes perhaps his strongest argument for *Auroras.*

49. Helen Vendler, *On Extended Wings* (Cambridge: Harvard Univ. Press, 1969), p. 296.

50. Vendler, *Extended Wings,* p. 269.

51. Lucy Beckett, *Wallace Stevens* (London: Cambridge Univ. Press, 1974), p. 92.

52. C. G. Jung, "Aion," in *Psyche and Symbol,* ed. Violet S. de Lazlo (Garden City, N.Y.: Doubleday, 1958), p. 19.

53. Theodore Roethke, "A Rouse for Stevens," in *Collected Poems* (Garden City, N.Y.: Doubleday, 1966), p. 266.

2

The Ocean Gods
of Robert Lowell

Whatever tribute Roethke would ultimately pay Stevens, it was the persistent voice of Eliot that rang most dramatically in the ears of poets starting out in the forties. If "Sunday Morning" and "The Red Wheelbarrow" were well known then, Stevens and Williams in general were less clearly in view. When Lowell's poetry found publication in the early forties, critics tended to regard him as Eliot's apparent heir, though his poetic tone (and even his theology) were conspicuously his own. Less sure of his poetic voice than Lowell, Roethke would fall into imitation of Eliot more often than he wished. But if they are both in odd ways Eliot's descendants, they hardly seem brothers in poetry. Lowell himself has insisted on their differences (though "we share . . . the exultant moment, the blazing out" of epiphany),[1] and at least one critic has used the two poets to typify the opposition between Christian mystical poets, like Donne and Eliot, and romantic mystics like Wordsworth and Stevens. The Christian mystic postulates a distinction between nature and "supernature," while the romantic experiences a merging; Lowell "is a poet of distinctions and definitions, not a poet trying to merge with nature."[2]

Like many earlier summaries of Eliot's sense of the world, this description of Lowell owes more to the abstractions of theology than to his actual poetry. There is more of Roethke in Lowell than meets the ear. When he wrote of Roethke, "The black stump of your hand / just touched the waters under the earth," especially when he revised the final line to read "touched the waters of the offing" (*N*, 22), he could have been describing his own poetic territory. "Offing," which specifically means the ocean water visible from the land, may in fact more accurately describe Lowell's world than Roethke's river realm. At any rate it is always in watery places that both poets indulge their preoccupation with death, often death in the context of the mother. And if all this is, as Harold Bloom calls the shore poem, merely the stuff of the romantic tradition, the two poets' fish and reptile poems are not; they form a unique connection. Roethke more often imagines becoming such creatures, but Lowell constantly celebrates immersion in their moist world. As he writes in "For the Union Dead":

> I often sigh still
> for the dark downward and vegetating kingdom
> of the fish and reptile.
>
> (*UD*, 70)[3]

The immediate tragedy of that poem is the destruction of the downward kingdom, source of evolution in the past and ecological vitality in the present, by "yellow dinosaur steamshovels," mechanical reptiles which parody the natural. Such destruction, in "Union Dead," leads to a vision of apocalypse.

The preoccupation with apocalypse — which was to become almost a cultural commonplace before Lowell's death — was not something he shared with Roethke, but it was clearly an inheritance from Eliot. As usual Lowell shares the abstract idea with Eliot, but not particular words and images; the apocalyptic visions they actually see differ radically. Eliot imagines fire or desert ("This is the dead land / This is the cactus land," *CPP*, 57) and describes it in a tone of flat liturgical repetition. Lowell depicts more flood than fire ("When the whale's viscera go and the roll / Of its corruption overruns this world," *LW*, 12) in a style that ebbs and flows with violent energy. Lowell's mode tends to imply greater ambivalence about the nature and source of divine energy, the energy behind apocalypse considered as revelation as well as apocalypse considered as general death. He imagines transcendence and a transcendent deity somewhat less than Eliot, and depicts mystical immersion in a physical flow a good deal more.

The earthly mergings characteristic of romantic mysticism appear in the Catholic Lowell's *Lord Weary's Castle* as well as his post-Catholic *Notebook,* his first significant collection of poetry and one of his last. Particular attention to these two collections, separated by over two decades, will indicate how much remains constant in the developing poet's vision, how much Lowell remained preoccupied with the same large questions, often examined through the same developing images. Always, water dominates, and in *Notebook* the underlying imagery of flow fits the mystical sense of immersion. For instance *Notebook's* version of the dark night of the soul poem "Night Sweat" ends by defining death in terms suggestive of ultimate union with the downward kindom. As the salt waters of the body emerge, "the downward glide / and bias of existing wrings us dry — / one universe, one body" (*N,* 175-76). But similar imagery causes conflict in *Lord Weary,* as the theoretically transcendent mysticism of "The Quaker Graveyard at Nantucket" and other poems finds actual definition in a vision of immersion in water and this world, the poet less "upward angel" than "downward fish"; Lowell's articulation of the traditional human desire for transcendence becomes oddly contradictory. In *Notebook* Lowell remembers his youth in a line that suggests more the mysticism of union than "distinctions and definitions": "whatever object I looked at I became" (*N,* 212). "Quaker Graveyard," if we can see its putatively Catholic theology in the right light, bears this statement out.

ii

Perhaps the point, as it must be with Eliot, is to de-emphasize the doctrinal protestations and look at the experience of the poems. Lowell would not remain technically Catholic for long, but the strange intensity of his religious passion in *Lord Weary* implies another similarity with Eliot that is more basic than religion, though hardly separable from it. Lowell achieves what Eliot apparently desired, a virtual late medieval apprehension of the world. More successfully than Eliot, he feels his way into the medieval brain without wholly losing his own time. This in part explains his oddly dark mysticism, his fascination with death and the negative way, in general his sensibility apocalyptic both in its openness to revelation and its awareness of imminent doom. That combination — an interest in mysticism and a preoccupation with apocalypse — is not unique among contemporary poets; in more cases than Lowell's the habits of mind of medieval Catholicism provide an interesting starting point for approach to the poet. The modern lyric seldom sounds medieval, as Lowell's (given the linguistic changes) sometimes do, but it often voices concerns that would strike, say, an eighteenth-century rationalist as oddly archaic. This is not simply because medievalists have rediscovered the past — though doubtless the existence of an easily available text of *The Cloud of Unknowing* had something to do with the shape of Roethke's mysticism — but because we are in some ways repeating it. Comparisons between the fourteenth and twentieth conturies must begin with humble apologies for simplifying both, but one or two similarities are evident. For instance, the expectation of Doomsday that was a matter of faith for the medieval Catholic has now, in another time of radical cultural upsets, become a statistical probability for everyone. What God has not yet wrought, human science can. In 1945 the dream of apocalypse found a new basis in history.

Lowell has more literally a medieval mind than most of his contemporaries, not only because of his preoccupation with the new forms of doom, but because of his adoption of a deliberate facsimile of medieval Catholicism. His critics have occasionally noticed his medieval orientation: Randall Jarrell's early and basic essay points out that Lowell's "present contains the past — especially Rome, the late Middle Ages, and a couple of centuries of New England — as an operative skeleton just under the skin."[4] But those centuries of New England have tended to obscure the fourteenth in the collective critical imagination. And most Lowell critics apparently imagine that the apocalyptic sensibility, along with most other spiritual excesses, is properly characteristic of Protestantism. So Marius Bewley finds in *Lord Weary* "a head-on collision between the Catholic tradition and an Apocalyptic Protestant sensibility,"[5] and John Crich expresses the same sense of conflict of worlds: "many of Lowell's lines give one the frisson of being at a revival meeting in a great medieval cathedral."[6] Such observations imply contradictions in Lowell's poetry that are not really there. They come from a mistaken idealization of what went on in (or just outside) medieval cathedrals, in fact including scenes wilder and more primitive than revival meetings.

Critics in the fifties and early sixties tended to speak of "the Catholic tradition" and "great medieval cathedrals" in excessively reverent tones, apparently unaware of the unromantic but fascinating understanding of the late medieval vision that had been available since the twenties, when Huizinga wrote the still authoritative *Waning of the Middle Ages*. He depicts a life which was emotionally extreme in strangely erratic ways, "violent and high-strung,"[7] obsessed with death and the last things, fond of images of rotting bodies (or of display of the bodies themselves), and deeply pessimistic about cultural and spiritual possibilities. Other commentators echo his dark vision: "the great theocratic age of England sends down the centuries an image of a society dominated by Death the Skeleton."[8] So in discussing Lowell, the Catholic confronting death and ambivalent about salvation, it is hardly necessary to imagine him as some improbable mix of glowering Jonathan Edwards and cheerful Chaucer. Edwards, himself the product of a crude and violent society, would doubtless have found preachers to his taste in medieval England; hellfire is no more a Calvinist invention than the apocalypse. Huizinga records "a popular belief, current towards the end of the fourteenth century [that] no one, since the beginning of the great Western schism, had entered Paradise."[9] Not only was "dethis wither-clench"[10] an ordinary reality in that perilous time, but beginning in 1348 England (like the rest of Europe) experienced an extraordinary foretaste of the apocalypse, when the Black Death danced off with about a third of the population.

For Lowell, moneyed urban American, the times were not so conspicuously perilous, but a more sudden collective death is featured in *Lord Weary;* the hellfire military bombing of civilian populations first (after Dresden) moved Lowell to his antiwar position, then (especially after Hiroshima) became one of the prime metaphors for his apocalyptic vision. "The Literary Life, a Scrapbook" is Lowell's retrospective description of himself as mad prophet, with blazing eye and "too much live hair":

> In those days, if I pressed an ear to the earth,
> I heard the bass growl of Hiroshima. No!
>
> (*N*, 86)

Perhaps he is thinking of his early poem "The Slough of Despond," which, with its visceral evocation of struggle through a swamp, suggests medieval imagery more than Bunyan's comparatively abstract allegory. It ends with an End:

> Now how the weary waters swell, —
> The tree is down in blood!
> All the bats of Babel flap about
> The rising sun of hell.
>
> (*LW*, 62)

The last line of the poem, published before Hiroshima, was probably intended to suggest the Japanese flag; to us now, ironically, it directly evokes the atomic sun-flash that ended that flag's imperial war. The image reverberates prophetically, evoking a greater terror than Lowell could then have known.

Despite its faith in imminent apocalypse, the medieval imagination was of course not consistently grim; Chaucer was not unique in his humor, or his celebrations of sexual love or the coming of spring. But even in medieval celebration, there persists an undertone of cynicism, as in the famous "Somer is i-comen in," with its refrain about the infamously symbolic "cuckow": "Bulluc sterteth, bukke uerteth, — / Myrie syng cuckow."[11]

The medieval lyric may occasionally seem childish (modernized, that buck is farting) but seldom carefree, or innocent. The world is too dark for that, and man too sinful; even children are touched by Adam's stain. One of the medieval poems Lowell chooses for *Imitations,* a book of the dead throughout, is "Children" by Der Wilde (vagabond) Alexander, a thirteenth-century German. The poem juxtaposes scenes of children playing in a meadow, and suddenly threatened by a snake, with a semi-biblical scene of virgins carelessly caught in the outer darkness when "the king slammed his diningroom door" (*I,* 7). Stripped naked, the virgins are left awaiting some unspecified horror. The imagery delicately suggests the Fall, always resonant with sexual guilt, then the Fall's terrible consequences, for children, virgins, all, the innocent caught in the general guilt.

Having gained a sort of domination through Adam's sin, the devil seems to control the medieval world and the flesh. So it is only right that life is grim and the grave — or the numerous charnel houses — close. As Huizinga puts it, "the true future is the Last Judgement, and that is near at hand."[12] Death is the only cure for the sinful man: "Of felthe thou art isowe — /weirmes mete thou suelt ben."[13] Likewise, the apocalypse provides the only answer to the evil of mankind, even though the Last Judgment may begin an eternity of fiery suffering for most individuals. In the Doomsday plays of the Corpus Christi cycles, the saved (and the audience) laugh as the damned are dragged away to hell, sometimes by slapstick-comedy devils. Presumably the laughter reflects not only the pleasures of vengeance, but pleasure in the absolute triumph of divine justice. This is precisely the pleasure Lowell finds, horrifying some critics, in imagining the apocalyptic destruction of devil-dominated Boston in "A Plane Tree by the Water." His misanthropy runs closest to medieval misanthropy, which was more universal and so finally more sympathetic than the misanthropy of Calvin and Jonathan Edwards, because it presupposes no elect, no dependable way out for the prophet and his company.

The medieval way out, not predictable for an elect but possible for anyone, is a transcendence of human nature through invocation of a magic power, a force like a totem animal or a pagan divinity, earthly but touched by heaven. The force is Mary. Lowell's "In Memory of Arthur Winslow," which initially reveals that grim medieval satisfaction in the death of the sinner, ends with an indicative reversal: "A Prayer for My Grandfather to Our Lady" suggests that Mary's mantle of grace may cover any sinner. In *Imitations* also, the preoccupation with death (especially with dead women) that marks Lowell's selection of poems by the late medieval

Francois Villon is to some extent balanced by hope in the Virgin. "Villon's Epitaph" (from *Ballade des pendus*) contains the usual rotting corpses, swollen by life, then death:

> the flesh we overfed hangs here,
> our carrion rots through skin and shirt,
> and we, the bones, have changed to dirt.
> Do not laugh at our misery:
> pray God to save your souls and ours!
>
> *(I, 23)*

The actual prayer that appears in the poem is addressed not to God the Father but to his human-divine son, invoking his fully human mother: "Oh Child of Mary, pity us." Even those of simple faith in the Middle Ages had the sense to pray more to the suffering and merciful Mary than to that awesome Creature who came to her as a dove, or a Word, but who comes to generally sinful men with the justice they deserve.

Not only is Mary, as Lowell's version of Villon's poem puts it, "my house and fortress / against the ills and sorrows / of life" (*I*, 21), she also functions as the prime antagonist of death and the devil, from here to apocalypse:

> To hire that ber the heuene kyng,
> of merci hire bysoghte:
> Ledy, preye thi Sone for ous
> that vs duere bohte,
> ant shild vs from the lothe hous
> that to the fend is wrohte.[14]

Predictably, her place in Lowell's apocalyptic scenario is conspicuous, as in "The Dead in Europe," a rather limited invocation poem. Partly because of its incessant punning on Mary's name, it sounds like something out of *Land of Unlikeness*, Lowell's mannered and often manic first collection. But its central plea is clear enough, and very medieval: "When Satan scatters us on Rising-day / O Mother, snatch our bodies from the fire" (*LW*, 68). This is no prayer against the apocalypse, only against hell. Like the medieval lyricists, Lowell often depicts Mary as sharing his eagerness for the End. If she seems then more misanthropic than maternal, we must remember that the medieval apocalypse was the time of triumph for the Son of Mary's body, and for those faithful to him. In "As a Plane Tree by the Water" corrupt Boston-Babylon has reduced Mary to a crumbling statue; she lives only in the miracle of Bernadette, and waits only for the "resurrection of the King," when Boston will fall like Jericho, and "The grave / Is open-mouthed and swallowed up in Christ" (*LW*, 47). "Plane Tree" is a more impressive invocation and curse than "The Dead in Europe," though history has undercut its admiring reference to Lourdes, which was, when Lowell wrote, becoming a showplace for the spiritual excess connected with the mid-century cult of Mary. In fact Lourdes became an embarrassment to modern Catholicism because it turned into exactly the sort of gaudy carnival of superstition that many shrines were in the Middle Ages, when religion was not expected to be restrained and tasteful. Mary the miraculous, the totem healer, seems to revert to the archetype of the Great Mother from which she probably derived in the deep history of human mythology; she puts on the Mother's gaudiness with her power.

iii

A more dignified Mary, fascinating even to the unbeliever, forms one mystical center of the confused and violent masterpiece of *Lord Weary*, "The Quaker Graveyard in Nantucket." The confusion revolves around the poem's deity as well as its mysticism. Not only does Lowell use imagery of immersion to serve a theoretically transcendent theology, he also inspires a concomitant doubt about the nature of the deity at the end of the mystic search, sometimes Christ, sometimes a savage ocean god. Recent critics have tended to irritation over this confusion, and the densely allusive surface of the poem is no longer fashionable after Lowell's own *Life Studies,* in a time of what Alan Williamson has unhappily characterized as "current disesteem for *Lord Weary's Castle*."[15] But the voices for the poem are still strong; the poet-critic Robert Hass, whose own fine poetry shows a classical restraint, describes "Quaker Graveyard" as "brilliant," and finds Lowell more "passionately" in the poem than in his later poetry, which is presumably more personal but actually more calculated and "magisterial." The early poem's "brilliance seems neither dictated nor wrought; it is headlong, furious, and casual."[16] Its energy makes up for failings that would ruin the weary later poems. I find it, still, perhaps the most vital of Lowell's major poems, with a power, if not authority, seldom apparent in his recent work. Clearly the poem's vitality exceeds Lowell's ability to control it, but uncontrolled energy can produce explosive results; some of the excitement of "Quaker Graveyard" comes precisely from its excesses, from the chances it takes.

In some of those excesses it becomes the most medieval of Lowell's poems. The boldness, even arbitrariness, of the symbolic imagination that could in one line establish an equation between Moby Dick and Christ directly recalls the medieval figural imagination, which interpreted everything sublunary in terms of the cosmic drama of Creation, Fall, Redemption, and Second Coming. Not only most of the characters in the Old Testament but most of the creatures of this world became symbols, frequently types of Christ. Ironically the figural tradition usually casts the whale in a radically different role from Lowell's. In medieval bestiaries he is a type of the devil, and in the fourteenth-century "Patience" Jonah in the whale's belly is in the guts of hell. What is confusing about Lowell's god-whale is that he has demonic aspects too; in imagining so ambiguous a deity, the implicit theology of "Quaker Graveyard" carries the medieval world view out of the bounds of Catholic orthodoxy.

The poem is medieval not only in its figural boldness and in some aspects of its style (extreme alliteration, the occasional Old English kenning), but in its tendency to depict the major events of man's long history with God as occurring in a timeless present. As in the Corpus Christi nativity plays the angels announcing the birth of Christ appear to fourteenth-century English shepherds, so in "Quaker Graveyard" "the time / When the Lord God formed man from the sea's slime" (*LW*, 14) is still present in the Nantucket wind, like the time of Crucifixion of Christ and whale. Not that time is illusion, but for God and mystic time passes in the white shadow of timelessness; certain enormous events, like the materialization of Christ out of eternity, or the creation or extinction of time, which cannot be held fast in any temporal matrix, remain undiminished by time's distances. Where Lowell departs from the Christian vision of cosmic history, throwing into question the nature of the Power within and behind Christ, is in regarding the redemption of mankind as a continuing act, not completed, and perhaps not destined by the Power that Is.

If medieval poems and sermons frequently give the impression that the devil presides over the earth, medieval Christians (except, of course, numerous Manichean heretics) remained aware that literal belief in such a limitation of the power of God was sinful. In "Quaker Graveyard" the issue is seldom so clear; sometimes the poem's divinity takes the shape of the savage god. The image of the Christ-whale of section V is obscurely related to the "hell-bent deity" of the first section of the poem, a divine sea monster who seems, as Alan Williamson puts it, "a devil (or what is often the same thing, a displaced chthonic or nature-divinity)."[17] Later the central line "Hide, / Our steel, Jonas Messias, in Thy side" (*LW*, 12) seems to cast both Jonah (traditionally) and the whale (not) as Christ. "The introduction of the biblical parallel between Christ's descent into hell and the story of Jonah complicates matters enormously, for it revitalizes the whole infernal aspect of the whale symbolism."[18] But the complexity, due in part to Lowell's practical need to use Jonah as a symbolic link between whale and "Messias," can be resolved in terms offered by the cosmic vision of the poem.

Between the initial Poseidon-like sea monster and the suffering whale-Christ, there appears another deity in the poem's third section, "IS, the whited monster" (*LW*, 10). Though he recalls the vengeful I Am Who Am of the Old Testament, he is the God of no Judaeo-Christian orthodoxy. He lives "in the nowhere," in what for man is nothing ("Ahab's void"), because for man this fierce ocean god is alien, cut off. All the gods of the poem finally blend, but this one is most clearly connected with the indescribable god of section VI, "Our Lady of Walsingham," also defined by negation. Lowell describes the statue of Mary:

> This face, for centuries a memory,
> *Non est species, neque decor,*
> Expressionless, expresses God: it goes
> Past castled Sion. She knows what God knows,
> Not Calvary's Cross nor crib at Bethlehem
> Now, and the world shall come to Walsingham.
>   (*LW*, 13)

Her union with God is the end of the way of unknowing, as the unorthodox Lowell limits God's omniscience, imagining a God too remote from humanity even to remember his own human birth and death as Christ. Mary becomes the model for the mystic (and in the End all men) who to know God must forget all that is human, even death and redemption.

Finally this divinity moves even further away than the Old Testament God: "The Lord survives the rainbow of His Will" (*LW*, 14). This oracular last line of the poem has been variously interpreted, but most critics now read "rainbow" as the traditional figure for God's post-deluge covenant with man.[19] As Randall Jarrell observed long ago, this and the reference to "the rainbow's epitaph" in "Where the Rainbow Ends," "are inexpressibly menacing, since they show the covenant as something that binds only us, as something abrogated merely by the passage of time."[20] The fear is not simply that apocalypse lies ahead — "When the whale's viscera go and the roll / Of its corruption overruns this world" (*LW*, 12)

— but that this apocalypse will mean not the second coming but the final departure of divinity. No "Rising-day" approaches; the poem begins with a clear parody of the resurrection of the body, and warns, evoking still another medieval type of Christ, "ask for no Orphean lute / To pluck life back" (*LW*, 8).

Despite his medieval mind, Lowell is only semi-Catholic. To understand him in orthodox Catholic terms, as Jerome Mazzaro does when he somehow reverses that final line to "suggest a wilful renewal of God's hopeful covenant with man now that World War II has ended,"[21] is to imagine an easy traditional affirmation and misunderstand the poem. Even on the safer grounds of original sin, in both Catholic and Calvinist theologies the root cause of disruption of the natural world as well as human suffering, we cannot simply assume orthodoxy in the poem. This is not just an antiwar but a proto-ecological poem (the first of many that have focused on the destruction of whales) against that human arrogance that claims "dominion over the fishes of the sea" and other beasts. At times it may seem that Lowell postulates original sin or something like it, an original violation of natural relationships, as a cause of violence among men as well as against animals. But "Quaker Graveyard" suggests that natural or even divine violence precedes human violence, that man was born into a world embattled before human sin was possible. Again, the poem's end:

> You could cut the brackish winds with a knife
> Here in Nantucket, and cast up the time
> When the Lord God formed man from the sea's slime
> And breathed into his face the breath of life
> And blue-lung'd combers lumbered to the kill.
> The Lord survives the rainbow of His will.

So man starts out as victim in a primal conflict, and ends up abandoned by God. It hardly seems fair. But, Catholic orthodoxy and the cult of Mary notwithstanding, the real medieval mind never expected fairness.

Though his ethical concerns are conspicuous, fairness is not what Lowell is finally after, either. The most basic mystical experiences involve not ethics but energy, and the poem abounds with that. Like Roethke's its vision is animistic and frequently surrealist, as one form of matter or energy flows into others in ceaseless and often violent transformation. Ocean, ocean's beasts, and land live and change and do battle; with the beach "Sucking the ocean's side," the "high tide / Mutters to its hurt self" (*LW,* 11) as if it were the whale. In the enormously vivid description of the sea in section II, nothing resists the flow for long; in one brief

passage the hunting *Pequod*'s sails become gull wings (through a pun on
the nautical term "beat") which in turn become waves which break into
water and land:

> The Pequod's sea wings, beating landward, fall
> Headlong and break on our Atlantic wall.
>
> (*LW,* 15)

Such rapid transformations move through the whole poem, as men and
their artifacts merge with the world of water, not just metaphorically as
in Roethke's "steady storm of correspondences," but almost literally:

> This is the end of running on the waves;
> We are poured out like water.
>
> (*LW,* 11)

If this human transformation into water means death, it also suggests
essential union with the flow of turbulent energy that is the final reality of
this poem. No such contact can now be achieved in the old meditative
style of the Walsingham pilgrims who come "Like cows to the old shrine"
(*LW,* 13). Here Lowell departs from the medieval vision, though it is a
medieval shrine he describes, using the words of the Catholic medievalist
E. I. Watkins (see his acknowledgment, *LW,* vii). It is a modern eye that
perceives the expressionless crudeness of the shrine's statue of Mary as a
symbol of the distance between divinity and man. Of course that distance
was a medieval problem too, but not an insoluble one. The remoteness of
Lowell's Mary from human concerns echoes the remoteness of the dead
and beatified daughter in *Pearl* from her father's suffering over her death;
at least she takes the trouble to appear to him, but finally human emotion
is irrelevant to heavenly ecstasy. Similarly the *via negativa* of *The Cloud
of Unknowing* (and of the medieval Eliot's *Four Quartets*) depends on a
complete emancipation from human thought; to "know what God knows"
one must forget what man knows, in the words of "Plane Tree," "put out
reason's eyes." If that is possible "the world shall come to Walsingham."

But if there can be any mystical contact in a time of cosmic violence and
divine distance, it cannot come, Lowell suggests, through the transcendence
of the world aspired to in *The Cloud of Unknowing,* but through that
dangerous immersion depicted, often less literally than in Lowell, by
Roethke and the other contemporary poets of death and mysticism. Here
as usual the immersion is described as drowning; the sanctified man must
lose more than his mind to the savage god. As Williamson points out, the
eye imagery of "Quaker Graveyard" connects Mary's "heavy eyelids" with

the drowned sailor's "staring eyes . . . Heavy with sand." Like the eyes of the sea gulls, which "blink their heavy lids / Seaward," these "images convey a sense of inscrutability, of immersion in the heaviness of matter, of inward or remote, as opposed to ordinary, seeing."[22] So there appear intimations of mystic vision not through meditation and transcendence but through descent into the violent storm of matter. Occasionally these intimations are confused or contradicted by Lowell's allusions to a transcendent theology, but in general the poem's vision remains consistent, though incompletely developed. If the traditional God no longer reaches man, perhaps a more primal divinity can be reached by what is no longer man. So the reified body opens to the stream of matter, as death provides the only metaphor extreme enough to embody immersion in the dark waters of primal divinity. Perhaps the ultimate problem with "Quaker Graveyard," from the viewpoint of the living, is that metaphorical death is not enough. The only real answer to Lowell's angry theology may be, not the mystical death of the self imagined by Eliot, but the collective actual death of apocalypse. Something anti-human in the young Lowell — something he moved away from as he moved away from the Church — echoes Eliot's final pleasure in the "purgation" of the London blitz, and anticipates a poetic fascination with death not always spiritually admirable. Sometimes the anticipation is very literal. In the apocalyptic "Where the Rainbow Ends," "I am a red arrow on this graph / Of Revelations" (*LW*, 69). In Sylvia Plath, who would more obsessively explore the death-revelation equation, the line would expand in the final stanzas from "Ariel."

> And I
> Am the arrow,
>
> The dew that flies
> Suicidal, at one with the drive
> Into the red
>
> Eye, the caldron of morning.[23]

"Rainbow" ends with a similarly suicidal ascent to sun-fire, couched in more traditional figures but also, as in "Ariel," ambiguously sexual:

> The victim climbs the altar steps and sings:
> "Hosannah to the lion, lamb, and beast
> Who fans the furnace-face of IS with wings:
> I breathe the ether of my marriage feast."
>
> (*LW*, 69)

In the fire of the savage god, amid the usual cluster of images, "the dove of Jesus" brings apocalyptic wisdom and new life. But first, all men have had to die; the poem begins "I saw the sky descending." ("Chickadee" appears four lines later; wouldn't it be pleasant to think that amid the welter of biblical allusions there appears an intentional echo of Chicken Little's "The sky is falling!")

But death is not always as literal as it is in "Quaker Graveyard" and "Rainbow"; sometimes it functions only as a metaphor for the violent vision that flares up in life. In "Colloquy in Black Rock," full of Roethke-like images of immersion in mud, "the mud-flat detritus of death" spreads everywhere, but the speaker seems to suffer revelation alive. Here there occurs an explicit dramatization of the frequent conflict, in "Quaker Graveyard" and the whole of *Lord Weary's Castle,* between transcendent Christian mysticism and the mysticism of earthy immersion. Christ is traditionally imagined as a bird of prey like Hopkins's windhover, clad in Mary's blue and presumably bringing the word from heaven: "The blue kingfisher dives on you in fire" (*LW,* 5). But the kingfisher comes out of mud, not sky: "In Black Mud / Darts the kingfisher . . . the mud / Flies from hunching wings and beak—." Despite theology, revelation comes from earth, as it comes in "Quaker Graveyard" from deep sea.

iv

The theology would change, as would Lowell's style, though his major preoccupations and his favorite images (usually marine) would remain remarkably consistent through the change. The vision behind "Quaker Graveyard" was not only too dark, but also too earthbound to sustain any transcendent system, Catholic or Protestant. Such theology was contradicted by the imagery, the surest clue to "vision," and finally the imagery won. "Beyond the Alps," Lowell's farewell to the aspirations and excesses of Catholicism, was written in "1950, the year Pius XII defined the dogma of Mary's bodily assumption" (*LS,* 4). Ironically, in view of Lowell's earlier reverence for Mary, the poem subjects that dogma to special ridicule, focused on the act of transcending.

> The lights of science couldn't hold a candle
> to Mary risen — at one miraculous stroke,
> angel-winged, gorgeous as a jungle bird!
> But who believed this? Who could understand?

Appropriately, the pious vision that provoked Lowell's break with the

Church was a treasured medieval belief even though it would not become official doctrine for centuries. Discussing the medieval fascination with "the putrefying corpse," Huizinga explains that "the Assumption of the Holy Virgin exempting her body from earthly corruption was on that account regarded as the most precious of all graces."[24] Lowell's comparatively affectionate mockery makes it seem precious in quite another sense.

Leaving Catholicism behind, Lowell kept faith in the apocalypse, at least in his "public" poetry. "Alps" is somewhat atypical of *Life Studies,* which is in turn somewhat atypical of Lowell, despite its renown; there his concern with death becomes private and familial, with little of the more general resonance that would inform even the personal poetry in *Notebook.* But, as its title poem indicates, *For the Union Dead* recreates the apocalyptic sense in a secular, often political, context. There Lowell persists in an ambivalent fascination with the idea of apocalypse, not now imagined as revelation but as just desert. In "For the Union Dead" his Colonel Shaw, having long ago chosen his own honorable death, "Waits / for the blessed break" (*UD,* 70) that will put his country out of its modern misery.

The poem's images also remind us of an earlier Lowell. Fish abound. As the sudden appearance of Moby Dick in an elegy for a dead sailor seems almost shockingly arbitrary, so it seems very odd to begin an elegy for Civil War dead with an image of the old South Boston Aquarium. But each image, by a series of ingenious and confident metaphorical leaps, is gathered into the organic center of its poem, is in fact revealed as the organic source of the unifying pattern of (fish) imagery. Through a series of subtle connections, Colonel Shaw himself turns fishy. Originally a figure in a bas-relief, he "is as lean / as a compass-needle" and his monument to lost honor "sticks like a fishbone / in the city's throat." As these apparently simple images resonate, "compass-needle" links "fishbone" directly with the figure of the Colonel, and prepares for his transformation into aquatic rider, representative (opposed to the "giant finned cars" which parody fish as the "dinosaur steamshovels" parody reptiles) of the values of the downward kingdom, the Aquarium, the buried past. In the end he seems to partake of the visionary immersion hinted at in "Quaker Graveyard," and the truth he knows is also one of imminent destruction:

> Colonel Shaw
> is riding on his bubble,
> he waits
> for the blessed break.

The blessed break will be apocalyptic, visionary but also violent, with a necessary violence that must follow human destruction of "the dark downward and vegetating kingdom / of fish and reptile," the ground of vitality.[25]

Lowell is strongest, as has long been evident, when he connects his own depths with the movement of history. This happens in another explicitly post-Christian apocalyptic poem, "Waking Early Sunday Morning," which like Stevens's "Sunday Morning" implicitly revolves around the experience of not going to church. Like the Stevens poem it shows some nostalgia for the simplicities of traditional faith, but traditional theology does not here confuse the basic issues, as it often does in *Lord Weary*. Here the apocalypse is more immediately convincing, neither Second Coming nor the almost equally romantic nuclear holocaust feared in "Union Dead," but an ongoing process which has already begun, the terminal erosion of our values and lives. The poem ends with a cosmic vision of the planet as "a ghost / orbiting forever lost" after "our children . . . fall / in small war on the heels of small war" (*NO*, 24). As usual in Lowell there appears no way out of this, only temporary escapes. "O to break loose. All life's grandeur / is something with a girl in summer" offers only a rather pathetic reduction of Matthew Arnold's "Ah, love let us be true / To one another!" — the line Lowell quoted at the opening of "The Mills of the Kavanaughs" — presumably addressed to a woman for more than one season.

But the other "O to break loose" passage comes at the powerful start of the poem, where Lowell imagines a transcendence of human destructiveness through immersion in an animal process which quite literally leads to death and new life, not afterlife but new earthly creation. Appropriately the image that suggests this involves both physical immersion and physical transcendence.

> O to break loose, like the chinook
> salmon jumping up and falling back,
> nosing up to the impossible
> stone and bone-crushing waterfall —
> raw-jawed, weak-fleshed there, stopped by ten
> steps of the roaring ladder, and then
> to clear the top on the last try,
> alive enough to spawn and die.
>
> (*NO*, 15)

In "Waking Early" an undefined God is even more remote than in

"Quaker Graveyard": "Each day, He shines through darker glass" (*NO*, 19). And man's habitual bloodshed is recorded with a more helpless resignation: "Only man thinning out his kind / sounds through the Sabbath noon" (*NO*, 23). But in this salmon passage Lowell can at least envision an alternative to human and divine failure, an animal union with the violent flow of being which answers death not through fantasies about heaven and hell but through what has always answered death, life. Philip Cooper may be too ingenious when he sees the "ten / steps of the roaring ladder" as a reference, via Eliot, to the ten stairs of John of the Cross, but he is right to see non-transcendental mysticism in the passage, and even to emphasize its suggestion of sexuality.[26] Lowell's links between sex, death, and mystical immersion in the world of matter will grow more pervasive in *Notebook* and *The Dolphin*. "Waking Early" embodies the final stage of the transition between the mysticism of *Lord Weary*, implicitly imminent despite its transcendent orthodoxy, and the explicitly earth-bound mysticism of *Notebook*.

V

Notebook 1967-1968, and the cluster of books that eventually superseded it, have provided serious problems of evaluation for most sympathetic Lowell critics.[27] Sometimes it seems that as Lowell's vision becomes more mature, which for him means more balanced and fatalistically accepting, his poetry suffers — in *Union Dead* and afterwards — from more frequent failures of energy. Originally in a posture of struggle with theology, or philosophy, or self, Lowell seemed energized by unresolved internal conflict, as well as conflict with the sinning world. In *Lord Weary* this produced strengths often inextricable from poetic weakness or confusion. The later poetry, having mastered conflict, often loses force; sometimes the mature Lowell seems the weary lord of a poetic territory conquered at too great a loss. It is not until *Day by Day*, published in the year of his death, that Lowell will recover much of his old force, partly because he returns to the type of accounts of personal struggle — with mother, lovers, madness — that energized *Life Studies*. As its title warns us, *Day by Day* is in part an extension of the resolutely mundane poetry of *Notebook*, and its poems are at times equally random and disconnected. But at best it recaptures Lowell's old scope and intensity.

Despite *Notebook*'s failures it too offers sporadic riches, poetic riches surprisingly traditional for such an open form of poetry. What emerges most definitely is not the sense of the poet's daily life and thought, but a larger concept of existence — or at least a consistent set of preoccupations — expressed through movements of the poet's mind remarkably similar to those of the much younger, God-crazed Lowell. There is the same swirl of personal, political, historical, and mystical perspectives, the same flow from one context to another. Correspondingly, despite obvious changes in verbal style, there appears the same almost surrealist leaping from one image to another. Often the images originate in the downward kingdom, which inevitably suggests the unconscious sources of surrealism; whales and immersion in water still predominate. As Alan Williamson has pointed out, the free association in parts of *Notebook* is as close to surrealism and as far from *Life Studies*' "rationalized description of consciousness"[28] as is the flow between conscious and unconscious in *Lord Weary*. Though the uncontrolled energy of *Lord Weary* is radically opposed to the failures of energy in *Notebook* and *Day*, many similarities make these temporal extremes in the line of Lowell's development circle toward each other, enclosing the unities of the poet's mind.

Those unities appear most conspicuously in thematic similarities, despite the theological distance between the young Lowell and the old. He remains one of the party of death, not simply the elegist, but the fatalist who sees that death will overpower life because it lives at life's heart. Death is not simply seen as the termination of individual lives, as in *Life Studies*, though Lowell's *History* is primarily a tissue of individual fates. Rather it is general death, suggestive of the old apocalypse, garbed in secular images but clearly recognizable. Francis Parker's frontispiece for the 1970 *Notebook* sets the tone with a piece of medieval iconography, a skeletal equestrian Death, transported to a girder-modern cityscape. Lowell's poem about this drawing, "Death and the Bridge," carries the old vision of Boston as Hell, the realm of "God's universal capital punishment," death. The slightly flippant, wryly fatalistic tone persists in references to apocalypse in *Day by Day*.

With the wry cynicism and the tendency to deflate his own large visions and formulations, Lowell in *Notebook* and *Day* conveys a sense, still, of a mystical opening to the world. In fact one reviewer described *Notebook 1967-1968*, with a flippancy it often invites, as a collection marked by "a shuttling between the reporter's view and the mystic's, at an erratic pace designed to surprise us into binocular vision."[29] This early response to the book leaves "mystic" undefined, and definition remains a problem. Lowell is no longer a Catholic mystic, even unorthodox, though he continues to play with terms like "God"; nor is his a mysticism of transcendent identification with all humanity, though he is still capable of tossing off a line like "I am Whitman, I am Berkeley . . . all men" (*N,* 168, his ellipsis). His mysticism is more eccentric than that, though it remains traditionally death-oriented. Like Roethke's it involves not only death but intimations of the vital energy of the world whirling in violent storm, the storm the secular mystic must penetrate, usually in the company of a woman. True vision resides in the vortex. As the first poem of *Notebook* puts it, "things whirl / in the chainsaw bite of whatever squares the universe by name and number" (*N,* 21). One depiction of this whirl comes in Parker's drawing for *The Dolphin:* a naked woman spins down into a whirlpool of air or water, apparently shaped by her turning body. Both *Notebook* and *Dolphin* contain several images of such whirling, like the one in "Winds," which mentions a woman caught in "This whirlwind, this delirium of Eros" (*N,* 160).

But the woman in the drawing may as well be drowning as experiencing sexual or visionary ecstasy; her face is spun away from us, unreadable. As Lowell consistently associated mystical experience with death, so in his late poetry he usually writes of sex in the context of death. All three frequently blend together, as sex triangulates the initial connection between death and mysticism. Now revelation comes from human love, not divine. Lowell's women, especially Caroline, are often depicted as deadly fish, but in the realm of their danger there can be illumination, even new life. Once Caroline is described as "a baby killer whale" (*D,* 36), and even in her more customary role as dolphin she can eat men alive, as she does in "Angling."

> I am waiting like an angler with practice and courage;
> the time to cast is now, and the mouth open,
> the huge smile, head and shoulders of the dolphin —
> I am swallowed up alive . . . I am.
>
> (*D,* 55)

In gauging the type of sexual magic operating in this death and rebirth to self, it is helpful to remember (as well as contemporary erotic slang) the traditional symbolic role of the fish, as in Lowell's earlier Christ-fishing poems. "The Drunken Fisherman" in *Lord Weary* caught apocalyptic rainbow trout, bloodied like Christ. In "1968" similar imagery connects an earlier love of Lowell's with death as well as Christ and apocalypse. First Ann Adden becomes "Hammerheaded Shark, / the rainbow Salmon of the world"; then the poem jumps to an image that expands her power even further, as Lowell evokes Pascal's mystical definition of God as a circle with its center everywhere and circumference nowhere.

> We ski-walked the eggshell at the Mittersill,
> Pascal's infinite, perfect, fearful sphere —
> The border nowhere, your center everywhere.
>   (*N,* 148)

Landscape and woman blend into divinity before the contemplative lover. Eternity is near, at the juncture of love and death.

Sometimes, especially in *The Dolphin,* love is seen rather as a force against death, as Lowell slips rather too comfortably into the conventional responses of the older man in the throes of intimacy with a woman young enough to carry his child. But if he tends to be less than compelling on the subject of immortality through love, he is more convincing in his equally traditional images of sexual love as temporary defiant freedom from immortality, a way of breaking loose like the salmon:

> still this is something, something we can both
> take hold of willingly, go smash on, if we will:
> all flesh is grass, and like the flowers in the field;
> no! lips, breasts, eyes, hands, lips, hair.
>   (*N,* 80)

Only one step beyond this is Lowell's elevation of the mystique of sex into mystical revelation, a sense of which is conveyed, again through imagery of the downward kingdom, in "Serpent." Here Lowell dreams himself a snake, a more pleasant and realistic one than in his early visions (for instance the hissing adulterers of "Between the Porch and the Altar"), but still the reptile suggests guilt. "My fall was elsewhere — / how often I made the woman bathe in her waters" (*N,* 99). The ambiguity of "waters" nicely suggests the connection between sex, tears, and birth, but the final images of this wandering meditation emphasize not only guilt but revelation. The context is somewhat unclear, but the phallic and liquid imagery suggests sex as mystic immersion:

> I see me . . . the green hunter leaps from turn to turn,
> a new brass bugle slung on the invisible baldric;
> he is groping for trout in the private river,
> wherever it opens, wherever it happens to open.
>   (*N,* 100)

Still the mystical fisherman, Lowell fishes not in the waters of Christ, but "her waters." In *The Dolphin* and *Day* he frequently describes Caroline in mythic terms that suggest a theology of love, and a time (to take another Lowell line out of context) "when Cupid was still the Christ of love's religion" (*Day*, 21). But more often the woman is the divinity. In "Logan Airport, Boston," Caroline boarding a plane first presents a "limitless prospect on the blue," then ascends to disappear in "consuming fire" (*Day*, 74). Her departure evokes the luminous paradoxes of mystical contact with the supernatural: "I see you, you are hardly there," and

> I cannot touch you —
> your absence is presence,
> the undrinkable blaze
> of the sun on both shores of the airport.

Witness to these illuminations, the poet is "blind with seeing."

A darker but more explicit evocation of Caroline's divinity comes in the final poem of the "Mermaid" sequence, a late sonnet that includes many of the habitual devices and conceptual patterns of the Lowell of *Dolphin*. The older Lowell looks back to the Renaissance roots of the sonnet tradition, as well as to the visions and revisions of the young medievalizing Lowell. The first poem in this brief sonnet sequence describes the mermaid's "conjunction of tail and grace" (*D*, 35); the physical structure imagined by her infatuated lover recalls his earlier description of the drowning sailors in "Quaker Graveyard" as "upward angel, downward fish." But the fourth sonnet casts Caroline in a radically different role by describing her as the largest of the Delphinidae: "I see you as a baby killer whale" (*D*, 36) recalls the dying chthonic divinity of "Quaker." So Caroline enters the final sonnet in the sequence trailing images that define her as both hunter and victim, human and divine; throughout she has presence in both worlds, as dolphins symbolically tend to do. Mammals masquerading as fish, they live in water and air, and they combine the incongruous breasts and tail of the mermaid.

The poem begins, after its deliberately commonplace and colloquial first line, with another symbolic conjunction of worlds, the world of love imagined as the world of the hunt, as a situation of danger. The ancient iambics of the sonnet have often carried such imagery; love tends to appear as a hunt in Wyatt or Sidney, the loved one a hunted animal (though usually one with feet rather than flippers) who may turn hunter in the convolutions of mating. The romance of the hunt is intensified by another

transformation, as flashes of divinity burst intermittently from the loved
one's countenance. With occasional iambic pentameter lines (and even a
conventional combination of allegorical high style and colloquialism that
recalls Sidney) Lowell submerges this old drama in black water:

> One wondered who would see and date you next,
> and grapple for the danger of your hand.
> Will money drown you? Poverty, though now
> in fashion, debases women as much as wealth.
> You use no scent, dab brow and lash with shoeblack,
> willing to face the world without more face.
> I've searched the rough black ocean for you,
> and saw the turbulence drop dead for you,
> always lovely, even for those who had you,
> Rough Slitherer in your grotto of haphazard.
> I lack manhood to finish the fishing trip.
> Glad to escape beguilement and the storm,
> I thank the ocean that hides the fearful mermaid —
> like God, I almost doubt if you exist.
>
>   (*D*, 37)

The casual speculations and mundane description of the initial sestet lull
the reader into a feeling of everydayness effectively shattered by the leap
into allegory in the seventh line. The allegory of the obsessive, dangerous
hunt for the mythic more-than-fish (echoes of Ahab inevitably intrude) introduces the central images: the danger of the quest, drowning, and the
need to grapple with this slithering mystery.

When the ordinary shoeblack-eyed woman of the sestet turns allegorical
mermaid, she also turns divine. Even without the backhanded comparison
in the last line, the final octave creates a theological vision. Creating calm
at the center of the storm, enshrined in a grotto, fearful and mysterious
but perhaps a source of salvation, the loved woman takes on many of the
characteristics attributed to Mary in Lowell's Catholic poetry. But here
is a force both more dangerous and more vitally immediate than the Mary
of "Quaker Graveyard." Her ability to quell the storm shows a Christ-like
power, but "drop dead" implies that such power can be ominous. Then
"Rough Slitherer" suggests something more reptilian, and therefore more
satanic than divine. Like the whale in "Quaker Graveyard," the loved one
has demonic attributes; no wonder Lowell's harpoon has its limp moments: "I lack manhood." What "the fearful mermaid" offers, like the
sirens of another grotto, is "beguilement and the storm," a revelation po-

tentially as violent as Lowell's earlier mystical visions. But she is inescapable; despite the crisis of lover's faith implied by the last line, the poet understands that he must confront her divinity.

Such ambivalent theological references persist throughout the dolphin poems; Caroline is both sweet mother Mary and the dangerous whale. As the Renaissance sonneteers saw their loves as divine, the medieval lyricists often referred to Mary in terms appropriate to sexual love, as in fact Lowell does when in a moment of despair he writes, "The Queen of Heaven, I miss her, / we were divorced" (*Day,* 115). But more often Lowell the more-than-courtly lover elevates his love to a secular divinity existing in the stormy ocean of revelation. This vision intrudes on the most mundane accounts of love; in "Redskin" what begins as a semi-comic meditation on sexual characteristics ("Women looks natural in herself, not man, / equipped with his redemptive bat and balls") suddenly opens into apocalyptic tremors, as the woman at penis's end turns whalish:

> your icy, poorly circulating fingers
> trickle all night from heaven to the skin;
> they will be warm today and we will be warm —
> at wrath-break, when the earth and ocean merge,
> who wants to hold his weapon to the whale?
> (*N,* 152)

It would be unwise to make too much of such free associating sexual apocalyptics, but clearly Lowell's deification of women is done with heart in mouth as well as (occasionally) tongue in cheek. "Europa" also makes the woman an overwhelming deity, reversing the mythic roles by describing "Jupiter, / daring to raise his privates to the Godhead" (*N,* 152). Such imagery, along with Lowell's poems about death as "the Mother" (*N,* 221) and orgasmic death (in "The Duc de Guise" *le petit mort* actually becomes the big sleep), creates an appropriate context for *Notebook*'s impotence poetry. But more significantly it parallels the dark visions of the Mother that were appearing in the poetry of Sylvia Plath and Robert Bly, as intimations of apocalypse spread and gathered in the sixties.

vi

Like the philosophy implied by Roethke's late poetry, Lowell's myth is incompletely formulated, revealed in hints and fragments, less defined though also less contradictory than the myth of *Lord Weary. Note-*

book and *Dolphin* form not a systematic record of mystical exploration, but
an account of the examined life lived in the shadow of death and the
sporadic illuminations of mystical insight. The vision is no longer based
on transcendent aspiration but on "love of the body, the only love man is"
(*N*, 152). *Day by Day* reaffirms this commitment to this world, no other:
"We took our paradise here — / how else love?" (*Day*, 57).

But *Day by Day* is full of the intuition of imminent death, "the shadow
of the crow." As in the medieval vision life is short: "We are things thrown
in the air / alive in flight" (*Day*, 22). And death is especially near for
Lowell personally. Though he was not right, when he wrote "Home," in
predicting his death within six months, he was not far wrong; in retrospect
we must accept his hints and statements as somehow prophetic. Now that
death is closer and more personal than it can have been even in the war
years of *Lord Weary* or *Near the Ocean,* Lowell tends to demythologize it.
Death means the end of life, not the beginning of any revelation: "It's
an illusion that death or technique / can wring the truth from us like
water" (*Day*, 39). Eternity, too, often loses its magic in the cold eye of
the passing Lowell: "we are designed for the moment" (*Day*, 118) suggests no eternal moments, only fleeting ones. When something like an
everlasting now does appear in the culture or in Lowell's life, it tends to
parody the peace of eternity. "Since 1939," the most apocalyptic poem in
the collection, creates a feeling of unpleasant suspension when it describes
"our unfinished revolutionary now" when "everything seems to end and
nothing to begin" (*Day*, 30). Like Sylvia Plath, Lowell also describes his
illness in mockingly theological terms; his deadly detachment from human
emotion establishes *"my little strip of eternity"* (*Day*, 110).

In the end Lowell is less concerned with the mystical stopping of time
than he is with time's inexorable passage: "After fifty, / the clock can't
stop" (*Day*, 22). But visions do not wholly stop either; there is "paradise
here" with the increasingly divine (but apparently less threatening) Caroline, and there is always the past, which "changes more than the present"
(*Day*, 92). "The Day" obscurely celebrates an Edenic past, personal as
well as racial, of revelation ("like lightning on an open field," *Day*, 53)
and cosmic union, for once not *dies irae* but *dies illa:*

> They fly by like a train window:
> flash-in-the-pan moments
> Of the Great Day,
> the *dies illa,*
> when we lived momently

.together forever
in love with our nature —

But this feeling of being together forever with self, with lover, with the
flow of the world, must give way to "the marriage with nothingness,"
really and absolutely nothingness this time.

In *Notebook*, Lowell allows himself more celebration of the Great Day,
the intuition of unities not entirely vanquished by death. The poems that
succeed in this collection frequently have the luminosity of a spiritual
quality perhaps more genuine, certainly less forced to extremes, than that
of *Lord Weary*. Occasionally Lowell articulates the underlying mystical
intuition with unusual directness, as in "Obit," one of many meditations
on death and the final poem of *Notebook*.

> Before the final coming to rest, comes the rest
> of all transcendence in a mode of being, stopping
> all becoming. I'm for and with myself in my otherness,
> in the eternal return of earth's fairer children,
> the lily, the rose, the sun on dusk and brick,
> the loved, the lover, and their fear of life,
> their unconquered flux, insensate oneness, their painful "it
>   was . . ."
> After loving you so much, can I forget
> you for eternity, and have no other choice?
>
> (*N*, 261)

Here the mystical definition of the experience of love, "insensate oneness,"
is explicitly grounded in the larger paradoxes of the earthly mystical vision.
Having outgrown transcendence and becoming, the poet is completely
himself but also other, completed by his identification with the beautiful
things of the world. The answer to his final question is probably "yes,"
but the knowledge of "eternal return" establishes a hopeful resonance.

In its talk of an otherness at the end of becoming, "Obit" is strongly
reminiscent of the Roethke of "North American Sequence," especially this
passage from "The Rose":

> And I stood outside myself,
> Beyond becoming and perishing,
> A something wholly other,
>
>   . . .
>
> And I rejoiced in being what I was:
> In the lilac change, the white reptilian calm.[30]

Some of Lowell's words echo this, but primarily the similarity is one of tone. "Obit" is not a limp poem like *Notebook*'s failures, but a calm one. At their best, both the late Lowell and the late Roethke achieve a calm in the face of death and life seldom evident in their early poetry of furious revelation. Here Lowell finally accepts death as a "coming to rest," purged of the violence that always attended it when it was the locus of *Lord Weary*'s stormy visions. Always the poet of death, Lowell at his richest manages to suggest that from the mystical perspective death is more positively a part of life than it is ordinarily possible to imagine. His final rejection of transcendence allows, even in apocalyptic times, a type of peace based not on heavenly evasion but post-Christian acceptance of the imminence of mortality.

NOTES

1. "Robert Lowell, as Interviewed by Frederick Seidel," *Robert Lowell,* ed. Thomas Parkinson (Englewood Cliffs, N.J.: Prentice-Hall, 1968), p. 31.
2. G. E. Powell, "Robert Lowell and Theodore Roethke: Two Kinds of Knowing," *Southern Review,* n.s. 3 (Jan. 1967), 181.
3. Lowell collections will be identified in the text. Those cited include *Lord Weary's Castle* (New York: Harcourt, Brace, 1946), hereafter *LW; Life Studies/For the Union Dead* (New York: Noonday, 1964), *LS* and *UD; Imitations* (New York: Farrar, Strauss, and Giroux, 1961), *I; Near the Ocean* (Farrar, 1967), *NO; Notebook,* revised and expanded edition (Farrar, 1970), *N; The Dolphin* (Farrar, 1973), *D; History* (Farrar, 1973), *H; Day by Day* (Farrar, 1977), *Day.*
4. Randall Jarrell, "From the Kingdom of Necessity," in Parkinson, *Robert Lowell,* p. 43.
5. Marius Bewley, *The Complex Fate* (London: Chatto and Windus, 1952), pp. 159-60.
6. John Crich, *Robert Lowell* (Edinburgh: Oliver & Boyd, 1974), pp. 24-25.
7. Johan Huizinga, *The Waning of the Middle Ages* (London: Lowe and Brydone, 1924), p. 6.
8. Brian Stone, "Poems of Sin and Death," in *Medieval English Verse* (London: Penguin, 1964), p. 60.
9. Huizinga, *Waning of Middle Ages,* p. 21.
10. *English Lyrics of the XIIIth Century,* ed. Carleton Brown (London: Oxford Univ. Press, 1932), p. 15.
11. *XIIIth Century,* p. 13.
12. Huizinga, *Waning of Middle Ages,* p. 28.
13. *XIIIth Century,* p. 16.
14. *Religious Lyrics of the XIVth Century,* ed. Carleton Brown, 2d ed., rev. G. V. Smithers (London: Oxford Univ. Press, 1965), p. 11.

15. Alan Williamson, *Pity the Monsters* (New Haven: Yale Univ. Press, 1974), p. 8. Perhaps a measure of Lowell's importance is the number of opposed types of critics that have been drawn to write and disagree about him; the differences begin to suggest the amount of disagreement about *Hamlet*. (I intend no direct comparison.) All of his collections have their strong and logical attackers and strong and logical defenders, though *Life Studies* — which caused the greatest resistance when it appeared — seems now accepted as a major success by almost everyone. For the rest, critics like Williamson are most taken by the romantic, rather impassioned, mystical and prophetic Lowell; as Williamson himself suggests, his contemporary opposite is the Irish Patrick Cosgrave, who in *The Public Poetry of Robert Lowell* (London: Victor Gollancz, 1970) praises the classical, restrained, somewhat distant Lowell, inferior to Samuel Johnson but definitely interesting. My own sympathies lie with Williamson, and I find myself irritated, perhaps enjoyably, by Cosgrave, an Yvor Winters man who has inherited not only many of the master's rules (e.g., romantic poetry is generally unfortunate, mysticism is not really a possible subject for poetry, etc.) but also something of his authoritarian tone.

16. Robert Hass, "Lowell's Graveyard," *Salmagundi*, 37 (Spring 1977), 60.

17. Williamson, *Pity the Monsters*, p. 38.

18. Williamson, *Pity the Monsters*, p. 42.

19. Some either resist or seem unaware of the reference. Cosgrave, who predictably dislikes the poem, claims without explanation that "rainbow" stands for "appearance" (*Public Poetry*, p. 99).

20. Jarrell, "Kingdom of Necessity," in Parkinson, *Robert Lowell*, p. 42.

21. Jerome Mazzaro, *The Poetic Themes of Robert Lowell* (Ann Arbor: Univ. of Michigan Press, 1965), p. 54. Mazzaro also pays excessive attention to Quaker orthodoxy, and so emphasizes the "pacifism" of the Quakers of the poem, again turning a symbolic pattern upside down. In "Death by Water: The Winslow Elegies of Robert Lowell," *ELH*, 34 (1967), 128-29, Marjorie Perloff presents the textual evidence to show the limitations of Mazzaro's interpretation. But Perloff suggests, I think incorrectly, that the poem is almost exclusively concerned with "man-made" violence.

22. Williamson, *Pity the Monsters*, p. 40.

23. Sylvia Plath, "Ariel," *Ariel* (New York: Harper & Row, 1966), p. 27.

24. Huizinga, *Waning of Middle Ages*, p. 128.

25. It is essential to realize the vitality of this kingdom in Lowell's imagination, and the consequences of its destruction. Like "Quaker Graveyard," "Union Dead" has conspicuous ecological implications. Several critics seem to ignore this; for instance Charles Altieri speaks of Lowell's being tempted to "submit to the utter prose of 'the dark, downward and vegetating kingdom.' Again pure prose is linked with Freud's *thanatos*" (*Enlarging the Temple* [Lewisburg, Pa.: Bucknell Univ. Press, 1979], p. 70). Again Altieri sees a pathological death wish in the dark imagery of the negative way of immersion. In fact in "Union Dead" this imagery (like Roethke's vegetable imagery) carries vitality and a primal energy suggested by "vegetating." It is in any case hardly "pure prose."

26. Philip Cooper, *The Autobiographical Myth of Robert Lowell* (Chapel

Hill: Univ. of North Carolina Press, 1970), pp. 121, 108. Interestingly, Cooper refers to Erich Auerbach's "Figura," an analysis of typological thinking, mostly medieval, to explain the way Lowell makes connections, even in this very contemporary poem.

27. Any critic more interested in poetry than bibliography must begin with some irritation at having to plough through so many versions of the same poems, often insignificantly or unwisely revised. For this reason and simply for convenience, I have tried to use the versions in the 1970 expanded *Notebook* whenever possible.

28. Williamson, *Pity the Monsters,* pp. 8, 10.

29. William Meredith, "Looking Back," *New York Times Book Review,* June 15, 1969, p. 1.

30. Theodore Roethke, *Collected Poems* (Garden City, N.Y.: Doubleday, 1966), p. 205.

3

Roethke, Water Father

"All night you wallowed through my sleep," Lowell writes in "For Theodore Roethke":

> You honored nature,
>
> helpless, elemental creature.
> The black stump of your hand
> Just touched the waters under the earth
> and left them quickened with your name . . .
>
> Now, you honor the mother.[1]

This image, drawn sharp out of the liquid darkness of sleep, celebrates not similarity but kinship. Here the cool "neoclassical" Lowell of *Near the Ocean* properly discovers the romantic Roethke in his unconscious if not in his poetic style. In the references to "water under the earth" and "the mother," Lowell fixes not only his own thematic connections with Roethke but links with several other poets of immanence. Beneath radical differences in verbal approach, Lowell and Roethke shared a mystical ambivalence. In different ways they were torn between a traditional God and an often medieval transcendence, and the secular (and often sexual) mysticism of immersion in earth water. Their particular forms of tension between orthodox transcendence and a new immanence recall Eliot before them, as they anticipate the tensions of the later poets of immanence like Sylvia Plath and Robert Bly. Roethke in particular seems a pivot between generations, an inheritor but also a source.

There remains little question that he was a rather muddled source, as he was a sometimes graceless heir. His uneven greatness was marked by consistent exploration of new poetic territory undercut by consistent re-

treat into the security of old and often secondhand styles. As an explorer
of the abstract ideas of mysticism he was often Lowell's "helpless, elemental
creature," but his visions, elemental in fact, became a dominant influence
on many recent oracular poets. Finally it seems impossible to understand
Roethke outside the current of poetic influence. (It comes as no surprise
that at least two of the monographs on Roethke are dominated by consideration of influence.)[2] Attention to his affinities with Plath and Bly,
in particular, clarifies some of his mystical complexities, as well as demon-
strating the continuing importance of his voice in contemporary poetry.
These two poets who most obviously echo Roethke are themselves now
centers of influence. Though they tend to occupy narrow and deep
poetic areas, like Roethke returning (often with mixed results) almost
obsessively to one subject or cluster of subjects, they function as models
for a wide variety of younger poets.[3]

   Even on the immediate level of similarity of sound, tone, it is evident
that analysis of Roethke's mysticism logically involves, may in fact depend
on, the study of poetic correspondences. These are created not only by
conscious imitation but by the flow of those underground waters (a constant image in mystic poetry) that seems to connect poets occupied with
unearthing the deepest visions. What is initially striking, though, is not the
deep convergences but the shallow ones, exact similarities in phrase, word,
image. Robert Bly may not have read Roethke's "Journey to the Interior"
when he wrote "Some petals are living on the other side of the light" in
"Looking at Some Flowers,"[4] but the line (and Bly's constant use of "the
body" instead of "the mind") echoes Roethke's

> And I roam elsewhere, my body thinking,
> Turning toward the other side of light
>
> . . .
>
> Neither forward nor backward,
> Unperplexed, in a place leading nowhere.[5]

Roethke himself here echoes T. S. Eliot's "Neither from nor towards; at
the still point, there the dance is, / But neither arrest nor movement . . . ,"[6]
which in turn derives from the mystical paradoxes of John of the Cross.
As Roethke says, "Eliot said, 'Bad poets imitate; good poets steal.' "[7] Eliot
steals with a light heart, but Bly is more concerned about the originality
of the deep image. Especially because he prefers Spanish to domestic
surrealism, such obvious borrowing from Roethke would make him un-
easy. The evidence suggests not conscious imitation here, but convergence.

Either way, Roethke's work abounds in lines that anticipate Bly's animistic surrealism, like "I want the old rage, the lash of primordial milk" (*CP*, 56) or "A dead mouth sings under an old tree" (*CP*, 59). The point is not that Bly imitated, but that he operates, at his best, in a poetic world sought and often found by Roethke.

Like Bly, Plath shows the effect of other voices, in her case especially Lowell's, as well as the influence of Roethke. In *The Colossus* she is a constant and superb imitator; her early poetry perfectly supports Roethke's argument, in "How to Write like Someone Else," that conscious imitation is no aesthetic sin if it produces real poetry. Significantly it was Roethke whom Plath was imitating while she was moving from the experimentation of *Colossus* to the mature style of *Ariel*. Somehow Roethke's distinctive tone helped to release Plath's, and his influence continues to be evident not simply in her traditional poetry, but throughout *Ariel*. In "Ariel" itself there appears a conspicuously literal connection. "The child's cry / Melts in the wall"[8] seems almost a direct reference to "the ghost of some great howl / Dead in a wall" (*CP*, 79), an image frequent in Roethke, and usually occurring in a sexual as well as mystical context, as Plath's image does in "Ariel."

But even with Plath, the most conscious imitator of Roethke, the salient fact is not simply the fact of imitation. Plath was predisposed to Roethke's influence because she participated in certain aspects of his visionary consciousness before ever reading his poetry. Ted Hughes has written that in 1959 she was reading "closely and sympathetically for the first time — Roethke's poems";[9] what she must have experienced then was a sense not so much of discovery as of recognition. Perhaps she felt what James Dickey later wrote in *Poetry* about his response to *The Lost Son*: "I had the illusion (perhaps not an illusion) that I had been looking for the book all my life without knowing it."[10] Indeed Plath's affinities with Roethke are retrospectively evident in poems she wrote before contact with Roethke's work, if Hughes's chronology is accurate. He places her "Disquieting Muses" in late 1957 or early 1958, but the deep image of three leathery ladies which dominates that poem is strangely suggestive of Roethke's "Frau Bauman, Frau Schmidt, and Frau Schwartze," surely not its source. Evidently the two poets are dipping almost together into Jung's dream pool.

After Plath actually read Roethke, the sounds of their lines would be similar too; her characteristic assonance and child's play with the language echoes the idiom he developed in *Praise to the End!* In the Roethkean rebirth sequence "Poem for a Birthday," her use of phrases like "mummy's stomach," "dead heads," and "rusty tusks" (all in a single stanza in "Who") or names like "Mumblepaws, teary and sorry," and "Fido Little-soul, the bowel's familiar"[11] seem like a very literal response to Roethke's expressed preference for internal rhyme and Mother Goose.[12] His sounds released her visions as she, like him, created a poetic sequence about death and rebirth, one of the first in which the myth of her mature poetry would be mysteriously revealed.

ii

Upon examination, the convergences deepen. But Roethke is not simply a source of influence; he is also influenced, one who struggled through the complexities of Eliot's negative way to his own vision of immanence. To specify the type of revelation sought by Roethke and those who followed, we must follow the steady stream of correspondences back into the past. Despite Roethke's professed admiration for Williams, and his late identification of Stevens as "our father," it was obviously Eliot with whom he had to contend. Partly the simple fact of Eliot's reputation dictated this, for both Lowell and Roethke. Lowell, though stylistically unique, operated in Eliot's sphere of influence at the beginning of his time as a poet; Roethke showed Eliot's obtrusive presence in his mind and ear more toward the end. Over the barriers of conflicting mythologies, Eliot spoke more directly to Roethke. For Lowell he was a more abstract force, an earlier prophet of the old religion and the new apocalypse, a precedent-setting maker of symbols in need of footnotes. For Roethke he was a voice to be resisted, but it turned out to be Roethke who wrote lines Eliot might have written, as Lowell found the permutations of his own distinct style.

Roethke tended, of course, not only to alter but to reverse Eliot; his intimacy with the older poet begins in conflict. As Karl Malkoff points out, "the points of direct contact with Eliot seem to indicate . . . a direct opposition rather than imitation."[13] Not only are there, almost always, clear differences in dogma and mystical approaches, but Roethke deliberately resists Eliot's constant tendency to abstract, for instance to make journeys and destinations into transcendent symbols. To Eliot's "Old men ought to be explorers" (*CPP*, 129), Roethke responds, in "North American Sequence": "Old men should be explorers? / I'll be an Indian. / Ogalala? / Iroquois" (*CP*, 189). Each successive line alters the definition of the term, making it more specific, reducing its symbolic content by grounding it in a more immediate reality.

Eliot's habitual movement away from images toward general conclusions, his tendency to define mystical experience in terms of pure logic and the paradoxes that pull logic apart, is consistent with a theology that ends in a burning away of the world and the flesh, as well as the word. As Kenneth Burke indicates in his basic essay "The Vegetal Radicalism of Theodore Roethke," what results is largely a poetry of abstract terms.[14] But the abstraction involves not only the "essayistic" language Burke mentions; when the things and places of the world do enter Eliot's poetry, they also come in the service of abstractions, eventually abstracted themselves. For instance the river that opens "The Dry Salvages" exists to introduce ideas more than experiences. We seldom feel our way to understanding in the *Quartets;* the understanding is announced, and if it is announced with sufficient precision the feeling follows, but it is seldom, like Roethke's, a feeling for things. The rivers of his "North American Sequence" appear in such physical detail that we wonder at times whether physical description may be the primary aim of the poetry. In a way it is; Roethke wants us to feel the objects in his poem as he leads us to the visionary revelations he will not always articulate, or cannot articulate, lacking Eliot's precision with abstract language.

Roethke's uneasiness with stylistic abstraction corresponds to his resistance — at times ambiguous — to the orthodoxies of transcendence. But if some critics have understood "North American Sequence" too much in terms of the orthodox mystical opposition between spirit and matter, Roethke's imprecision is at least partly at fault. Hugh Staples, in his explication of the sequence, writes that Roethke begins by "mapping the strategies whereby man can at least partly escape the life of the senses."[15] But, in "The Longing," "How to transcend this sensual emptiness?" (*CP*, 187) may be more a complaint against emptiness than against sensual existence. Actually Roethke seeks an interpenetration of sense and spirit, "A body with the motion of a soul" (*CP*, 188), the body fully itself with its own spiritual grace, immersed in the flow of being where "All finite things reveal infinitude" (*CP*, 201). Like Bly Roethke is a very earthbound mystical poet, a champion of the senses. So for Eliot's traditional *via negativa* — "In order to arrive at what you do not know / You must go by a way which is the way of ignorance" (*CPP*, 127) — Roethke, though he had also read John of the Cross, substitutes a more instinctive animal unknowing. In "Her Becoming" the meditating old woman says of her awakening, "My breath grew less. I listened like a beast" (*CP*, 166). Final knowledge is to be sensed, not spiritually intuited. In describing the end of the mystical progression in "The Far Field," Roethke suggests something like Eliot's "still point of the turning world," but he does it with a realistic physical image: "I have come to a still, but not a deep center, / A point outside the glittering current" (*CP*, 201).

However Roethke is not always so firm in his resistance to that transcendence which implies separation from the physical. If Roethke's influence somehow liberated Plath's most distinctive voice, Eliot's influence on Roethke, always poetically less sure of himself than Plath, may not have been so beneficial. As Roethke's characteristically aggressive-defensive references to "Tiresome Tom, the Cautious Cardinal" suggest, Eliot may have intruded more into his consciousness than he liked.[16] Often, especially in his last poems, he seems to accept the tenets of Eliot's otherworldly mysticism, and the concomitant tendency toward abstraction, the use of purely symbolic terms to define a non-sensual state. But his abstractions lack the subtle force of Eliot's. In *Four Quartets* the image of the rose, though it lacks any real sensual referent, concentrates the force of the entire poem. When Roethke, in "The Rose," writes of "the rose in the sea-wind," the image not only derives too obviously from Eliot's symbol, it seems contrived and flat, an oddly dead flower in the otherwise beautifully vital sequence.

Roethke's problems with abstract language and symbolism cannot, of course, all be blamed on Eliot, who is too often held personally responsible for most of the academic excesses of modern American poetry. Roethke's tendency toward abstraction and symbolic overload appears even in the Williams-influenced flower poems in *The Lost Son*, for instance, "Cuttings (later)," which unlike the first "Cuttings" loses its rich suggestiveness when Roethke plugs it into theological concepts both trite and vague. Even without Eliot's influence, the temptation toward such vitiating symbolism would probably have increased as Roethke's theological imagination became more complex, more pedantic. But he remained, partly because of Williams's influence, at least theoretically aware of the dangers of abstraction. As in 1944 he had praised Williams's fight against "the conceptual boys," so in a 1958 letter to Williams he wrote, "I took your advice about making my old lady less lit'ry."[17]

Of course Roethke could on occasion be successfully "conceptual" himself; no poet can avoid the abstraction of concepts, if only because words are abstracted from things. Even "The Red Wheelbarrow," that archetypal imagist poem, begins with a highly abstract phrase. And some of Roethke's finest lines can be as abstract as anything in Eliot. But in general he is less comfortable with logical argument than Eliot; this weakness is especially evident in his last poetry, in the highly "lit'ry" and artificial language of the "metaphysical" poems in *The Far Field*. Since his abstractions tend to accompany an uncharacteristic yearning for transcendence from the world of sense, it is hardly surprising to find Eliot's ultimate abstraction, "God," in much of this poetry. Not the metaphorical and immanent God who appears (once) in "Meditations," this seems to be the God of orthodox Christianity, distant from man and that vale of tears from which only sacrificial suffering can provide escape. One of the devotional cliches in "The Marrow" reads "From me to Thee's a long and terrible way" (*CP*, 246). "Infirmity," a somewhat grimmer reformulation of the idea behind George Herbert's "The Pulley," occasionally sounds like an earlier, more vital Roethke, but is on the whole shot through with an otherworldliness which does not affirm but denies the life of this world. "The eternal seeks, and finds, the temporal" (*CP*, 244) is a radically different proposition from "All finite things reveal infinitude" in "The Far Field," especially since "the eternal" or "divinity" is to be achieved "By dying inward, like an aging tree." Now unhappily preoccupied with actual death, Roethke turns away from life. And with a poetic logic that seems inevitable his language, unsuited for transcendence, suffers its own loss of sensual vitality.

Even the celebrated "In a Dark Time," which confronts the difficulties of transcendence more directly than most of these poems, is finally marred, as Stanley Kunitz has suggested, by the final lines' "clinically analytic tone, which jars on the ear that has been listening to a stranger music."[18]

> Which I is *I?*
> A fallen man, I climb out of my fear.
> The mind enters itself, and God the mind,
> And one is One, free in the tearing wind.
> (*CP*, 239)

This is the first appearance of "God" in the poem, and as usual he brings unconvincing comfort and mystical cliches. The divinity that an earlier Roethke worshipped could not be so described as a God who, separate at first, deigns to visit the mind and the world only after they have suffered sufficiently. Despite his history of mental illness Roethke was not usually so much a manic-depressive as John of the Cross, who experiences first the absolute despair of the dark night, then the sudden absolute ecstasy of union. For Roethke, that dichotomy, like the opposition between "God" and the world, could not convincingly be sustained. The imagery of his strongest mystical poetry, poetry not of transcendence but of physical immersion, combined darkness and light in a union ambiguously beautiful, and it was that dark revelation which Roethke's descendants had begun to explore even as he himself was falling away from its difficult truths.

iii

When Roethke's last poems fail it is often because they seek — through abstract statement and the cliches of orthodoxy — too easy a resolution of his ambivalence toward the mystical experience. But the final abstractions of "In a Dark Time" are partly redeemed by its deeply suggestive closing phrase, "free in the tearing wind" (*CP*, 239). In the *New World Writing* symposium on the poem Roethke explains this passage by saying that the mystical experience is "no moment in the rose garden," that "God himself, in his most supreme manifestation, risks being maimed, if not destroyed."[19] The mystic who participates in the divine consciousness must suffer the same danger. This unusually contemporary version of mysticism, in which dark night and ecstatic vision are simultaneous, inextricable from each other, recalls the final stage of the "ten-day voyage" into madness and vision taken by Jesse Watkins in R. D. Laing's *Politics of Experience*. Watkins participates in the being of a god evolved from humans who "was a madman . . . because he's got this enormous load . . . he was the one [transcendent man] that was taking it all at that moment."[20] Unlike the traditional transcendent mystic the contemporary visionary often locates himself not in an imagined area of cosmic peace, but at the center of the storm, Roethke's "steady storm of correspondences," but also the storm of irreducible particulars. The locus of vision is the point of maximum tension among all the world's dualities, the breaking point of a pattern constantly threatening to fly apart. The turmoil that characterizes this aspect of Roethke's vision anticipates Bly's plunge "Into the wilds of the universe" (*Light*, 21), or Plath's electroshock revelation in "Mystic"; she is "Used, utterly, in the sun's conflagrations."[21]

The conception of revelation as an experience of being pressured or storm-battered or devoured comes naturally from that visionary experience which — like Watkins's or Lowell's or Roethke's or Plath's — is often inextricable from experiences of psychological disintegration. In Plath loss of self, no matter how illuminating, is inevitably perceived as damaging; mystic ecstasy is cut with terror. Roethke confronted terrors too, as even the most romantic interpretation of his visions must concede. But Roethke achieves a peace momentarily beyond terror, and throughout his poetry there appears a separation between the poems dominated by psychic struggle and the poems of peaceful union. A few key poems, including some from the central sequences, can be used to illuminate this separation and to suggest some of the general characteristics of all of Roethke's mystical states, dark or light. The peaceful explorations include "A Field of Light," "Her Becoming" (the center of "Meditations of an Old Woman") and "The Far Field" (from "North American Sequence"). The darker visions, more abstract and in general more characteristic of the later poetry, include "The Pure Fury," "The Abyss," and "In a Dark Time."

The tortured poems tend to consist of meditations on the dark night of the soul and the psyche, abstractions about experience recollected. The poems of union tend to begin with landscape, a field or a body of water suggestive of "the eternal" or "infinity"; in this terrain the poet first appears passively, in the dark night of the body, then rises to transforming union with the flow of his surroundings, usually after a period of meditation on death. Following confrontation with the darkness of the eternal, stasis gives way to ecstasy, union characterized by motion as well as immersion. Water dominates. Even meadows become shores, as Roethke seeks the point where worlds meet, "in a country half-land, half-water" (*CP,* 201), or "where sea and fresh water meet" (*CP,* 202).

The poems of deep struggle and dark night tend to avoid specifically rendered landscape in favor of general statements about phases of consciousness. Fragments of landscape may be used as metaphor, as in "In a Dark Time," but internal conflict tends to exclude the world, or to make it foe: in "The Abyss" "the world invades me again" (*CP,* 220) in a grim parody of mystical plenitude which prompts a plea for help from the poet who became the master of plenitude: "Be with me, Whitman, maker of catalogues" (*CP,* 220). When the world becomes enemy, a desperate transcendence is the only response, as the poet looks up and out to "the Lord God." As peace within the self leads to immersion in the world, psychic terror leads in the opposite direction.[22] As "The Pure Fury" puts it, "I live near the abyss" (*CP,* 134), and "The Abyss" makes it clear that this chasm leads not down into earth, but up to "the slippery cold heights," ultimately up to something reminiscent of the young Lowell's terrible deity: "A terrible violence of creation, / A flash into the burning heart of the abominable" (*CP*, 221).

But Roethke constantly alternates between terrible revelation and the vision of peaceful immanent union. To the extent that his philosophy is formulated, it involves a combination of these near-opposites. Even "The Abyss," despite its desperate turn to the Lord, ends as a poem of "luminous stillness." "I have merged, like the bird, with the bright air" (*CP*, 22) implies a combination of animal immersion and transcendence, a condition, finally, of peace. Correspondingly the predominantly peaceful poems seldom exclude the dark night and the storms of fearful revelation. And if death is not confronted directly, as in the dead animals of "The Far Field," it invariably shadows the adjectives, often quite bluntly, as in "dead water" and the constant darks. The darkness often gives way to chaos, "the wild disordered language of the natural heart" (*CP*, 166), before the peaceful flow to integration. The field poems move to a different spirit, but their calm wholeness includes enough tumult to harden both poetry and implied theology to radiance.

In these ultimately peaceful poems, which depict a comparatively visceral experience, the way out of the self is as often the way into beasts, who tend to represent ways of knowing uncorrupted by rational consciousness, as it is into the landscape. Often speaker and landscape meet at the animal level. After the old woman describes herself as listening "like a beast" in "Her Becoming," she goes on to ask, "Was it the stones I heard?" (*CP*, 166). As her knowing recedes to the instinctual, the land rises to animation, sounding out of silence to meet her in the territory of beasts somewhere between human and inanimate. In "A Field of Light," as the speaker falls into a "watery drowse," the "dead water" comes alive. Here animism verges on surrealism, though the eye that "tilted" in the water may simply be attached to a fish, and a change in perspective can explain "A stone's shape / Became a clam" (*CP*, 62). Later the stone acquires skin which the poet kisses to begin his movement from stasis toward flowing union; the ground for this ritual affection has been established by the initial animation.

The animated landscape moves even more dramatically to meet the human descending to unknowing. The downward kingdom moves upward not only in changes of shape and sound, but in the production of a "voice" that responds to the speaking being of the body, itself surreally animated: "From the folds of my skin, I sing." In response there comes a voice perhaps inside, perhaps outside: "A voice keeps rising in my early sleep, / A muffled voice, a low sweet watery noise" (*CP,* 165). Perhaps because the old woman who recounts this later speaks of dreaming "a jauntier principle of order," this voice suggests the mysterious voice that dominates "The Idea of Order at Key West," part human, part sea sound, promising some curious union. A voice which more definitely comes "from outside" (as Stevens would say of a sound also heard on the edge of sleep in "Not Ideas about the Thing but the Thing Itself") speaks to the drowsing poet in "The Rose," which immediately follows the searching "The Far Field":

> I return to the twittering of swallows above water,
> And that sound, that single sound,
> When the mind remembers all,
> And gently the light enters the sleeping soul,
> A sound so thin it could not woo a bird.
>
> (*CP,* 204)

As in Stevens, this voice of revelation seems to recall an ancient union, before the separation of mind and world, inside and outside.

When the Roethkean speaker wins that union he does it not in the complete stasis of orthodox mysticism, but in motion in and out of the "watery drowse." The end of "A Field of Light" announces a perception of "the separateness of all things," but carries an overriding sense of union: "I moved with the morning" (*CP,* 63). Variants of this line, like "I rock with the motion of morning" (*CP,* 191), imply a liquid immersion, and balance the motion with a sense of stillness, as the separateness of things balances union. The speaker moves, flowing, but he also remains still, rocking. In "Meditations of an Old Woman," Roethke uses the same verb to dramatize the fluctuation between the feeling of union and the feeling of separateness, as the voice of the self and the world's voice sing together, then apart.

> The body, delighting in thresholds,
> Rocks in and out of itself.
> A bird, small as a leaf,
> Sings in the first
> Sunlight.
>
> (*CP,* 163)

Finally, as in "Her Becoming," self is lost in the outside, as the sound and flow of being shape a new self defined totally by response.

I am benign in my own company.
A shape without a shade, or almost none,
I hum in pure vibration, like a saw.
The grandeur of a crazy one alone! —
By swoops of bird, by leaps of fish, I live.

     . . .

I dare caress the stones, the field my friend;
A light wind rises: I become the wind.

       (*CP,* 167)

  The terrible poems suggest that being "a crazy one alone" is seldom so grand. Moving toward "God" instead of "the mother of us all," these poems naturally draw very literally on the tradition of the dark night of the soul. Sometimes, as in "The Pure Fury," the sense of debt to the literature of mysticism is too strong for the poetry. The essential characteristics of Roethke's mystical experience — the "fearful night," the stones "with my own skin," the sense of immersion in "a denser shade" when the original "pure fury" is achieved, the inspiring presence of a woman, the "dream of faith" (*CP,* 134) — all of these are reduced to elements in an essay about psychologically violent mysticism. In "The Abyss" similar images are presented in a less studied fashion, as Roethke makes the negative tradition his own. As Rosemary Sullivan points out, with corroboration from Roethke's notebooks, the "not-knowing" that comes in silence "bearing being itself" in "The Abyss" obviously derives from *The Cloud of Unknowing.*[23] Roethke's use of this negation, which paradoxically provides a positive answer to the terrible negative of the dark night, acquires a visceral immediacy. As in the peaceful poems of flow to union, darkness and negation achieve that immediacy because embedded in landscape, surrounded by imagery of vegetation and flowing water. Even the old abstracter Eliot used similar techniques.

  The end of flow, in the poems bright and dark, is usually not only union but transformation. When the abyss opens to "luminous stillness" and the poet, once more moving still, begins to "rock between dark and dark" what sings is "my dead selves" (*CP,* 221). "Her Becoming" is more explicit about death; confronting "The holy line," the old woman wonders "Did my will die? Did I?" (*CP,* 167). What dies may simply be all in the self that is not pure response to the radiant now, but "death" leads to the birth of a new self, mysterious. "North American Sequence" defines this self most clearly, at least once in terms reminiscent of the poet Roethke called "our father." As Rosemary Sullivan has noticed, "The Rose" "closes with an image of the final man which owes much to Wallace Stevens' conception of the central man."[24]

> The lost self changes,
> Turning toward the sea,
> A sea-shape turning around —
> An old man with his feet before the fire,
> In robes of green, in garments of adieu.
>
>   . . .
>
> He is the end of things, the final man.
>
> (*CP*, 201)

Like the watcher on the shore at Key West, this man confronts by the sea "the murmur of the absolute." Naturally this passage immediately follows Roethke's "thought of my death" and evocation of "a dying garden in September," akin to the autumn fields and gardens of "Sunday Morning," as well as the autumn rose garden of "Burnt Norton." Thoughts of the absolute are autumn thoughts.

Such climactic descriptions of transformation suggest that despite its vocabulary of immanence "North American Sequence" shares some of the fascination with transcendence evident in Roethke's more theologically conservative late poetry. "The Long Waters" even ends with a dream of something Christlike, "The eternal one, the child, the swaying vine branch, / . . . The friend that runs before me on the windy headlands, / Neither voice nor vision." But immediately the suggestion of an actual supernatural visitant is balanced by imagery of immersion, acceptance of this world.

> I, who came back from the depths laughing too loudly,
> Become another thing;
> My eyes extend beyond the farthest bloom of the waves;
> I lose and find myself in the long water;
> I am gathered together once more;
> I embrace the world.
>
> (*CP*, 198)

Though this transformation pushes at the edges of the physical, it is still contained in water and world. In "The Abyss" Roethke may complain, "How can I dream except beyond this life?" (*CP*, 211), but his dreams of transcendence are usually contained by the reality of immanence, union at the watery heart of this earth, this life.

The conviction of eternity within immanence, infinity within time, is seldom more effectively conveyed than in the unabashedly eloquent pas-

sage in "The Far Field" that immediately precedes Roethke's meditation
on the movement of rivers:

> I learned not to fear infinity,
> The far field, the windy cliffs of forever,
> The dying of time in the white light of tomorrow,
> The wheel turning away from itself,
> The sprawl of the wave,
> The on-coming water.
>
>   (*CP*, 200)

As usual paradoxes abound. Time dies, but tomorrow approaches; the
wheel turns away from itself (as in the next stanza "The river turns on
itself") but never escapes itself, transcends itself. Paradox is inevitable
because Roethke confronts, more simply or directly than Eliot or Lowell,
the basic contradictions of all poetic mysticism. Not only is the other world
present in this world, so that the language of transcendence must describe
the condition of immanence, but the one who speaks that language is presumably on the way to losing the knowing and speaking self in the unknowing whole, either actually or in a poetic fiction that must be sustained. "A
Field of Light" deserves close attention because it deliberately stresses the
balance between the quest for self and the thrust toward loss of self in all.
To begin with, it describes no self, almost no action in a static landscape
described in heavily and appropriately end-stopped lines. The speaker
elides his "I" so, though his acts cause responses in the surrounding land,
the source of action often remains unclear.

> Came to lakes; came to dead water,
> Ponds with moss and leaves floating,
> Planks sunk in the sand.
>
> A log turned at the touch of a foot;
> A long weed floating upward;
> An eye tilted.
>
>   (*CP*, 59)

Here the poet's body seems to reveal itself, even assemble itself, part by
part, but the owner of that tilting eye could as easily be a fish as a poet.

If the eye is the beginning of "I," what it catches is discrete particulars,
as fragmented as the parts of his own body, his own psyche. But "a fine
rain fell," and it becomes possible for the poet, still "in a watery drowse,"
to proclaim "I" and to begin the descent into healing immersion that will
climax in rising. The poem's rhythm quickens, as a series of prepositions

carries him "Under, under . . . Under . . . Behind . . . In . . . Along" a low glide path to vegetable moisture.

> Along the low ground dry only in August, —
> Was it dust I was kissing?
> A sigh came far.
> Alone, I kissed the skin of a stone;
> Marrow-soft, danced in the sand.

This rhythm and the animistic trope implicit in "skin" suggest that some deep union between self and nature comes from this redemptive gesture at the end of the dark night descent.

Then much of the vision of the first section of the poem undergoes precise reversal, as everything rises and converges. Again the natural scene acts for the speaker, takes on human characteristics, but now to imply union, not surreal distortion and psychic fragmentation. "A path went walking" with the poet. The stone that disconcertingly "Became a clam" in section I was mollified by the kiss in section II; now "The salt laughed and the stones." While awareness of the separateness of things caused the speaker to feel fragmented and isolated in section I, now it becomes paradoxically consistent with a conviction of union: "With," not "alone," becomes the dominant word.

> I saw the separateness of all things!
> My heart lifted up with the great grasses;
> The weeds believed me, and the nesting birds.
> There were clouds making a rout of shapes crossing a
>   windbreak of cedars,
> And a bee shaking drops from a rain-soaked honeysuckle.
> The worms were delighted as wrens.
> And I walked, I walked through the light air;
> I moved with the morning.

Animal vitality (beating, singing, laughing, pulsing, nesting, delighted) has replaced the initial vegetable inertia. Unlike the earlier ones, the simple declarative sentences of this section are allowed as much line length as they need; a flowing ease results, bolstered by constant movement and energy.

In the simplest physical terms, the speaker has only lifted his head, changed the direction of his attention from down to up. But the rhetoric describes a passage through dark night to union. The landscape, transformed by the change in vision, almost carries the speaker into the sky. But still the rhetoric of immersion persists. "I moved with the morning" barely conceals the buried trope of a man carried by, immersed by, flowing with a wave.

iv

The union here experienced is most often defined by metaphors of death and flow, usually combined. Those who follow Roethke would insist even more on the idea of immanence, and their imagery would with uncanny constancy describe mystical immanence in terms of immersion in dark water. In "Poem in Three Parts" Bly describes himself as "Bathed in dark water, like any blade of grass."[25] Here the immersion is metaphorical, as night air turns liquid, but at times it becomes literal, as in "A Field of Light." Often not only air but the solid earth is imagined as water, as in Roethke's "I rise and fall in the slow sea of a grassy plain" (*CP*, 194). But intimations of the earth in watery flux are not always so soothing, especially when the poet confronts the final implications of unifying immersion. In this context, Plath's mortal terrors are only extensions of what the other poets suggest. But for Plath even literal death held a breadth of resonance often obscured by the grim particulars of her suicide. For her, as for Bly, death can involve a spiritually fulfilling immersion in the heart of the corporeal world. Bly writes constantly, in a tone that suggests a reality deeper than metaphor, about "the death we love," and, in "The Far Field," so does Roethke:

> I am renewed by death, thought of my death,
> The dry scent of a dying garden in September,
> The wind fanning the ash of a low fire.
> What I love is near at hand.
> Always, in earth and air.
>
> (*CP*, 201)

Predictably, in poetry of liquid landscapes, death is usually death by drowning, burial in a watery earth. Drowning forms a constant metaphor in Bly and Plath; Plath, at least, carries the mystic metaphor to a strange conclusion by imagining literal drowning with the same melancholy ecstasy that dominates Roethke's descriptions of immersion in the flow of existence. This characteristic tone can be heard in her "Lorelei." Roethke seldom used the image so literally as the younger poets; he tended to stop with suggestions of immersion. But he characteristically described "infinity" as "The sprawl of the wave, / The on-coming water" (*CP*, 200).

Throughout "North American Sequence" water that does not already surround the poet threatens and promises to submerge him, as he correspondingly internalizes it; in "The Far Field" as the water approaches the poet feels within himself "a weightless change, a moving forward / As of water quickening before a narrowing channel," and there follows the meditation on the "thought of my death."

This immersion, the flow into water or into earth, "flying like a bat deep into a narrowing tunnel" (*CP*, 199), implies a mysticism opposed to the mysticism of transcendence not only because it is described in immediately physical terms and because it contains a deep ambivalence in its imagery of darkness and its more literal suggestions of death. Because the water which receives the poet is usually internalized, the image of movement into watery darkness also suggests, unlike the images of transcendence, a movement into the depths of the self, and "down into the consciousness of the race," as Roethke wrote in a 1946 letter to Kenneth Burke.[26] This idea, now almost a cliché, lies behind such Roethke-like images as "a tunnel softly hurtling into darkness" (*Silence*, 26) in Bly's "Awakening"; the darkness is the darkness of earth, but also of the deep mind, for the voyage to the heart of the world involves not loss of self but discovery of the most hidden self. Inevitably the mystical terminology appropriate for these poets comes as much from Jung as from John of the Cross. "Death" for them suggests not a severing of attachments to the physical world and the physical self, but a mythic transition through the depths of the earth and the depths of the unconscious to a more cosmic existence. The path appears in another darkness; as Bly's "Awakening" begins "We are approaching sleep," Roethke's "Waking" opens with "I wake to sleep" (*CP*, 51). In sleep the mind opens to the inner world, which is not beyond but within the ordinary world.

Almost as often as it has been noticed, Jung's influence on Roethke has been misunderstood, or understood too much in terms of logical dualities by critics who emphasize the orthodox aspects of Roethke's mysticism (though Sullivan's excellent study uses Jung with a corrective subtlety). Karl Malkoff, whose explications of individual poems are perhaps deeper than anyone else's, tends to hyphenate Jung and St. John of the Cross, and to describe Roethke's darkness simply as the "dark night" that must be confronted and fought through as the mystic hero struggles into the light.[27] Except in his last and most theologically conventional poems Roethke seldom falls into such simple progressions. Because he tends to discover a paradoxical light within the darkness, not beyond it, his poetry, like

Stevens's before him and Bly's after, constantly involves images of dark light, "bright shade," "shimmering" illuminations in shadow. Like Plath and Bly, Roethke's favorite light seems to be the shimmering moon, as coldly dark as it is light.

To achieve this illuminating darkness the poet can feel his way into beasts, but the more common route leads into the inanimate, not only the omnipresent water, but into impenetrable stone, the least animate form of the least animate element, earth. Sometimes stones are animated, like the laughing stones in "A Field of Light," but more often stones remain stones, dead but paradoxically heavy with spiritual resonance. Confronting this lithic preoccupation, critics tend to discover death wishes in Roethke as well as Plath. But identification with stones is not necessarily escapist or self-destructive; it can be the logical end of a particularly visceral sort of mysticism, mysticism which depends on physically experiencing spiritual abstractions. The lithic experience seems as close to the experience of unchanging timelessness as the resolutely earthbound poet can come, but at the same time stones, especially Roethke's and Plath's stream-washed stones, are physically part of the constant flow of matter, dissolving and dissolving in accord with the earth's deepest reverberations. In Roethke's "Praise to the End," where the end is ecstatic change, immersion in "ultimate waters," Roethke describes the final transformation partly in lithic imagery: "I lost my identity to a pebble" (*CP*, 88).

Before this participation in "the stone's eternal pulseless longing," the poet has evoked the name "Father" and the voice of the Mother. In retrospect, at least, the female spirit seems the more crucial, for throughout the work of these three poets there recurs a loose constellation of traditionally feminine images. Stones associate with darkness, dim moons, water, death, and maternal women who become the signs or causes of transformation. To understand one culmination of the mysticism of immersion, one of the final meanings of ecstatic death in this poetry, we must examine these women as carefully as the dark world they guard.

V

Like women in Lowell, Roethke's women often play a mythic and implicitly mystical role. As mystical union with nature was the way out of sexual turmoil and guilt in such early poems as "The Lost Son," so in his late poems Roethke often seeks the way through sexual fulfillment into mystical illumination. Throughout, Roethke stresses the linkage between psychological and spiritual development, as do Plath and Bly. Each is capable of using mystical experience as a sort of ultimate therapy, responding to psychological questions with spiritual answers. But one difference comes in their treatments of the archetypes of the female, in all three poets usually imagined in some psychic tension with the male. "Words for the Wind," which involves "That woman I saw in a stone" (*CP*, 123), exemplifies the frequent visionary overtones of Roethke's romantic poetry. Unlike Bly's archetypal women, or Plath's mysterious elementals, Roethke's often seem ill suited for the task of guarding the dark secrets. Instead of being powerful they often appear childishly vulnerable, soft and furry like the baby animals and plump birds which quiver about them. Though some of Roethke's love poems are evident triumphs, many, especially toward the end, degenerate into pop love-song cliches, frequently involving the wind; as his words go limp, heavily precious sentimentalism takes over. Like the "essayistic" language of much of the philosophical poetry, the sentimental language creates the effect of excessive abstraction, and the vitality of individual experience becomes lost in generalizing triteness. It remains clear what Roethke is trying to do with his women; as the poet James McMichael writes, Roethke uses women — as he uses animals in his meditations — as "mediators" in his journey to spiritual union with nature.[28] But to make this work — even if we disregard the probability that women may be less appropriate for such an instrumental role than animals — requires more control of tone, and more psychological self-assurance, than Roethke usually possesses.

The second stanza of "The Pure Fury," which could be offered in evidence of the awkwardness of Roethke's philosophical abstractions, also exemplifies the inadequacy of his abstract women, though here the problem is not exactly sentimentality. Again thinking of Jung, Malkoff sees the woman described in this poem as an anima figure,[29] but she seems entirely too foolish and insignificant for that rather heavy role, more stereotype than archetype:

> I love a woman with an empty face.
> Parmenides put Nothingness in place;
> She tries to think and it flies loose again.
> How slow the changes of a golden mean:
> Great Boehme rooted all in Yes and No!
> At times my darling squeaks in pure Plato.
>
> (*CP*, 133)

Here perhaps with a try at affectionate humor, Roethke attempts to create a woman with the spiritual receptivity of a holy beast, a more than human embodiment of the *via negativa;* what he actually depicts seems more a sexist cliché, a mindless woman to whom any man can safely condescend no matter what spiritual attributes he grants her.

Perhaps inevitably, Roethke's most genuinely forceful enlightened woman is not the figure of a lover but a mother-figure, and an intelligent one. "Meditations of an Old Woman" not only contains an attack (in "Fourth Meditation") on spiritually pretentious clichés about woman, but it creates a clearly female being who is fully individuated and as human as her creator, even when becoming "like a beast" (*CP,* 166). She is a convincing representation, partly because not simply archetypal, of a basic female force that Roethke successfully evokes in few of his poems. She is the "mistress of lost wisdom" whom he describes in the only half-comic "Lost Words," where she may be mother or wife or both:

> Come out of a cloud, angel with several faces,
> Bring me my hat, my umbrella and rubbers,
> Enshroud me with Light! O Whirling! O Terrible Love!
>   (*CP,* 48)

Reduced to archetype, this woman becomes the fulfilling natural force Roethke will later seek in "North American Sequence," where, as W. D. Snodgrass has written, the final aim is entry "into water as woman, into earth as goddess-mother."[30] The actual means of that entry remains ambiguous; as "Enshroud" and "Terrible" suggest, Roethke's female is as potentially ominous as she is enlightening, when he confronts her fully. In this she resembles Bly's women who guard the secrets of dark waters under the earth, the Great Mothers whose current violent reappearance in our racial psyche he describes at length in his essay "I Came Out of the Mother Naked."[31]

Though Roethke never actually depicts such elemental conflict as Plath and Bly do, he does describe some sort of archetypal female force whose ultimate effect is to transform the self and perhaps the world. In "The Dream" the speaker dreams or "remembers from a deeper sleep" a woman who, changing herself, is "A shape of change," who transforms him and "turned the field into a glittering sea" (*CP,* 119-20). Though it anticipates Plath's "I / Foam to wheat, a glitter of seas" in "Ariel" (*Ariel,* 26), the alteration here is simply the opening of vision. But in "The Shape of the Fire," with its overtones of evolutionary change,

Roethke addresses the strange "Mother of quartz" who will reappear as "mother of pestles" in Plath's "The Stones" or as "Mother of otherness" in "Who," two sections of "Poem for a Birthday."

For Plath, the Mother becomes a death mother; the illumination comes with the dying. At times her fascination with actual death seems only an extension of Roethke's deepest knowledge, which is that vision — at times unbearable — will unalterably change those who achieve it, that death may be the only word extreme enough to reflect that change, that in any case the proper end to all human change is really and finally death. But as Bly says (for them all), we discover "nourishment in death" (*Light*, 44). The paradox is inescapable: mystical experience is the terminal stage in the development of the self, but this end is only another beginning. Like Plath, Roethke writes in "The Long Waters" "I . . . / Become another thing" (*CP*, 198), and in "The Rose":

> A something wholly other,
> As if I swayed out on the wildest wave alive,
> And yet was still.
> And I rejoiced in being what I was:
> In the lilac change, the white reptilian calm,
> In the bird behind the bough, the single one.
>
> (*CP*, 205)

Here, amid the usual paradoxes — stillness in motion, the discovery in otherness of "the true ease of myself" — the "other" is more clearly defined. To see the world truly is not simply to internalize it as in Stevens but to become it; the final immersion leads to a more than romantic or animistic exchange of identities with things and beings.

But how literal can such an exchange be? If the idea of immersion in the flow of existence, of dying into the "steady storm of correspondences," is to have any realistic basis, the theoretical structure that supports the vision of orthodox mysticism with literal belief in an ubiquitous God and an afterlife outside of time must be replaced by another, more physically oriented theory of final union. So Darwin's vision of the flow of all corporeal reality becomes as important to these poets as Jung's theory of the unifying sea of the collective unconscious. By thinking in terms of evolution, an idea that will become as pivotal as the idea of apocalypse, Roethke can imagine immersion in and expansion through the fields of time, which adds the resonance of fact to his images of expansion through space and objects. In "The Far Field" the speaker is described sunk in sand "Fingering a shell, / Thinking: / Once I was something like this, mindless" (*CP,* 200). The past is experienced in the body as well as the imagination; in "River Incident" "Sea water stood in my veins / . . . And I knew that I had been there before" (*CP,* 49). In the *Praise to the End!* sequence Roethke writes "By snails, by leaps of frogs, I came here, spirit" (*CP,* 89) and "I've traced these words in sand with a vestigial tail; / Now the gills are beginning to cry" (*CP,* 92). Here he anticipates such poems as Bly's "Evolution from the Fish," which describes the "nephew of snails," a man in present time who "Moves, dragging a great tail into the darkness" (*Light,* 59).

But Bly's poem, unlike Roethke's, ends with a suggestion of further evolution, beyond this particular human condition. Those who followed the paths Roethke had explored through much of his life ended, inevitably, by going further than he even as he retreated at the end to the comfort of simpler answers. While Roethke was writing such hymns to the orthodox God as "Infirmity," Bly and Plath (and W. S. Merwin) were confronting the more terrifying implications of evolutionary mysticism. While Roethke was giving way to a fear of death that resulted in certain spiritual evasions, the others were accepting death and exploring its vital implications (each in his own way; Plath, who died the year Roethke died, accepted with deadly literalism).

Roethke does, once, imagine evolution into the future. In "Fourth Meditation" the old woman says of the new people she hopes for:

> I see them as figures walking in a greeny garden,
> Their gait formal and elaborate, their hair a glory,
> The gentle and beautiful still-to-be-born;
> The descendants of the playful tree-shrew that survived the archaic
>   killers,
> The fang and the claw, the club and the knout, the irrational edict,
> The fury of the hate-driven zealot, the meanness of the human weasel.
>
>   (*CP,* 170)

A moving description, but perhaps too ideal; there seems an unbridgeable gap between "the human weasel" and these Edenic creatures, reminiscent of the spirit children in Eliot's "Burnt Norton," and equally removed from the dark physical flow which will presumably produce them. The poets who follow Roethke seldom idealize so; when they imagine further evolution they admit not only its moral ambiguity but the probability that it will occur, as evolutionary development always has, amid violence and strife. Ted Hughes and Plath imagine evolution primarily as an aspect of apocalypse, or at least cultural collapse, and Bly, whose vision is complicated by an awareness of political strife always sadly lacking in Roethke's poetry, is fully aware of the apocalyptic implications of evolution, the destruction of one world as another approaches.

Roethke could not, of course, be expected to travel so far into this surrealist vision, where even now it is often difficult to follow Bly and Plath. His unique value lies partly in his ability to develop much of the poetic and spiritual vocabulary they have carried further, and to articulate the vision at a time when it seemed far more eccentric than it seems now. That vision — the animism, the "body consciousness," the particularly corporeal approach to mystical contact, with the evolutionary and apocalyptic imagery that logically follows — has become almost commonplace in poetry now. This happens not entirely because of Roethke's influence; the vision is at least in its large outlines collective; fragments of it keep turning up. One logical extension of Jung's theory of archetypes is the idea that a particular cluster of images, and even a particular attitude toward those images, may dominate the psyches of the inhabitants of a given period of history. Unless we allow for more direct influence and imitation than the facts can probably justify, this seems to be the situation with these poets, and with various other spokesmen (mystical or apocalyptic) from the culture that produced them. In the darkness beneath the waters Roethke saw something extensive enough to touch us all, something ancient that calls forth both terror and ecstasy, but at the same time something new, and newly come to the deep dreams of our deepest poets.

NOTES

1. Robert Lowell, *Near the Ocean* (New York: Farrar, Strauss, and Giroux, 1967), p. 51. The ellipsis is Lowell's.

2. In *The Echoing Wood of Theodore Roethke* (Princeton: Princeton Univ. Press, 1976), Jenijoy LaBelle links Roethke with most of the American poets who existed up to a century before him — and many of the British (though, oddly, she ignores Stevens's influence). Closer to my own concerns is Harry Williams's *"The Edge Is What I Have": Theodore Roethke and After* (Lewisburg, Pa.: Bucknell Univ. Press, 1977), in which Williams discusses Roethke's influence on Robert Bly, James Wright, James Dickey, Sylvia Plath, and Ted Hughes. Because a much earlier version of this chapter appeared in *American Literature* before his book was published, Williams was able to comment on my "study along similar lines" (p. 203). He greets it "with enthusiasm," but points out that I draw "some different conclusions — less controversial perhaps." Well. This should not be taken as a critic's overstated defense of his own originality. We do indeed come to different conclusions, though Williams did convince me

that James Dickey's use of "the Roethkean mode" is essentially reductive, not worth the attention I originally paid it. About Bly and especially Plath, I find him less convincing (more controversial?), largely because the connections he sees ultimately depend on very large generalizations about "tragedy," "the search for identity in modern times" (p. 189), and the "invidious technology" of the modern age (p. 191). Roethke — like everyone else — may be concerned with "identity," but Williams finds in him a social commentator I cannot see, though I would like to.

3. Without historical distance "influential" is almost as difficult to define as "great." Unquestionably the disproportionate popularity Plath now enjoys implies a concomitant influence. In fact Marjorie Perloff ends *The Poetic Art of Robert Lowell* (Ithaca: Cornell Univ. Press, 1973) by suggesting that in the poetry of the seventies Lowell's mode may be giving way to Plath's, "the tradition of oracular or visionary poetry" (p. 183), which Perloff traces back to Rimbaud as well as Roethke. Bly is less conspicuous than Plath in bookstores, though he has won a National Book Award (in 1967, after Roethke in 1965). But his voice too is often evident in the work of younger poets. And he enjoys considerable importance as a theoretician, primarily because of a few brief essays he has published in his journal *The Sixties,* now *The Eighties,* when it appears.

4. Robert Bly, *The Light around the Body* (New York: Harper & Row, 1967), p. 50. Hereafter identified as *Light.*

5. Theodore Roethke, *The Collected Poems* (Garden City, N.Y.: Doubleday, 1966), p. 195. Hereafter *CP.*

6. T. S. Eliot, "Burnt Norton," *The Complete Poems and Plays 1909-1950* (New York: Harcourt, Brace, 1952), p. 119. Hereafter identified as *CPP.*

7. Theodore Roethke, *On the Poet and His Craft, Selected Prose,* ed. Ralph J. Mills, Jr. (Seattle: Univ. of Washington Press, 1965), p. 62.

8. Sylvia Plath, *Ariel* (New York: Harper & Row, 1966), pp. 26-27.

9. Ted Hughes, "Notes on the Chronological Order of Sylvia Plath's Poems," *The Art of Sylvia Plath,* ed. Charles Newman (Bloomington: Indiana Univ. Press, 1970), p. 192.

10. James Dickey, "Theodore Roethke," *Poetry,* 105 (Nov. 1964), 119.

11. Sylvia Plath, *Crossing the Water* (New York: Harper & Row, 1971), p. 52. Hereafter *Crossing.*

12. Theodore Roethke, "Some Remarks on Rhythm," *Selected Prose,* p. 71.

13. Karl Malkoff, *Theodore Roethke* (New York: Columbia Univ. Press, 1966), p. 14.

14. Kenneth Burke, "The Vegetal Radicalism of Theodore Roethke," *Sewanee Review,* 58 (Jan.-Mar. 1950), 68-108.

15. Hugh Staples, "The Rose in the Sea-Wind: A Reading of Theodore Roethke's 'North American Sequence,'" *American Literature,* 36 (May 1964), 193.

16. Theodore Roethke to Kenneth Burke, Sept. 6, 1949, *Selected Letters of Theodore Roethke,* ed. Ralph J. Mills, Jr. (Seattle: Univ. of Washington Press, 1968), p. 154.

17. Roethke, *Letters,* pp. 111, 221. Roethke was usually willing to acknowledge Williams's influence: in a 1946 letter to him Roethke said of "The Lost Son," "In a sense it's your poem — yours and K. Burke's" (p. 122).

18. Stanley Kunitz, "The Taste of Self," rpt. from the *New World Writing* (19) symposium on "In a Dark Time," *The Contemporary Poet as Artist and Critic,* ed. Anthony Ostroff (Boston: Little, Brown, 1964), p. 47.

19. Roethke, in *Contemporary Poet,* p. 47.

20. R. D. Laing, *The Politics of Experience* (1967; rpt., New York: Ballantine Books, 1968), p. 158.

21. Sylvia Plath, *Winter Trees* (New York: Harper & Row, 1972), p. 4. Hereafter *Winter.*

22. Rosemary Sullivan, probably the most perceptive and thorough analyst of Roethke's mysticism so far, argues that "he began his 'drive toward God' under tremendous pressure and out of psychological more than spiritual necessity." She questions whether his sense of "God" "was ever a coherent philosophy or whether such a philosophy might have been possible," but she feels that his notebooks suggest that his notion of divinity "owes much to the medieval mystic Meister Eckhart." *Theodore Roethke: The Garden Master* (Seattle: Univ. of Washington Press, 1975), p. 178.

23. Sullivan, *Theodore Roethke,* p. 176.

24. Sullivan, *Theodore Roethke,* p. 161.

25. Robert Bly, *Silence in the Snowy Fields* (Middletown, Conn.: Wesleyan Univ. Press, 1962), p. 21. Hereafter *Silence.*

26. Roethke to Burke, 1946, *Letters,* p. 116.

27. Malkoff, *Theodore Roethke,* pp. 64-65, 199.

28. James McMichael, "The Poetry of Theodore Roethke," *Southern Review,* n.s. 5 (Winter 1969), 10.

29. Malkoff, *Theodore Roethke,* p. 136.

30. W. D. Snodgrass, " 'That Anguish of Concreteness' — Theodore Roethke's Career," in *Theodore Roethke: Essays on the Poetry,* ed. Arnold Stein (Seattle: Univ. of Washington Press, 1965), p. 87.

31. Robert Bly, *Sleepers Joining Hands* (New York: Harper & Row, 1973), p. 6.

4

Sylvia Plath, God's Lioness
and the Priest of Sycorax

Poets deep and mysterious can too easily become mirrors, their central obscurities burnished to reflect our cultural preoccupations. So popular categories falsify. We are invited to understand Sylvia Plath as feminist, despite the rather strong animosity to women in *The Bell Jar* which led Harriet Rothstein (writing in *Ms.*) to question "her falsely assigned role as feminist heroine."[1] And in a culture fascinated by the spectacle of its own gradual self-destruction, there is perhaps even more preoccupation with Plath as suicide, despite various brave but questionable critical assertions that suicides have little of general importance to say to us.[2] Clearly it is impossible to deny that the feminist and suicidal categories touch on Plath's vision of sexual destruction, but those classifications fail to take us deeply enough into her poetry; even taken together they suggest too simple a direction for the violence she evokes, too reductive a preoccupation with Plath as victim. Victimizer as well, she achieves a strange mythic power. Even more clearly than Lowell's, her poetry illuminates the anti-human side of the negative mysticisms.

The problem of interpretation is compounded by the extreme and unevenly obscure nature of her poetry, which invites extreme critical responses. The most basic judgments about the significance and value of her central poems vary enormously according to the preoccupations of her critics. The difficulty is nicely exemplified by two critical books about the poet in which David Holbrook and Judith Kroll describe two radically opposed Sylvia Plaths. In fact these critics agree that the poems dramatize a basic duality in the poet, but their accounts of the fruits of that duality have little to do with each other. Holbrook, who has nothing but heartfelt scorn for the "Women's Liberation fanatics" who glorify Plath,[3] orchestrates a Freudian case study which concludes that almost all of Plath's poetry is the record of "paranoid-schizoid" delusions, worthwhile primarily as a documentation of the nature of madness. With a very different sort of ingenuity, which I find more sympathetic but equally extreme, Kroll makes the poet a priestess in search of absolute transcendence. Her Plath dies (not before seeing God) because of a "religious crisis," after producing poetry which seems morbid only to a culture inordinately afraid of death and suspicious of mysticism.[4]

The radical contrast between these critical approaches inevitably appears in their reactions to the very late poem "Edge," which is fortunately only in part prophetic in its depiction of a woman accompanied to death by her two children. Holbrook finds the poem "beautiful but psychotic" and argues that it "idolizes infanticide."[5] Kroll, who sees Plath's actual suicide as an attempt to liberate her true self and to achieve some (undefined) immortality, seems to invite Holbrook's accusation, precisely by justifying (poetic) infanticide. "The dead woman . . . has reabsorbed her world and her children, an act which emphasizes the perfectedness of her life." This is done "in a way that goes beyond judgement or blame."[6] Neither critic entertains the possibility that Plath may present the whole tableau, including the initial line "The woman is perfected," with some irony, that she is not necessarily idolizing anything here. Surely that irony is suggested by the description of each child as "a white serpent," and especially by the reference to "the *illusion* of a Greek necessity" (*Ariel*, 84, my emphasis), which — instead of genuine fate — seems to govern the action.[7] The discussion of Plath's attitudes toward death, and even more of Plath herself as a mystic — a term which appears not only in Kroll but repeatedly in the critical collection *The Art of Sylvia Plath*[8] — must never lose sight of her pervasive irony. She does, finally, write visionary poetry, and it will be essential to determine what myth informs her mysticism. But first it is important to define the limits of that mysticism. The problem is not the degree of her morbidity, or fascination with death for its own simple sake, but her cynicism; mystics are often fascinated by death, but seldom so given to callous jokes about transcendence.

Like Roethke, Plath is at times a mystic of immanent union. But like Wallace Stevens she is quite capable of using religious terminology for her own sometimes devious purposes. Like Stevens she rejects the traditional mysticism of transcendence; "I am not mystical" (*Winter*, 28), one poem says in reference to belief in spirits. In "Love Letter" Plath, like

Lowell, uses the vocabulary of transcendence to describe romantic love, but she does it more playfully than he. The lover has resurrected the "dead" speaker:

> I started to bud like a March twig:
> An arm and a leg, an arm, a leg.
> From stone to cloud, so I ascended.
> Now I resemble a sort of god
> Floating through the air in my soul-shift
> Pure as a pane of ice. It's a gift.
>
> (*Crossing*, 27)

Less playful and more mocking is the imagery of rising in "Fever 103°," which deflates both transcendent mysticism and its source, orthodox Christianity, by using them to describe a sickness. Plath becomes the central figure in a tawdry holy picture of the Assumption defaced by images of modern mechanical flame:

> I think I am going up,
> I think I may rise —
> The beads of hot metal fly, and I, love, I
>
> Am a pure acetylene
> Virgin
> Attended by roses,
>
> By kisses, by cherubim,
> By whatever these pink things mean.
>
> (*Ariel*, 54)[9]

Amused by her own rising, she is flippant about the myth of Christ's Ascension; "Years" describes him as "Christus . . . Dying to fly and be done with it" (*Ariel*, 72).

Even the specific images of the *via negativa* are irreverently manipulated, though here Plath's frequent irony fails to conceal a terminal longing. She imagines not the cloud of unknowing but a sky of forgetting: "the black amnesias of heaven" (*Ariel*, 17). But such blankness draws her. The temptation is explicitly dramatized in some of her poems of sickness, among her most humanly appealing because they show her resisting the powerful pull. How sweet, as well as saintly, to turn from the complexities of ordinary existence to the simple blankness at the end of her version of the negative way. Plath will ultimately confront a divinity that offers little peace, but in "Tulips" she allows herself a wistful parodic use of mystical terminology to describe a confrontation with nothingness un-complicated by savage deities. "I am nobody," Plath writes:

> I didn't want any flowers, I only wanted
> To lie with my hands turned up and be utterly empty.
> How free it is, you have no idea how free —
> The peacefulness is so big it dazes you,
> And it asks nothing, a name tag, a few trinkets.
> It is what the dead close on, finally; I imagine them
> Shutting their mouths on it, like a Communion tablet.
>
> (*Ariel*, 11)

The loss of self, the hands posed to fit the traditional inconography of mysticism, the evocation of death, the reference to the union with God in Communion — all these signs of ecstasy accompany a mental state pre-sented as a dead end and finally resisted. Similarly in "Paralytic" the speaker achieves an enforced and empty transcendence, like a "buddha," asking "nothing of life" (*Ariel*, 78). In both poems the equation between sickness and mystic peace suggests how easily the negative way can turn perverse, the deadly self-involvement of the suicide only one step beyond the ecstatic death to the world of the mystic. As W. S. Merwin will at times demonstrate, mysticism may reveal a psychological deficiency as well as psychic power, inability to accept ordinary human life and death.

Some of Plath's mocking references to the way of unknowing imply that the deficiency is an attribute of "the big god," who meets the mystic's emptiness of self with his own: "The white gape of his mind was the real Tabula Rasa" (*Winter*, 32). When Plath does allow herself to write straight descriptions of peaceful loss of self in unknowing, she tends to leave the transcendent God out. In fact these poems allow very little of man, either; the context is nature. In "Two Campers in Cloud Country" the purity of the landscape is defined, as it will be in Merwin's poetry of icy mysticism, by its distance from the human: "It is comfortable, for a change, to mean so little, / These rocks offer no purchase to herbage or people: / They are conceiving a dynasty of perfect cold" (*Crossing*, 32). Under the spell of these clouds unknowing ("No gesture of yours or mine could catch their attention,") the campers drift into an ancient union:

> Around our tent the old simplicities sough
> Sleepily as Lethe, trying to get in.
> We'll wake blank-brained as water in the dawn.

This occasional poem is not fully typical of Plath. In her later work "the old simplicities" will be defined by a strange and far less peaceful combination of ancient myth and new magic, but the early poems of mystical contact are frequently dominated by a simple loss of self in landscape or animals, Lowell's "dark downward kingdom." As Robert Phillips puts it, "Always in these first poems one observes Plath's identification with the lower forms of existence — mushrooms and moles, snakes and insects, stones and bones."[10] Sometimes the imagined union comes, as in "Blue Moles," in the depths of sleep, more dream vision than mystical vision in any exact sense.

Whether the result of dream or meditation, the evocations of natural union in the early landscape poetry are marked by an uncharacteristic gentleness, even when they describe that ultimate union, death. In Plath's more mature poetry, mystical contact is usually characterized by a mysterious violence. Here the connection between Plath and Lowell may supplement the comparison between Roethke and Plath. Because her mysticism is ultimately dominated by a violent anthropomorphic deity, it is directly comparable to the mythology of the younger Lowell. His influence on her has less to do with confession than communion with a savage god. Initially, she internalized the violence of his world by copying the violence of his imagery. In direct imitation of him she wrote shore poems marked by what he called, in introducing her later poetry, "Massachusetts' low-tide dolor" (*Ariel,* ix). "Point Shirley" is more characteristically a Lowell poem than many of Lowell's own, if only because of an image like "The sun sinks under Boston, bloody red," or the rhythms of "Against both bar and tower the black sea runs" (*Colossus,* 25, 26). Specifically reminiscent of "The Quaker Graveyard at Nantucket" is imagery that describes "a dog-faced sea" as an animal in mortal combat with the shore. (Similar imagery appeared in T. S. Eliot's Massachusetts North Shore poem "The Dry Salvages"; like Lowell, Eliot concentrates on the sea's voices when the sea is caught in "the granite teeth" of the shore.)

As the sea, which both "Quaker Graveyard" and Plath's "Finisterre" describe as "exploding," becomes a source of savage violence, the consolations of traditional belief recede. In "Finisterre" the ocean expands to infinite "nothing": "With no bottom, or anything on the other side of it, / Whitened by the faces of the drowned" (*Crossing,* 3). At land's end Plath describes a statue of "Our Lady of the Shipwrecked," as intent on eternity and ignorant of human concerns as Lowell's Lady of Walsingham. Supplicants sculpted and real pray to her, but "She does not hear what the

sailor or the peasant is saying — / She is in love with the beautiful formlessness of the sea." Sometimes in Plath, as in "Quaker Graveyard," the
way to union with that beautiful formlessness is a literal drowning; under
the coldly maternal "full moon" of "Lorelei," the speaker is tempted to
join the "great goddesses of peace" who call to her from "the great
depths" (*Colossus,* 23). But in the later poems to the great goddess, peace
is far away, a forgotten and boring condition.

Even more than the early Lowell, the late Plath scorns the peace that
passes understanding, or presents peace as sterile though tempting passivity. Only occasionally does she celebrate the type of revelation that happens
to the traditionally passive recipient, and the revelation is presented as a
relief from passivity. The epiphany poem "Black Rook in Rainy Weather"
describes her jolted out of "neutrality" by a miracle of ordinary vision ("If
you care to call those spasmodic / Tricks of radiance miracles"). But the
revelation received passively leads nowhere; afterwards she can only wait
for recurrence, "for the angel, / For that rare, random descent" (*Crossing,*
42). Like "The Moon and the Yew Tree," "Years" rejects peaceful mysticism and the transcendent theology that advocates it.

> O God, I am not like you
> In your vacuous black,
> Stars stuck all over, bright stupid confetti,
> Eternity bores me,
> I never wanted it.
>
> > (*Ariel,* 72)

To this transcendent God, "great Stasis," is opposed the worldly ecstasy of
motion and violent flow:

> What I love is
> The piston in motion —
> My soul dies before it,
> And the hooves of the horses,
> Their merciless churn.

The hint of sexual movement, as well as the horse in flight and the soul
dying of excitement, also appear in Plath's ultimate hymn to the mystical
flow, "Ariel." The basic reality for her is not peace but the storm, sometimes Roethke's "steady storm of correspondences," often "a wind of such
violence" that "I break up in pieces that fly about like clubs" (*Ariel,* 15).
Like "Years," "Getting There," a strangely hallucinatory poem also driven
by "these pistons," gives up on an Eliot-like transcendence ("Is there no

still place / Turning and turning in the middle air"). Instead, there is the
earthy drive of "these wheels / Fixed to their arcs like gods" (*Ariel,* 36).
Whether with reluctance or excitement, Plath must seek her true mystic
perceptions not in the stasis of traditional faith, or eternity, or even death,
but in a myth of ecstatic and violent kinesis, in a transforming progression
of which death is only a part.

ii

The deity involved in her myth is seldom clearly described by
Plath. To understand her final secret we must look to a more intimate
influence than Lowell or Roethke, to the poet who inhabited her life and
participated in her mystic search as well as her poetry. But to mention
Ted Hughes with Sylvia Plath is to risk a long and ultimately tedious
descent into biographical and sexual controversy. "Ted" and "Sylvia"
threaten to become the Scott and Zelda of our time, though Ted has
fewer defenders than Scott, despite feminist poet Robin Morgan's tritely
phrased assertion that "the entire British and American / literary and
critical establishment / has been at great lengths to deny" that Hughes is
responsible for "the murder of Sylvia Plath."[11]
Somehow the denial seems more reasonable than Morgan's glib accusation, but who knows? Hughes's psychological influence on Plath must
inevitably remain partly hidden; if her poetry is "confessional" it is often
the most abstract and evasive of confessions. More obvious and interesting
is the great stylistic and philosophical influence each exerted on the other.
From the beginning they shared a vision of elemental mythic conflict,
which should not be oversimplified by too rigid a concentration on their
biographies. Plath's death and Hughes's emergence as a survivor and,
in A. Alvarez's term, a "survivor-poet," tempt us to see them in simple
opposition. As Phyllis Chesler writes, "traditionally, the ideal female is
trained to 'lose,' and the ideal male is trained to 'win' (i.e., psychologically
females are trained to die, males to survive)."[12] Sometimes their poetry
about each other seems to reinforce this dichotomy. Most conspicuously,
"Daddy" has popularized the image of Hughes as "A man in black with a
Meinkampf look," the "vampire" who "drank my blood for . . . / Seven
years" (*Ariel,* 51), presumably the same ambiguously destructive honey-
moon Hughes gives his account of in "Crow Improvises" (*Crow,* 53). But
even in "Daddy" the female speaker is as much manipulator as victim;
she creates the man in black — "I made a model of you" — and she finally

destroys him — "If I've killed one man, I've killed two." Of course this murder is metaphorical; except herself, Plath never actually killed anyone. But neither, as far as we know, did Hughes.

They did shape each other's work. We can easily discover characteristic Plath images in Hughes's later poetry, and his images in hers. Even more striking is the probability that each anticipated imagery characteristic of the other. Although we have Hughes's precise dating of the composition of much of Plath's poetry, and therefore it seems safe to assume that *Lupercal* (1960) influenced the imagery of *Ariel* (composed 1961-63) more than *Ariel* influenced *Lupercal*, that assumption is open to question. For instance Hughes's "Cleopatra to the Asp" in subject (a woman's vengeful suicide), imagery (a mirror, waters, the moon), and even tone ("the devil in it / Loved me like my soul, my soul," *Lupercal*, 60) sounds so characteristic of the later Plath that Hughes seems here to be influenced by her unwritten poetry, to be working in her vein before she herself has fully discovered it. They lived and worked together, probably choosing to do so partly because they shared the same vision from the start; neither created the other, each constantly influenced the other. That influence probably began — through publications — before they met, and it continues after they have parted; if Sylvia Plath is still somehow fully alive in *Ariel*, she is at least a presiding spirit in *Wodwo* and *Crow*. If we are to discover the final resonances of her mythology, we must look not only to the posthumous publication Hughes the editor gives us in her name, but also to the poetry he wrote in the years after her death.

Despite the pervasive similarities between the two poets, there are clearly certain areas which one seems to occupy more fully than the other, and in those areas the direction of influence is obvious. When Plath ends "Watercolor of Grantchester Meadows" with the sudden and rather arbitrary suggestion that "The owl shall stoop from his turret, the rat cry out" (*Colossus*, 41), she has projected herself with some effort into Hughes's territory. When, with more success, she envisions a gull with "The whole flat harbor anchored in / The round of his yellow eye-button" ("A Winter Ship," *Colossus*, 44), she seems directly influenced by Hughes's hawk, who "hangs his still eye. / His wings hold all creation in a weightless quiet" (*Hawk*, 11). So in "Zoo Keeper's Wife" the cold eel immersed in the dark "like a dead lake" with a belly "Where the heads and tails of my sisters decompose" (*Crossing*, 38) specifically suggests his "Pike," though here as in "Elm" Hughes's projection becomes her internalization.

While Hughes's explicit influence shows more clearly in Plath's early work, her clear influences on him, his excursions into her territory, are more evident in his later collections. In at least one of the poems in *Wodwo,* Plath as presiding spirit is perhaps more than metaphorically present. "Cadenza," according to M. L. Rosenthal, "has precisely the type of dynamics that Sylvia Plath at her best achieved, especially in her poem 'Ariel.' "[13] Remarkably like a Plath poem, it echoes not only "I am the arrow" from "Ariel" but these lines from "Fever 103°":

> . . . I
> Am a pure acetylene
> Virgin
> Attended by roses.
> (*Ariel,* 54)

> . . . I am the cargo
> of a coffin attended by swallows.
> (*Wodwo,* 20)

Presumably this is what Robin Morgan refers to when she accuses Hughes of "malappropriating" Plath's imagery, but perhaps there is something more here than stylistic imitation. Rosenthal describes "Cadenza" as a "lament" for Plath; in fact it seems an attempt to conjure her up, and to reexperience some basic union with her, to join with her spirit and to see with her eyes. The attempt leads to a dream of descent into a realm of elemental force. The poem begins its impressionistic fantasy by connecting the coffin with "a woman walking water," the act of a god; the coffin returns to violate the silence of "The loaded estuary of the dead" with some message or accusation. The one who dreams or speaks the poem identifies himself not only with the coffin's cargo but with the dark rising water that carries it: "And I am the water / Bearing the coffin that will not be silent." Given water and the presence of death, the will toward dark union in these lines suggests Roethkean immersion mysticism, but the poem is more magic spell than mystic meditation and it ends not in peace but in hallucinations of apocalyptic violence. As the coffin rises, the sky falls, "dives shut like a burned land"; the woman who walks the estuary of the dead brings visions not of peaceful death but of cosmic turbulence. What Hughes makes clear about Plath is that despite her popular reputation death is not so much the center of her poetry as violence. She herself says of her poetic terrain (showing a casual blunt humor usually ignored) "It isn't England, It isn't France, It isn't Ireland. / It's violent" (*Winter,* 17). If there is mystical revelation to follow the magic more or less seriously practiced by Plath and Hughes, in general that revelation will come, like the early Lowell's, out of the heart of violence.

That "Cadenza" is in fact intended as a sort of magical spell seems probable; it would not be Hughes's first attempt to invoke a violent spirit. Responding in an interview to the charge that his poems about jaguars are "celebrations of violence," Hughes replies that he considers them "invocations of a jaguarlike body of elemental force, demonic force." Lest we interpret this talk of "real summoning force" as metaphor he continues, "Lots of people might consider I'm overrating the powers of these two poems, but I'm speaking from my own evidence."[14] The "evidence" is not described, but according to Hughes the role he plays as poet must be understood literally in terms of the activity of the shaman. He uses the same term to describe Plath's poetic activity: "Her poetry escapes ordinary analysis in the way that clairvoyance and mediumship do: her psychic gifts, at almost any time, were strong enough to make her frequently wish to be rid of them. In her poetry, in other words, she had free and controlled access to depths formerly reserved to the primitive ecstatic priests, shamans and holy men, and more recently flung open to tourists with the passport of such hallucinogens as LSD."[15] Whether or not we can fully assent to the implications of the analysis Hughes offers here, we have a certain amount of evidence that Plath did. For instance A. Alvarez, who tends to dismiss Hughes's "black magic" as "a metaphor for . . . creative powers," writes that in describing to him her final rapidly productive period Plath made it sound like "demonic possession."[16] Later Hughes would speak of the poems of *Crow* in similar terms. "Most of them appeared as I wrote them. They were usually something of a shock to write. Mostly they wrote themselves quite rapidly . . . arrived with a sense of having done something . . . tabu."[17]

But where, really, did they come from? It is difficult to imagine that this "demonic possession" depends on a literal belief in devils, especially in view of various early poems on the subject by both authors. In the late fifties both wrote on the contemporary failure of myth. In "Fourth of July" Hughes says "The right maps have no monsters" (*Lupercal*, 20), and in "The Death of Myth-Making," Plath writes that "lantern-jawed Reason, squat Common Sense" have "minced the muddling devil."[18] The undertone of complaint here would become more explicit a decade later, when Hughes would lash out at "rational skepticism"; his response is not to revive the devil, but to find "completely new Holy Ground, a new divinity, one that won't be under the rubble when the churches collapse."[19]

The argument here is more developed, but something of the underlying vision is already there in 1959, in Plath's "On the Decline of Oracles."

> In the Temple of Broken Stones, above
> A worn curtain, rears the white head
> Of a god or madman.[20]

But here the god only communicates trivia, "tomorrow's gossip," and the poem carries little force.

The connection with Yeats is evident. At this time Hughes and Plath, perhaps simply searching for a framework for their poetic powers, felt the need of, and apparently genuine intimations of, a mystical theology both ancient and new. Though it seems unlikely that either of them anticipated how extreme, or how literal, it would eventually become, there emerge early suggestions of their ultimate myth. In "I Want, I Want," Plath imagines "a baby god / Immense, bald, though baby-headed" (*Colossus*, 39), whose suffering creates the world's suffering; he will be reborn, more clearly understood because linked to the Mother, in Hughes's "Logos." Another savage god appears — or almost appears — in Hughes's "Crag Jack's Apostasy," where he comes in a constantly elusive dream of "a wolf's head, of eagles' feet" (*Lupercal*, 55); similarly in "The Hermit at Outermost House" Plath evokes "The great gods, Stone-Head, Claw-Foot" (*Colossus*, 56). Very early "The Manor Garden" describes "a difficult borning" which is somehow the end of an evolutionary movement toward something ambiguously destructive.

> Incense of death. Your day approaches
>   . . .
> You move through the era of fishes,
> The smug centuries of the pig —
> Head, toe, and finger
> Come clear of the shadow. . . .
>   (*Colossus*, 3)

Still it remains unclear what is being born, whether man, or god, or something between.

Clearly the conditions of its birth are appropriate to the savage god. Plath's pleasure in its very alienness is first seductive, then chilling. Again her mysticism of extreme negation casts a strange light on all the mystic patterns that begin by rejecting the world. Often she turns Roethkean lines celebrating earth contact into evocations of something alien in the most innocent landscapes. In "Sheep and Fog" she speaks with Roethke's voice to the extent of an apparently unknowing anticipation of the title of his final collection of poems: "the far / Fields melt my heart" (*Ariel,* 3). The line cannot actually refer to Roethke's "The Far Field," which had probably (in 1961) not been written, and would not for three years give its title to the posthumous collection. Still the phrase seems to promise, in Roethke's own words, a Roethkean merging of internal and external. But since Plath feels more than Roethke the terrors of immersion in the flow of being, the following stanza gives "melt my heart" a dark coloration, suggesting not the enriching flow into the world that often lifts Roethke's heart, but a terrible dissolution of self in watery emptiness.

> My bones hold a stillness, the far
> Fields melt my heart.
> They threaten
> To let me through to a heaven
> Starless and fatherless, a dark water.
>   (*Ariel,* 3)

"Poem for a Birthday," which contains more of Roethke's spirit as well as his style, moves beyond dissolution toward some alien affirmation despite the fact that the experience behind the poetry — mental collapse and shock treatment — seems on the face of it far more terrifying than the experience of casual observation that produced "Sheep and Fog." The electric revelations of this sequence predict the final nature and direction of Plath's transformational mythology, still in images inherited from Roethke. In "Birthday" she operates partly in the potting shed world she had just seen Roethke describe as she studied his greenhouse poems for the first time. This is a world of immersion in a damp vegetable kingdom, "in the bowel of the root," among "little humble loves" (*Crossing,* 50). Not only do Roethke's words echo but the poems recall his excursions into loss of self and self-discovery. Further, "The Beast," about Plath's father, suggests Roethke's poetic versions of his father, and "Who" takes place in a potting shed. But again the correspondences will not go all the way. Plath's intimations of vegetable rebirth are deeply opposed to Roethke's, not so much because the creature that may emerge from her dark cocooned gestation would be radically different from his enlightened man — that creature is never really presented — but because of the alien force that presides over the gestation. Constantly there is the sense of a threatening, illuminating, and apparently conscious power which is described in most of these poems in similar terms, "Mother of otherness," "mother of

mouths," "Mother of beetles," "mother of pestles." Plath's interaction
with this "Mother" will become a dominant theme in *Ariel*, and finally the
same being will emerge at the center of Hughes's mythic vision.

Who is she? Of the poems in the sequence "Who" most clearly describes
the Mother, but as its title predicts it offers primarily suggestive ambiguity.
It recalls the memory of an event partially blotted out by shock treatment,
an event which involves experiencing the inertness of "a root, a stone, an
owl pellet" in a shed which Plath describes as "fusty as a mummy's stomach." The suggestions are double; she has been devoured, or she is
gestating in some ancient womb. To add complexity, she says "I am all
mouth," which may present "I" as baby, like the "foetus" who sucks "the
paps of darkness" in "The Stones," or it may imply that "I" devours, participates in the being of the savage devouring Mother. Finally it seems
the speaker wants to be both eater and eaten.

> Mother, you are the one mouth
> I would be tongue to. Mother of otherness
> Eat me. Wastebasket gaper, shadow of doorways.
> (*Crossing*, 49)

"Shadow of doorways," this Mother is "nothing," but she is also a spirit of
transformation into otherness, not simply death.

Never simply death. "Maenad" describes another movement into darkness, into the Mother's womb, "the moon's vat," a more frightening movement this time because it is more strenuously resisted at first. The speaker
wants to remain "ordinary," existing in the realm of "my father," "eating
the fingers of wisdom," but the time of a deeper wisdom is on her.

> A red tongue is among us.
> Mother, keep out of my barnyard,
> I am becoming another.
> (*Crossing*, 51)

The plea to this "mother of mouths," "devourer," is futile; time and
change unwind, and Plath writes "I must swallow it all." The poem ends
in mystery, with a question to the "Lady" that we must consider repeatedly
as we read Plath's poetry of madness and vision: "Tell me my name."
For Plath is herself united with the Mother, an eater, a tongue, another.
In her poetry, as in her life, her name was becoming "Mother" too.

iii

We think of "Daddy" as typical of her — far from her best poem, but surely her most sensationally memorable one. In a time when no one memorizes poetry, most of us could probably quote at least some of "Daddy." But like her suicide its dominance in our imagination may over-simplify our sense of what was dominant in her imagination; the poetry of the *Ariel* period is more often concerned with mothers and babies than with fathers and daughters. The birth of her children released in Plath not simply a generalized creative urge, but an urge to construct images which would allow her to explore herself as mother, her relation to her own mother, and her relation to some underlying elemental force which with Hughes she came more and more to understand in mythic terms as a terrifying but compelling female, not God but the Great Mother, her antagonist and her ally, an enemy and a self. Her ambivalence toward this figure, which often accounts for the real confusion at the base of some of her poetry, will never reach any resolution. The extremity of this ambiva-lence seems schizophrenic, or at least understandable in terms of what R. D. Laing calls "ontological insecurity."[21] One of the forms of this is the fear of "engulfment," the sense that one's own reality is so tenuous that a more vital other may swallow one up, creating a psychic parody of mystical im-mersion. Paradoxically, the insecure self may desire as well as fear this engulfment, because it allows the security of participation in the vitality of the other.

Another aspect of ontological insecurity Laing mentions is the fear of "petrification," of being turned to stone. Plath dramatizes this fear in "Medusa," a companion piece to "Daddy" which begins by evoking an apparently real person but rapidly expands into the mythic territory sug-gested by its title. Like "Daddy" it depicts a parent looming from the ocean like a massive head, still umbilically connected to the poet, still op-pressive as a womb, still constricting. But the "Bottle in which I live" of "Medusa" carries more present force than the "black shoe / In which I have lived like a foot" of "Daddy" (*Ariel*, 39, 49). "Daddy, daddy, you bastard, I'm through" may work as exorcism, but the end of "Medusa," "Off, off, eely tentacle! / There is nothing between us," has more the sound of a futile plea; the tentacle is the maternal umbilicus, which unlike the black telephone to daddy remains "in a state of miraculous repair." The connection is sustained by "Your stooges," the speaker's children, de-scribed in foetal terms. The children are so identified with the speaker's mother that "you" in the poem often suggests them more than her. "You steamed to me over the sea, / Fat and red, a placenta" seems to imply both, since the placenta, associated with the baby, remains a part of the mother. Caught up in a cycle of generation which "paralyzes" her, Plath the mother feels the oppression of babies as an aspect of some larger maternal force which winds into her own maternal mind along some ancient umbilicus.

This maternal force cannot be described simply as the poet's own mother, if only because of the mystic or divine context introduced by: "Who do you think you are? / A Communion wafer? Blubbery Mary?" As *The Bell Jar* and various poems suggest, Plath may have felt oppressed by her own mother, and in general by dominant older women interested in influencing her,[22] but the personal obsession only leads to something more fundamental. In "Medusa" as in other poems the Mother turns Plath to stone, in the "Birthday" sequence she devours the poet, in "The Moon and the Yew Tree" she is a terrible deity, "bald and wild," and again opposed to the orthodox goddess: "The moon is my mother. She is not sweet like Mary" (*Ariel*, 41). But the destructive or oppressive aspects of the devouring Mother seldom prevent Plath's willing or unwilling impulse to union with her. Even in "Ocean 1212-W," her short prose piece about her early childhood, the dangerously enticing sea is described not only as "maternal," but as a mirror. "I often wondered what would have happened if I had managed to pierce that looking glass. Would my infant gills have taken over, the salt in my blood?"[23] As we will see, this suggests the dominant pattern; in this terrible and oppressive Mother Plath sees a possible self, and from immersion in the Mother she hopes for transformation into a purer existence, a terrible rebirth.

Though Plath's poetry creates the most dramatic evocations of the Mother, Hughes's explanations indicate her origin, and her apocalyptic significance. His sense of impending apocalyptic or evolutionary change is more general and more explicitly articulated than Plath's. As she says, her "vision of the apocalypse" is seldom stated in her poems; "they are not about the terrors of mass extinction, but about the bleakness of the moon over a yew tree in a neighboring graveyard."[24] What she implies here is that the two are connected, and when Hughes does write about mass extinction his images recall her perception of elemental sexual conflict, of the terrible Mother. Hughes makes it clear in the *London Magazine* interview that his sense of our culture's collapse derives largely from his perception of its repression of certain natural forces, mythically defined as feminine in contrast to the mythically male forces of logic and "rational skepticism." The power of what he calls "the Goddess" cannot be repressed forever, and poetry's task is to describe her return, to become "the record of just how the forces of the Universe try to redress some balance disturbed by human error . . . the difficult task of any poet in English [is] to locate the force which Shakespeare called Venus in his first poems and Sycorax in his last."[25]

A number of other poets agree with Hughes about this force. Robert Graves, who discovered the Goddess in Welsh myth and in Frazer's *Golden Bough,* formed some of Hughes's and Plath's vision of her;[26] and Robert Bly discovered her in his own visions, as well as in the Jungian Erich Neumann's *The Great Mother.* All insist on a radical division in the figure: the Mother of Life as opposed to the Death Mother or the Stone Mother. According to Neumann's scholarship the archetype has from primitive times contained this opposition, but Hughes's stress on her dark side is so emphatic that, despite his avowed devotion to her, he seems never to present her in her nourishing aspect. Nor does Plath, and in Bly the Good Mother appears infrequently. Hughes explains that the darker forms of the archetype must inevitably dominate now, principles of violent rebellion in the psyche. Repressed for so long by our patriarchal culture, depicted as a destroyer, the Mother takes the destructive role to redress the blame. "When Christianity kicked the devil out of Job," Hughes explains, "what they actually kicked out was Nature . . . and Nature became the devil."[27] The opposition between aggressive Christianity and the primal purity of nature continues as a center of Hughes's poetry. "As I came, I saw a wood," from his "alchemal cave drama" *Cave Birds,* describes an "ecstatic" natural scene in which plants and animals are one with earth and sky outside of time "in sanctity." The speaker recognizes this place of mystic fullness as

> . . . the crowded crossroads of all the heavens
> The festival of all the religious
>
> But a voice, a bell of cracked iron
> Jarred in my skull
>
> Summoning me to prayer
>
> To eat flesh and to drink blood.
>
> (*Cave,* 42)

Here nature turns gentle, and Christianity is seen as red in tooth and ritual.

In the earlier *Wodwo,* however, the Goddess seems more a principle of original evil than an elemental forced into the role of devil. Hughes's appalling images suggest the fundamental destructiveness in Plath's will to union with her. Her reign is terror. Behind the earth-shaking suffering of the mild baby-God of "Logos" lies the indifference of the real power, the original maternal creator. "God's a good fellow, but his mother's against him" (*Wodwo,* 34). So too in "Karma" the pleas of suffering humanity ("At Dresden at Buchenwald") are directed to "the mother / Of the God / Of the World / Made of Blood" (*Wodwo,* 160-61). Finally in "Gog" the Mother becomes a dragon, her ancient mythic role.[28] But in this poem St. George loses. The knightly masculine consciousness that fights for "the octaves of order" seems to be the aggressor ("My feetbones beat on the earth / Over the sounds of motherly weeping") but against "the womb ... that is of stone / ... Against the fanged grail and tireless mouth" he is clearly impotent.

Hughes's belief that this Goddess is rising again is corroborated by a broad and very mixed assortment of thinkers. Neumann's assertion about the mother's "reascent in modern times"[29] is amplified by Bly in his essay "I Came Out of the Mother Naked."[30] Neumann has also been cited with approval by feminist thinkers like Adrienne Rich and Nancy Bazin, who might at one time have been concerned about the stereotypes lurking in Jungian archetypes, but who now use the idea of the Great Mother to define necessary psychic and cultural changes. Plath's sense of the terrible rising Mother must be shared by others if Hughes's statement that Plath's "emblematic visionary" experiences derive from "total biological and racial recall" is not just a glorification of a private, possibly psychotic, obsession.[31] She can truly be called visionary only if she sees something that touches us all. Hughes's statements suggest Neumann's master Jung, who defines the mystic as someone in unusually direct contact with the movements of our collective unconscious, and, unless we are willing to accept the older definition of mysticism as contact with an actual God or Goddess, Jung's definition seems the most useful alternative.[32]

iv

Plath herself never made such explicit statements about her "visions" as Hughes has, but given the extent to which they shared a general poetic vision, we may hypothetically assume that he speaks for her. This hypothesis is supported by the dominant imagery of her poems, imagery historically associated, according to Neumann, with the dark side of the Mother: the moon, the sea, poppies, stones ("among the oldest symbols of the Great Mother Goddess"),[33] even the lioness and bees that appear in *Ariel*. From the beginning, in *Colossus,* she often evokes the fundamental Mother image of women rising out of darkness to invite her into a deadly sisterhood. The mythic creatures of "Lorelei," whom Neumann associates with Medusa as "figures of fatal enchantment,"[34] sing to her not from their traditional rocks but from the watery depths: "these shapes float / Up toward me, troubling the face / Of quiet" (*Colossus,* 22). Though they rise, they seem living stone, "ponderous," "hair heavier / Than sculpted marble."

As these dark forces rise from mystic water and the unconscious, the poet often descends to ultimate union. In "All the Dead Dears," which begins with the image of a woman "with a granite grin,"

> Mother, grandmother, greatgrandmother
> Reach hag hands to haul me in,
> And an image looms under the fishpond surface.
> (*Colossus,* 30)

"Nick and the Candlestick" employs the image of descent into the earth to enact a darkly sacramental movement into the unconscious, now the realm of the savage Goddess. In the blue light which often illuminates visionary experience in Plath and Hughes, the poet sinks into the realm of the Mother, to immersion in "the earthen womb," "Old cave of calcium." There she finds "A piranha / Religion, drinking / Its first Communion out of my live toes" (*Ariel,* 33), as the distinction between human communicant and sacrificed deity grows dim. Awakening from her long fall she discovers her child ("O embryo") sleeping as if in a womb himself. She looks to him for human relief from her apocalyptic vision, but we know the comfort he provides cannot last, though it makes her bold in the teeth of doom:

> Let the stars
> Plummet to their dark address,
>
> Let the mercuric
> Atoms that cripple drip
> Into the terrible well.

Here as in "Medusa" the devouring Mother evokes from Plath not the desire for union but fear of engulfment, finally of annihilation. As Neu-

mann explains, the contemporary woman existing in a rationalist patri-
archy also has "a symbolically male consciousness and may experience the
unconscious as 'negatively feminine.' "[35]

But this fear only dramatizes a characteristic of mystical union, with
any sort of god, that has always existed. Plath only takes the stock imagery
of death and immersion to an extreme. The *via negativa* has always implied the destruction of self in the service of ultimate otherness, ultimate
power. As the opposition between the child and the ritual immersion in
"Nick" indicates, the pull of otherness can move the mystic away from
human concerns, away from the love of men into the primal whirl of
power. Even Christian mystics seem often to regard the love of humanity
as a distracting duty. What tends to emerge in visionary writing, despite
the rhetoric of love, is a God of power. (Even in St. Theresa's description
of the dart of love and spiritual marriage, the conspicuously sexual metaphors depict power more than love. Her intense pleasure in her "delicious
wound" and "delightful" pain reveal a masochism closer to Plath's than
most mystics'.)[36] So in the poetry of dark union, from Stevens and Eliot
through Plath and Merwin, few avowals of love for humanity balance
the desire for immersion in otherness. When Williams allowed people
realistically imagined (not simply metaphors for the Mother) into
Paterson, they tended to distract him and finally turn him away from the
mystic quest.

Ultimately Plath, seldom distracted by love for humanity, finds something like transcendence within immanence, within the physical world.
Her descent into darkness ends in a rising under the sign of the ascendant
Terrible Mother. Her poetry is unusual not for its preoccupation with
death, but in its references to a mysterious rebirth, ascension not to redemption but to vengeance. "It is inherent in the mysteries of the Great
Goddess and in her spiritual character that she grants life only through
death"; as in "Nick and the Candlestick," "rebirth can occur through sleep
in the nocturnal cave, [or] through a descent to the underworld realm of
the spirits."[37] More literal suggestions of rebirth and ascendance come in
"Lady Lazarus," the ending of which is inexplicable except in terms of
the devouring Mother, who is out to get not only "Herr Doktor," but also
"Herr God."

> Out of the ash
> I rise with my red hair
> And I eat men like air.
>   (*Ariel,* 9)

Plath's war against God the Father is not always so potentially successful, especially in those poems which apparently refer to her shock treatments, the most dramatic imaginable imposition of a mechanical otherness on the unconscious. But shock treatment, as in the "Poem for a Birthday" sequence, almost invariably assumes mystical resonance, as a metaphor for intimately violent contact between the boldest searchers and a god perceived as totally alien. If the mystic is not destroyed (as in Lowell) by contact with such otherness, union can bring painful revelation. By referring to Prometheus ("vulturous boredom") as well as the hanged man of the Tarot, punished for spiritual presumption, "The Hanging Man" suggests the arrogance of those who would put on the fiery knowledge of gods. For such mystical overreachers, revelation comes as punishment: "I sizzled in his blue volts like a desert prophet" (*Ariel*, 69), and later imagery describes eyes fixed open in a terrible excess of vision. But paradoxically, in a line as full of blunt authority as anything Plath wrote, the drive to know forbidden truth is described as something divine, though destructive, in man; the hanging mystic says of the god, "If he were I, he would do what I did."

This experience of elemental conflict is far from the peaceful orthodox mysticism it reflects and parodies. But the loving beatitude imagined by Eliot, or before him Juliana of Norwich, was itself a radical departure from an earlier way of knowing, reflected in Judaeo-Christian mythology (the Old Testament) as well as pagan. Unconvinced by the Christian story, Plath feels the need to confront the god who dwells in the whirlwind, who may put out reason's eyes, but who knows truths deeper than the pallid evasions of Christianity. "Mystic" suggests that this confrontation, as much as violent identification with Mother or land, constitutes Plath's most intense mystical experience, which nothing can top:

> Once one has seen God, what is the remedy?
> Once one has been seized up
>
> . . .
>
> Used utterly, in the sun's conflagrations, the stains
> That lengthen from ancient cathedrals
> What is the remedy?
>
> (*Winter*, 7)

The only remedy is further conflict. In words reminiscent of Hughes, the "Second Voice" of Plath's "Three Women" explains the reason for rebellion against the Father. She says of "the Father" and "the Son," "They are jealous gods / That would have the whole world flat because

they are" (*Winter,* 51), and she goes on to describe the response of her
Mother the earth as "now the world conceives / Its end and runs toward
it."

> She is the vampire of us all. So she supports us,
> Fattens us, is kind. Her mouth is red.
>   . . .
> Men have used her meanly. She will eat them.
> Eat them, eat them, eat them in the end.
>   (*Winter,* 53-54)

Many of Plath's bee poems turn on this idea that oppressed female nature
will escape and rise to destroy the constrictions of a masculine and mechanical civilization. In "The Swarm," escape fails, but "the man with
grey hands / . . . a man of business, intensely practical" remarks as he
shoots the swarm down, "They would have killed *me*" (*Ariel,* 65).
Mythically he speaks the truth; the matriarchal bees, who kill males after
mating, are "a favorite with the Great Mother."[38] In the strange poem
"Stings," the poet leaves the company of drudging women to find an
earlier identity as queen bee, elsewhere described as "murderess." "I /
Have a self to recover, a queen." As usual the matriarch ascends from
death, red and threatening:

> Now she is flying
> More terrible than she ever was, red
> Scar in the sky, red comet
> Over the engine that killed her —
>   (*Ariel,* 63)

The queen's "lion-red" body connects her with the woman in "Purdah"
who will "unloose / . . . The Lioness" against "the bridegroom" who owns
her (*Winter,* 42).

But the most striking lion image celebrates mystic motion but not mythic
violence: In "Ariel" "God's Lioness" reconciles male and female in a
phrase. If Hughes's "Cadenza" is an evocation not so much of the personal
spirit of Plath as of the underlying terrible Goddess, "Ariel" is an attempt
to imagine sexual and mystical interaction in a context so ecstatic that underlying sexual conflict is resolved in cosmic union. Like Roethke's more
still but no less ecstatic "A Field of Light" the poem begins in dark motion-
lessness, a condition dramatized by the perfect balance of syllables and ac-
cents in the brief end-stopped first line. As in "Field" the initial stasis gives
way to liquid flow before any subject, any "I" is defined or even mentioned.

Undefined stasis gives way to undefined motion, both subject and verb
withheld until the second stanza.

> Stasis in darkness.
> Then the substanceless blue
> Pour of tor and distances.
>
> God's lioness,
> How one we grow,
> Pivot of heels and knees! — The furrow
>
> Splits and passes, sister to
> The brown arc
> Of the neck I cannot catch.
>
> <div align="right">(<i>Ariel</i>, 26)</div>

Even as they begin to emerge the actors remain vague, looming out of the
darkness, defined in small detail by Plath's resonant monosyllables; but the
larger shapes continue to be ambiguous. "God's lioness" seems both above
and below the human, both divine and animal, perhaps a shape with lion
body and the head of a woman, perhaps simply brown horse, white rider.
But the sexual resonances become so conspicuous that they do more than
simply color the image of horse and rider; they cause the superimposition
of another image, of human lovers. The powerful monosyllables "How one
we grow" can be explained in terms of riding as well as loving, but the
specifically sexual interpretation seems necessary to explain a later image.
"The child's cry / Melts in the wall" can only happen in a bedroom, as
the imagery of lovemaking mixes with and then overcomes the fragmented
image of horse and rider.

Finally both sex and riding are overcome by a stronger force, as the
landscape/bedscape recedes and the passive rider is "hauled through the
air" like Yeats's Leda, caught up by "something else," some force of otherness that takes her beyond ordinary self and landscape in orgasmic rising.
After the suspenseful line "And now I," pausing before the final rush of
action, everything passes into unity as the poet internalizes the landscape
and wheat and seas exchange characteristics in another beautifully balanced line. The interlocking images shimmer with light both still and
moving in the heart of flow:

> And now I
> Foam to wheat, a glitter of seas.
> The child's cry

Melts in the wall.
And I
Am the arrow.

"And now I . . . And I. . . ." In the moment of loss of self, the moment of
orgasm/merging that extinguishes such ordinary sensation as the child's
cry, the "I" is still conspicuous, separate and indomitable. As in Roethke,
loss of self becomes the only complete self-assertion, here a self-assertion
which joins male (the arrow) and female (wheat, seas, dew) imagery not
in violent conflict but in a bold leap to ecstatic energy.

Am the arrow,

The dew that flies
Suicidal, at one with the drive
Into the red

Eye, the cauldron of morning.

In such a poem of sexual fulfillment, the devouring Mother cannot appear, so "Ariel" is Plath's most ecstatic dream of merging with various
others. But without murderous violence, the Mother's patterns are fulfilled: the female ascent from darkness and stasis into light and motion,
the sense of transformation and purification, and finally the death that is
also a rebirth in the cauldron of the Mother, a fall into cosmic rising.
Throughout the poem, the perimeters of union expand; first Plath is "one"
with horse or lover, both in the "pour" of landscape turned liquid, "sub-
stanceless"; the horse is "sister" to the road; and then Plath begins to
become everything, wheat, seas, and finally the dew which carries her into
the sun as the horse carried her into the world. Despite its emphasis on
air and fire the poem abounds with liquid, even to the "cauldron" of the
sun. Images of transcendence and immersion alternate as motion submerges violence in Plath's most fully realized poem of union. Only in one
word does the pervasive violence of her mythology remain; under the
circumstances we cannot simply read "suicidal" as ecstatic metaphor.

So even in a poem which rather beautifully suggests the white magic of
Ariel, Hughes's Sycorax, mother of Caliban, looms behind the ascent to
triumphant union. For Plath's identification with the destructive Mother
dominates her mystical imagination. At war with the archetypal Father,
and not finally able to remain in the world, much less to sustain mystical
immersion in the flow of being that is also an aspect of the Mother, she
followed the way of violence to the end. She was psychologically more

vulnerable than Hughes to the Great Mother because she was a mother, and imaged herself as prey, but also because she identified with the vengeful aspect of the archetype. For the vengeance was all inside, and from her death there was no rising. There the identification broke down, with inexorable logic. The female can no more survive destruction of the male principle than men can survive the ongoing destruction of the mythically feminine, whether imagined as mother earth, women, or their own unconscious. As Hughes projected his sense of cosmic violence onto the animal landscape, Plath internalized the apocalypse, became both avenger and victim. Out of the tension between these two roles came much of her most obsessive poetry, poetry often obscure or ambiguous, marked by flashes of genius but also by a certain amount of that oracular confusion that always attends struggle with mystery.

But her poetry is as deep as it is dark and narrow, and it goes to the heart of our time, not only in its psychodrama of sexual conflict but in its exploration of the darker reaches of mysticism. Though not aimed so conspicuously beyond the concerns of ordinary humanity as the mysticism of transcendence, immersion mysticism can be characterized by a coldness toward men and women which lives at the heart of visionary ecstasy. In the frame of eternity, in the poetry of death, the love and suffering of other humans can fade into exemplary abstraction. If humanity considered as a combination of self and others is elided from poetry and meditation, the mystical poet can become as lost in inwardness and morally insensitive as any of the mystics of the past who turned away from men to total concentration on a divinity hallucinated as an image of self in absolute otherness. The familiar otherness, immanent or transcendent, provides endless fascination, but even if it actually is some ultimate ground of goodness as well as power, the claims of human morality lead away from it, back to the world of men. Such claims are explicitly confronted by Robert Bly, like Hughes a poet not only of the Great Mother but of imminent apocalypse; they will have a curious effect on the poetry of W. S. Merwin, who discovers for himself a mystical territory even colder and more remote than Plath's, a place somehow full of that otherness never fully described by Stevens.

NOTES

1. Harriet Rothstein, "Reconsidering Sylvia Plath," in *Ms.*, Sept. 1972, p. 99.
2. For instance Irving Howe, "Sylvia Plath: A Partial Disagreement," in *Harper's*, Jan. 1972, pp. 88-91. Interestingly, Howe makes much the same judg-

ment about the Quentin Compson section of *The Sound and the Fury* in his *William Faulkner* (1952; rpt., New York: Vintage, 1962), p. 167.

3. David Holbrook, *Sylvia Plath, Poetry and Existence* (London: Univ. of London Press, 1976), p. 184. Later he says of feminists, "what they want to be liberated from is being female and being human" (p. 200).

4. Judith Kroll, *Chapters in a Mythology, the Poetry of Sylvia Plath* (New York: Harper & Row, 1976), p. 210. Kroll's ideas about Plath's use of the "Moon-muse" or White Goddess have, for me, the distinct advantage of making my own very similar ideas about Plath, Hughes, and the Great Mother sound considerably less eccentric than they did when I first published them, in an early version of this chapter printed as a 1974 *Contemporary Literature* article. Inevitably I find her account of Plath attractive, but in defending Plath (and probably in writing a book acceptable to Ted Hughes) she relentlessly discovers mystical affirmation in the poems, sometimes turning the bitterly ironic ones upside down to do so.

In the still more recent study *Sylvia Plath and Ted Hughes* (Urbana: Univ. of Illinois Press, 1979), Margaret Uroff correctly argues that "Kroll's discussion of the death in this poem as an intermediate step toward rebirth suggests the limitations of her effort to fit all of Plath's poetry into *The White Goddess* mythology" (p. 170n). Still, Kroll sees depths not adequately fathomed in Uroff's analysis of Plath.

5. Holbrook, *Sylvia Plath*, pp. 271, 272.

6. Kroll, *Chapters in a Mythology*, p. 147.

7. Primary sources will be identified by their first word in the text. Plath collections cited are *The Colossus and Other Poems* (New York: Knopf, 1962), *Ariel* (New York: Harper & Row, 1966), *Crossing the Water* (Harper, 1971), and *Winter Trees* (Harper, 1972). Hughes collections cited include *Lupercal* (London: Faber & Faber, 1960), *Wodwo* (Faber, 1967), *Crow* (Faber, 1970), and *Cave Birds* (New York: Viking, 1978), p. 42.

8. *The Art of Sylvia Plath,* ed. Charles Newman (Bloomington: Indiana Univ. Press, 1970).

9. Typically, Judith Kroll argues that these lines should be taken seriously: "The farce in a sense rises by its own levity above itself" (*Chapters in a Mythology,* p. 179). Worse, Uroff (*Slyvia Plath and Ted Hughes,* pp. 167-68) seems unaware of the possibility of farce.

10. Robert Phillips, "The Dark Funnel: A Reading of Sylvia Plath," in *Sylvia Plath, the Woman and the Work,* ed. Edward Butscher (New York: Dodd, Mead, 1977), p. 191.

11. Robin Morgan, "Arraignment," *Monster* (New York: Vintage, 1972), p. 76. Plath herself suggests a response to this accusation when in *The Bell Jar* she has Esther Greenwood laugh at Buddy Willard's assumption of responsibility for her suicide attempt and the successful suicide of another of his girls. After all, as *The Bell Jar* also indicates, Plath's first attempts occurred long before she met Hughes.

12. Phyllis Chesler, *Women and Madness* (New York: Doubleday, 1972), p. 294.

13. M. L. Rosenthal, *The New Poets: American and British Poetry since World War II* (New York: Oxford Univ. Press, 1967), p. 233.

14. Ekbert Faas, "Ted Hughes and *Crow*," interview in *London Magazine*, Jan. 1971, pp. 8-9.

15. Ted Hughes, "Notes on the Chronological Order of Sylvia Plath's Poems," *Triquarterly*, 7 (Fall 1966), 82. When this essay was reprinted in *The Art of Sylvia Plath*, the sentence about shamans and LSD was discreetly omitted.

16. A. Alvarez, *The Savage God* (London: Weidenfeld & Nicholson, 1971), pp. 24, 14.

17. Faas, "Ted Hughes," p. 18.

18. Sylvia Plath, "The Death of Myth-Making," *Triquarterly*, 7 (Fall 1966), 11.

19. Faas, "Ted Hughes," p. 19.

20. Sylvia Plath, "On the Decline of Oracles," *Poetry*, Sept. 1959, p. 368.

21. R. D. Laing, *The Divided Self* (1960; rpt., Baltimore: Pelican, 1965), pp. 39ff. Marjorie Perloff also notes the connection between Laing's "engulfment" and a Plath poem ("Parliament Hill Fields") in "On the Road to *Ariel*: The Transitional Poetry of Sylvia Plath," *Iowa Review*, 4 (Spring 1973), 96-97.

22. In "Reconsidering Sylvia Plath," Rothstein contends that Esther Greenwood's complaint that she is manipulated by "weird old women" is a rather "malicious" distortion of her actual situation (p. 49). About Plath's feelings for her own mother we can only speculate, drawing on a range of descriptions from Holbrook's "the poet had a happy relationship with her mother" (*Sylvia Plath*, p. 9) to biographer Butscher's "she was a monster, this sincere Aurelia Plath of Wellsley, a vampire of the unconscious" (*Sylvia Plath, Woman and Work*, p. 8). If the second opinion sounds extreme, the first seems almost willfully naive. Similar disagreements exist about everyone in the Plath cosmos, including Ted and (especially) Olwyn Hughes.

23. Sylvia Plath, "Ocean 1212-W," appearing in *Art of Sylvia Plath*, p. 266.

24. Sylvia Plath, "Context," *London Magazine*, Feb. 1962, p. 46.

25. Faas, "Ted Hughes," pp. 6-7.

26. Like Hughes, Robert Graves sees evidence of the Goddess and her mythic companions in *The Tempest*. See *The White Goddess* (New York: Creative Age Press, 1948), p. 98. According to Kroll (*Chapters in a Mythology*, p. 49), Hughes introduced this book to Plath in 1956.

27. Faas, "Ted Hughes," p. 8. Of course Graves saw this too, and in *The White Goddess* he made a prediction which Hughes must have appreciated. Our culture must reacknowledge the Goddess, he wrote, "But the longer the change is delayed, and therefore the more exhausted by man's irreligious improvidence the natural resources of the soil and sea become, the less placid and merciful will be the five-fold mask that the Goddess ultimately assumes" (p. 391). He also wrote that in this "Apollonian civilization" the Goddess cannot return "until women themselves grow weary of decadent patriarchialism, and turn Bassarids again" (p. 376).

28. See Erich Neumann, *The Great Mother* (New York: Pantheon, 1955), p. 38.

29. Neumann, *Great Mother*, p. 331.

30. Robert Bly, *Sleepers Joining Hands* (New York: Harper & Row, 1973), p. 48.

31. Ted Hughes, "Chronological Order," p. 81.

32. Plath's familiarity with Jung is evident. Not only does she use the term "archetype" (*Crossing*, 9), but in "Johnny Panic and the Bible of Dreams" she locates "those great originals" in a lake of dreams that clearly symbolizes the racial unconscious. *Johnny Panic and the Bible of Dreams* (New York: Harper & Row, 1978), p. 154.

33. Neumann, *Great Mother*, p. 260.

34. Neumann, *Great Mother*, pp. 80-81.

35. Neumann, *Great Mother*, p. 148.

36. St. Theresa, *The Interior Castle*, trans. "A Benedictine of Stanbrook," rev. Prior Benedict Zimmerman (London: Thomas Baker, 1930), p. 132. Theresa also compares her God to "a burning furnace," as Lowell does in "Where the Rainbow Ends." Finally her desire for total union with this fiery Love leads her to an "ardent" longing for death: "life becomes a painful though delicious torture" (p. 172).

37. Neumann, *Great Mother*, pp. 279, 292.

38. Neumann, *Great Mother*, p. 265. An example of the lion-bee-Mother connection is Cybele, whom Graves calls "the Mother of All Living" (*White Goddess*, p. 259). He initially identifies her as "the Lion and Bee Goddess of Phyrgia in whose honor young men castrated themselves" (p. 45).

5

Robert Bly Unknowing, Knowing

Not so much Roethke as the early Stevens, according to Robert Bly himself, is his American predecessor in the exploration of the mysterious energies of the physical world. Again the relationship is not one of direct influence, at least stylistic influence. Bly's rather special voice was touched not simply by American traditions but by foreign tones, especially that of the surrealist Pablo Neruda. Neruda's style, like those of many others Bly translates, blends with Bly's in the free and energetic translations, and the mixtures persist in the translator's own work. Bly cannot of course translate Stevens, but when asked for an essay about his own poetry for the collection *American Poets in 1976,* he replied with one primarily about Stevens. He regards Stevens not simply as the great poet of death and the Mother, but also as a far more sensual poet than current criticism tends to emphasize, one who aims to awaken the reader's senses and tune them to a high enough pitch for the reception of abstract ideas through sense impressions. In *Harmonium,* Bly says, "the thinking is expressed through odor and sound images, and the sense images become more intense through the thinking going on."[1] Bly follows Stevens in this philosophical sensuality, and here probably speaks for himself as well. His thinking is more overtly mystical than Stevens's, with transcendent longings, but partly because it is expressed through immediately sensual imagery his mysticism remains immanent, mysticism of the deepest immersion.

Bly may impose his own current concerns on Stevens when he goes on to describe him (along with Eliot and Williams) as a poet of the Jungian Shadow, and he seems insensitive to Stevens's visionary development when he claims that "the late poems are as weak as is possible for a genius to write; what is worse, most of them have the white nightgown mentality."[2] But his insistence on "the extraordinary richness of his sensual intelligence" and Stevens's intention to achieve "a union of all the five senses"[3] does much to characterize both poets. Each constructs an exchange between physical and spiritual that ends in a perception of the body and reality as interpenetrating fields of energy. Each is a poet of meditation, believing finally that the only true perception is visionary, that man's lost purity of seeing can now be achieved only through a mystical leap beyond ordinary vision. And each, despite a pervasive sensuality of language and image, is finally drawn to images so austere as to suggest not only purity but an underlying psychological distance, a coldness somehow related to each poet's romantic vision of death. In "Thinking of Wallace Stevens on the First Snowy Day of December," Bly makes the connection explicit.

> This new strength whispers of the darkness of death,
> Of the frail skiff lost in the giant cave,
> Just as in the boat nearing death you sang
> Of feathers and white snow.[4]

Stevens is surely a greater and more consistent singer than the often uneven Bly, but he does not necessarily touch deeper chords. Bly's poetry, like Roethke's, can be careless and even crude, it can assert a spiritual authority which it does not always earn, it can fall into mannerism or overstatement. But when it works, it cuts very deep, characterized by a fullness of energy seldom evident in poetry of philosophical or spiritual exploration. As Bly finds the spiritual world embedded in the physical, so he embodies the abstractions of poetry in physical reality viscerally rendered. He is a poet of dreams, of the unconscious, but the hero of his poetry is not the mind or soul but the body, the body thinking in its own difficult language. Bly's task has been to make this language clear, and though he insists on its independence from ordinary analytic thought, he is in poetry and out a born explainer, teacher, proponent of theories that will illuminate the paradoxes of a mystical vision both more overtly spiritual and more viscerally physical than either Stevens's or Roethke's. Like many mystical poets, Bly writes with large patterns in mind, and behind his explorations into darkness there stands not only a complex poetic theory but also a highly articulated mythology of the psychological development of civilization. This scheme, like that of other mystical poets (conspicuously Blake) is frequently based on logical antithesis suspended in paradox, and paradoxes simple and profound form the base of Bly's poetry.

He begins with the intention of creating a truly free associationalism, radically opposed to what he considers the calculated and artificially logical associationalism of Eliot and Pound. In an essay called "Looking for Dragon Smoke" he argues that the formalist obsessions of modern American poets (from Eliot to Charles Olson) have obscured the true psychic bases of poetry. Despite some exceptions, he says, "We have not yet regained in American poetry that swift movement all over the psyche, from conscious to unconscious, from a pine table to mad inward desires, that the ancient poets had, or that Lorca and others gained back for poetry in Spanish. Why not? Every time we get started, we get sidetracked into technique."[5] As this surrealist example suggests, Bly's poetry depends on the conception of the "deep image," a concept developed by Bly and James Wright. The successful deep image strikes with the force of a newly discovered archetype, minor or major, coming from the depths of the poet's subjectivity with a paradoxically universal force, his private revelation made ours. In Bly's "Depression," for instance, the poet describes his psychic state in images which despite their novelty seem more discovered than made.

> I dreamt that men came toward me, carrying thin wires;
> I felt the wires pass in, like fire; they were old Tibetans;
> Dressed in padded clothes, to keep out cold;
> Then three work gloves, lying fingers to fingers,
> In a circle, came toward me, and I awoke.
>
> (*Silence,* 37)

Bly describes such unusually concrete surrealist imagery as the result of "leaping" from conscious to unconscious mind and back again. In advocating the return of such leaping in "Dragon Smoke," Bly looks back with longing to the last period in Western poetry when such associative travel was possible. Ironically this is also the time dear to the hearts of Eliot and Lowell, hardly Bly's favorite modern poets. "Sometime in the thirteenth century poetry in Europe began to show a distinct decline in the ability to associate powerfully. There are individual exceptions, but the circle of worlds pulled into the poem by association dwindled after Chaucer and Langland."[6]

Primary among the separated worlds, as Bly explains in his essay on Stevens, are those of intellectual apprehension and physical apprehension; consciousness is distant not only from the unconscious but from the senses. This proves destructive spiritually as well as poetically, so "the majority of people in the West are worse off than they were in the Middle

Ages."[7] Bly tends to be irresistibly drawn to such sweeping statements; the odd thing about the thinking that led to this one is that it inevitably reminds us of Eliot on the "dissociation of sensibility," though Eliot places the fatal split in the seventeenth century. Both philosophers of the psyche describe a failure in poetic imagery which results from the loss of a unified view of the spiritual and physical world, and which can be healed by the visionary poet, transcending the limitations of his culture.

Bly differs from Eliot, of course. What Eliot applauds as "direct senuous apprehension of thought" in Donne[8] is quite different from what Bly admires in the illuminated Stevens of *Harmonium;* Stevens's imagery is more dramatically sensual, far less disciplined by ordinary logic, at times as surreal as that of Bly's foreign masters. Bly's own images imply a type of spiritual perception that is even more rooted in the physical world; where Eliot or even Stevens would write "the spirit," Bly will usually say "the body." Opposed to this spiritual body is the dissociated intellect, the mind of the Enlightenment, channeled away from the natural flow of existence by the rigid conduits of rationalism. At the center of Bly's poetry and poetic theory is the suspicion of rationalism always evident in mystical poets but articulated so bluntly by Bly that it evokes outraged critical response.

The older Bly has taken some pains to modify the excesses of the younger polemicist. In a general restatement of his position in *News of the Universe,* he argues that the importance of rationalist irony and dislocation in the modernist tradition has been overstated, and that we must pay more attention to the poetry of mystical connection and "swift association. Its aim is not to scant the modern world, but to approach the nourishment of night-intelligence."[9] The use of the term "intelligence" to describe intuitive knowledge, the unknowing knowledge of the unconscious, seems aimed to correct a false dichotomy assumed by many critics and sometimes implied by Bly himself, a complete dichotomy between logic or intelligence and intuition. In championing the poetry of visionary leaping against rationalist discursive poetry, in arguing the sterility of poetry of "the workshop" in the university, Bly has attacked rationalist analytic thought so energetically that he has often been perceived as a foe of intelligence entirely. Partly this is his own fault; feeling almost alone against the poetic establishment in the fifties and early sixties, he made a habit of overstatement, shouting loud enough to be heard, in fact to become a leader in one of the many revolutions of the time.[10] His most serious overstatements force a complete separation between vision and intelligence, the right brain and left brain functions that his poetry ("leaping about the psyche") seems specifically intended to connect. As Robert Hass put it, with an amused glance at Bly's habitual animal images, Bly tended to describe "imagination as a kind of ruminative wombat," hidden away from reason. "As everyone knows, the imagination is luminously intelligent," Hass writes; "this description, which is contradicted anyway by Bly's best poems and by other more plausible things he says . . . is typical of the hatred of intelligence that pervades puritan culture."[11] That culture, Bly's archenemy, resides also within him; as usual the strongest rebel is the one who has internalized enough established belief to power his rebellion with an energy derived from internal strife.

Though an older and gentler Bly has qualified many of his excessive positions (and some harsh judgments of such poets as Eliot), some critics still portray him as the assassin of intelligence. In a presumably sympathetic essay in *Of Solitude and Silence,* Patricia Goedicke goes so far as to suggest that Bly's "abandonment of reason" logically runs the risk of "encouraging philosophical and political totalitarianism . . . Jonestown and Auschwitz are ever present specters."[12] Perhaps Bly deserves such irrational "analysis" for his sins of overstatement, but any real thought about his own essays (always shaped by analytic reason, as well as intuition) would suggest that it is precisely the type of "reason" that produced Auschwitz that Bly attacks, that reasoning cut off from the ground of the body, where physical and spiritual meet. To repeat his own intentions again: Bly wants not "to throw reason out the window" (to echo Goedicke's cliché) but to join it with the forces defined as "unreason" by our mechanistic culture. The leaps in his poem intend to wed conscious reasoning and archetypal image in a union both felt and understood.

Examined closely, Bly's poetry celebrating visionary otherness appears carefully grounded in the logic and the ordinary sensations of this world. Its surreal images are logically orchestrated, its leaps beginning with, and often returning to, the reasoned perceptions of poet and later readers. Bly's conviction of the importance of the vision of the other world makes him all the more eager to ground it in plain speech and plain thought; for a surrealist poet of the negative way he remains surprisingly devoted to ordinary logic. (But so were Eliot and Stevens.) Such common critical statements as "Typically the coherences within the [Bly] poem are intuitive and associative rather than rational"[13] create a division not borne out by the poetry. Even Bly's most visionary utterances tend to begin with a blunt, plain style assertion of subject and attitude, and often his arcane images resist logical analysis only briefly and superficially. In his brand of surrealism, "associative" usually depends on "the rational." For instance the leaps of a poem like "The Clear Air of October" create somewhat mysterious images: "I know these cold shadows are falling for hundreds of miles," and "I know the horse of darkness is riding fast to the east, / Carrying a thin man with no coat" (*Silence,* 52). But the images are not only logically articulated, they are in the end made transparent by our realization that the poet is describing a sunset in imagery heavy with the sense of death traditionally inspired by the dying day.

In fact such code words as "reason" and "intelligence" seldom refer to the actual experience of Bly's poetry but to a basic argument about the nature of poetry rooted in a conflict about the nature of nature. As she chides the poet for his attacks on reason, Goedicke refers to Robert Pinsky's *Situation of Poetry,* an engaging and frankly "reactionary" and Wintersian plea for "discursive poetry," poetry with fewer surreal images and more of what Pinsky calls "the Prose Virtues." Pinsky is not particularly interested in Bly, except negatively; he presents Bly as a typical practitioner of forced imagery in an inadequately internalized surrealist style, and also as one poet (not identified by name) guilty of "a dated, sentimental 'imagism': the 'single raindrop' of the Iowa *haiku,* the snowflake in the horse's mane."[14]

When the proponents of reasoning are reasonable, it seems beastly to argue with them; what Pinsky stands for, though, is ultimately unreasonable given Bly's understanding of the world. This academic poet draws the line between himself and Bly very clearly, because his book really concerns the "problem" of the romantic's dangerous desire to merge with nature. "The problem can be summarized as a need to find language for presenting the role of a conscious soul in an unconscious world."[15] Bly could not have asked for a clearer declaration of what he calls "the Old Position." The Old Position is best described as Cartesian rationalism, the prime focus of Bly's attack in his most systematic, mature, and comparatively restrained position paper on poetry and the cosmos, the introductory material in his Sierra Club anthology *News of the Universe.* There he argues for a sort of ecological balance between reason and the more animal responses to existence. "The Old Position may be summed up, or oversimplified, this way: Consciousness is human, and involves reason. A serious gap exists between us and the rest of nature. Nature is to be watched, pitied, and taken care of if it behaves."[16]

The answer to this destructive assumption of alienation is not the abandonment of reason: Bly specifically praises the German romantics like Holderlin and Goethe for using reason against excessive rationalism, fighting "the battle of ideas" against the Enlightenment. The point is to open reason to other types of consciousness, to use it to unite, not divide. He quotes Basho: "The trouble with most poetry is that it is either subjective or objective."[17] He might have quoted Stevens or Williams to much the same effect. As J. Hillis Miller explains in *Poets of Reality* (from which Bly approvingly quotes in another context in *News*) Williams too opposes Descartes: "The resignation to existence which makes Williams' poetry possible is the exact reverse of the Cartesian Cogito. Descartes puts everything into question in order to establish the existence of his separate self, an existence built on the power of detached thinking. Williams gives himself up in despair and establishes a self beyond personality, a self coextensive with the universe."[18]

The mystical implications are obvious; union with the world's soul is imaginable if human consciousness is not "detached" by reason. Bly's attacks on reason simply suggest, like Eliot's mystical paradoxes or Stevens's desire "to catch from that / Irrational moment its unreasoning," that unknowing must open knowing to the patterns of a larger consciousness. The spiritual movement enacted or wished for in most of Bly's poems involves not only a wedding of mind and matter, a sinking into earth or dark water, but a blending of two consciousnesses. In *This Tree Will Be Here for a Thousand Years,* which Bly presents as a 1979 extension of *Silence in the Snowy Fields,* he specifically articulates concern with immersion in a "consciousness *out there* among plants and animals"; like Stevens at his most romantic Bly aspires to "a union of inner and outer in the same poem" (*Tree,* 9, 10). Like Stevens too, Bly often imagines that union in the context of images of death. Death achieves a constant immediacy that strongly suggests the omnipresent medieval devourer, who lurks in the abyss beneath the narrow way of life. In "Night" Bly dreams an image appropriate to a fourteenth-century sermon:

> Alive, we are like a sleek black water beetle,
> Skating across still water in any direction
> We choose, and soon to be swallowed
> Suddenly from beneath.
>
> (*Silence,* 55)

But if Bly's images of death are more explicit and immediate than Stevens's they also tend to be oddly cheerful; his response to death has an unaccountable joy in it, not the world-weary relief of Eliot or the vengeful satisfaction of Lowell. Lowell's medievalism is bleak, though profoundly energetic; Bly feels a different blend of ecstasy and pain, a mixture common to all times, but unusually extreme in the Middle Ages. In "Images Suggested by Medieval Music" life is again an ocean voyage, as "we plunge on into the sea of pain." But pain causes an unexpected joy:

> I have felt this joy before, it is like the harsh grasses
> On lonely beaches, this strange sweetness
> Of medieval music, a hoarse joy,
> Like birds', or the joy of trackless seas.

(Silence, 44)

The same ecstatic perception of death as inseparable from the vital energy of life forms the climax of the bright night vision of "To Live" in *This Tree:*

> To live is to rush ahead eating up your own death,
>   like an endgate, open, hurrying into the night.

(Tree, 25)

There sounds a curious excitement here, that is both more reasonable and more mysterious than anything like a death wish. If otherwise sympathetic critics have found Bly's love of unreason simply irrational, they have also found his fascination with death not only unreasonable but even self-destructive. Because he does not fully accept the negative basis of much of Bly's mysticism, seeing him simply as a poet of "presence" (as Lowell dramatizes "absence"), Charles Altieri is puzzled by his insistence on death: "its recurrence seems almost pathological; at best it manifests an attitude surprisingly alien from the activist voice of Bly's prose."[19] Perhaps it is only so alien as death is alien to life; in many perspectives, that opposition is only superficial.

But death cannot be dismissed, in Bly or in the medieval poetry that influenced *Silence*,[20] simply as a vital part of the circle of life, any more than passion over death in "Sunday Morning" can be explained away in logical or psychological terms. Something, to use a characteristic phrase of Bly's, is hidden here that we don't yet understand, and much of his poetry enacts an imagistic struggle to reveal the hidden more clearly. Especially in his early work the joy Bly describes is always dark, and often believable without being fully understandable. His celebration of the things of this world follows the negative way in more than one respect; his highest praise is usually reserved for states of consciousness and being ordinarily regarded with sorrow. He celebrates pain, spiritual turbulence, grief, and "the death we love." Predictably that death is often death by water, as spiritual immersion turns physical.

> We want to go back, to return to the sea,
> The sea of solitary corridors,
> And halls of wild nights,
> Explosions of grief,
> Diving into the sea of death
> Like the stars of the wheeling Bear.
>   (*Silence,* 12)

Bly's imagery of mystical immersion is not restricted to water, as he enacts in *Silence* and *Tree* an interpenetration of body and world. Animism ("The dawn stood there with a quiet gaze; / Our eyes met through the top leaves of the young ash" (*Silence,* 39)) is complemented by a sort of bodily surrealism ("Inside me there is a confusion of swallows" (*Silence,* 31)). As the psyche is crowded with arcane corporeal images, so the body contains the objects of the world. In the early Bly, such interpenetration is not struggled for, as in Stevens, but taken for granted, as in Williams. Bly feels his way into "the inner life of objects"[21] not because of a transcendental spiritual reality which infuses all nature with one Spirit, but because his body partakes of the energy immanent in the physical world. His animism stems from a perception of vitality in things which connects with the vitality of the self, but which is neither separable from states of physical being nor basically alien to consciousness. Dying into the darkness at the heart of Bly's poetry is not a transcendence of the body but an immersion in the body in turn immersed in the flow of things. If this elusive immersion is achieved the body in its fullness contains and is contained by "the inner world," which is this world, not illuminated but condensed to its deepest individual essence.

So behind the traditional mystical paradox — the praise of ordinarily negative states, grief and "the death we love," as avenues to holy joy — there exists in Bly, even more literally than in Roethke, the further paradox that spiritual union with the world must be sought in physical terms. Partly for this reason trees play a constant symbolic role in *Silence* and, of course, in *This Tree;* they are depicted as reaching toward emptiness, but always rooted in the earth. "Women We Never See Again" describes the cosmic emptiness of the tree: "Sometimes when you put your hand into a hollow tree / you touch the dark places between the stars" (*Tree,* 41).

In the earlier "Poem in Three Parts," a living tree leads toward the same ecstatic nothingness:

> The strong leaves of the box-elder tree,
> Plunging in the wind, call us to disappear
> Into the winds of the universe,
> Where we shall sit at the foot of a plant,
> And live forever, like the dust.
>
>   (*Silence,* 21)

The dust, which appears frequently in Bly's poetry, suggests the most corporeal vision of union with the cosmos, a union more simply meaningful than the traditional Christian dreams of death if only because of its physical inevitability. Bly compares the two visions in "At the Funeral of Great-Aunt Mary."

> The minister tells us that, being
> The sons and daughters of God,
> We rejoice at death, for we go
> To the mansions prepared
> From the foundations of the world.
> Impossible. No one believes it.
>
>   III
>
> Out on the bare, pioneer field,
> The frail body must wait till dusk
> To be lowered
> In the hot and sandy earth.
>
>   (*Silence,* 34)

The sense of death as physical union with everything becomes a spiritual or moral force in life because it celebrates a loss of self into the other which is more absolute than the ego-loss presumably implied by the death of transcendence; the traditional mystic soul united with God as often seems swollen in a higher egotism as lost in oneness. Also the sense of corporeal dissolution of self is, Bly suggests, always with us. Every sleep is a bodily premonition of death. Much of *Silence* concerns periods of transition between waking and sleeping, between light and darkness. During such periods the deep image comes close to the surface because the mind sinks to the depths of the body, the body opens to the world.

> The day shall never end, we think;
> We have hair that seems born for the daylight;

> But, at last, the quiet waters of the night will rise,
> And our skin shall see far off, as it does under water.
>
> (*Silence*, 15)

ii

In *The Light around the Body* (1967) and later in *Sleepers
Joining Hands* (1973), Bly moves from his usual territory of simple and
direct surrealist leaps into union to a conceptually more complex poetry.
He remains a visionary, but his mysticism is both enriched and diluted by
political and psychological theories as he joins cultural observation to the
records of private epiphany, sometimes describing and sometimes suffering
a pervasive tension between mystical and ethical or political perspectives.
The results are invariably interesting, and these two collections contain
some of Bly's richest poetry, although occasionally the poetry is swamped
by arcane theories. In *Light*, it is a sense of political turmoil that deepens
Bly's habitual paradoxes. Like various other American mystics, most conspicuously Thoreau but later Lowell and Merwin, Bly becomes interested
in the politics of American imperialism, a subject at least superficially un-
congenial to mysticism.

All but one of the sections of *Light* begin with quotations from Jacob
Boehme, the Protestant mystic who influenced Roethke as well as Emerson. "For according to the outward man, we are in this world and according to the inward man, we are in the inward world. . . . Since then we
are generated out of both worlds, we speak in two languages, and we must
be understood also by two languages" (*Light*, 1). The poems of *Light* embody the conflict between the two worlds, in the poet and in America. So
inevitably these poems bring together the two languages of which Boehme
speaks, doubling Bly's paradoxes, sometimes confusingly. *Light* still praises
grief and maps the progress of the body toward that death which is fulfillment, but while *Silence* emphasizes intimations of ultimate union *Light*
focuses on obstacles to the good death, one of which is, paradoxically,
another sort of death. "Smothered by the World" describes a purgatory
between life and death, marked not by union but an absolute isolation.

> Once more the heavy body mourns!
> It howls outside the hedges of life,
> Pushed out of the enclosure.
> Now it must meet the death outside the death.
> Living outside the gate is one death,

> Cold faces gather along the wall,
> A bag of bones warms itself in a tree.
>
> (*Light,* 7)

This death results from basic spiritual distortion in the world. Bly describes
it with the same animistic imagery he uses to link the body with the world,
but here the animism has turned grotesque.

Similar images are extended into greater complexity in "Those Being
Eaten by America," which also compares indicatively with Bly's earlier,
more innocent visions. Its rhetoric is more extreme than the style of poems
like "The Clear Air of October," but marked by the same balance between
logic and intuitive leaping, even the same underlying imagery of sunset and
animal transition. Some of Bly's most sensible critics have worried about
the collision, in *Light,* between mysticism and political commentary; as
Charles Molesworth says, "Satire and ecstasy make strange bedfellows."[22]
Yes, but strange bedfellows can energize each other in unpredictable ways
(as they did throughout the counterculture in 1967, when *Light* was published, and when mass political protest and mass drug ecstasies joined
their improbable forces to create the myth/reality of a psychopolitical
revolution). In any case Bly's rhetoric of ecstasy had from the start contained enough darkness and turmoil to accommodate any political anxiety;
the omnipresent dark night imagery had only to shift very slightly. "Those
Being Eaten" resonates with regret over vision lost, primal union fragmented like the images and lines of the poem, which like America is pulling
apart under the general strain.

The first couplets establish the tension; its populist ideals lost, America
at war is a devouring beast. Bly's tone sounds more fatalistic than angry;
here is little of the "shrillness" some critics find in *Light.*[23]

> The cry of those being eaten by America,
> Others pale and soft being stored for later eating
>
> And Jefferson
> Who saw hope in new oats
>
> The wild houses go on
> With long hair growing from between their toes
> The feet at night get up
> And run down the long white roads by themselves
>
> The dams reverse themselves and want to go stand alone in the desert

> Ministers who dive headfirst into the earth
> The pale flesh
> Spreading guiltily into new literatures
>
> That is why these poems are so sad
> The long dead running over the fields
>
> The mass sinking down
> The light in children's faces fading at six or seven
>
> The world will soon break up into small colonies of the saved.
>
> (*Light,* 14)

Although very strange, the surrealist image flashes begin in logical play as much as visionary intuition. Surely those "wild houses" derive much of their imagistic energy from the phrase "wild horses" presumably echoing in the mind of the reader (and certainly of the poet). Neither horses nor houses have toes; the word humanizes them to express domestic human fear and disintegration, and then allows a logical leap to the image of feet running alone. This becomes such a fine tragicomic image that pleasure in it must for a moment vanquish political anxiety in both reader and poet. The word "themselves" and the idea of pervasive denaturalization lead to the image of the dams reversed and standing alone, but the dams isolated in the desert also suggest the mystic peace of the old anchorites, so Bly's language of political terror seems almost indistinguishable from his language of vision. In fact both include hefty components of fear and awe; few twentieth-century revelations can be tranquil.

The final images of "Those Being Eaten" distantly echo the sunset imagery of "Clear Air," transposing its vision of apocalyptic transformation from the magic world of fairy tales to the more genuinely scary one of social conflict. "The long dead running over the fields" echoes "those cold shadows are falling," and "the mass sinking," "the light . . . fading at six or seven," which punningly conflates age and time of day, confirm the reader's sense of implicit sunset imagery. The slow dying of the light in America becomes almost a natural process, the gradual fading of empire. Far from being shrill or inconsistent with visionary images, the tone of this poem is more a tone of fatalism than anger or satire.

Not that Bly idealizes or romanticizes social collapse, as some sixties dreamers would. The sterile death that follows this despair is occasionally described in terms of whiteness, often snow, but even the darkness which in *Silence* was always the medium of visions has in *Light* become corrupted. "There is another darkness," Bly writes in "Listening to President Kennedy Lie about the Cuban Invasion." "There is a bitter fatigue, adult and sad" (*Silence,* 16).

Always, however individually, the poet reflects his time. Primarily *Silence* contains poetry written in the 1950s, a time of comparative political innocence (or naiveté) for American literature, when literary rebellion against America was usually considered a rather solitary and apolitical experience. *Silence* is a book of solitude, of Bly alone with the world; even its few love poems do not involve a recognizable other. *Light* is a book of the sixties, a politically conscious book, like many other books of poetry published since 1966 (the year Bly organized American Writers against the Vietnam War). But while Bly's development must obviously be understood in terms of our recent history, he might probably have undergone similar changes in any historical context, for in *Light* he is only dramatizing a tension implicit in the paradoxes of *Silence*.

Traditionally, mysticism has existed in potential or actual conflict with more earthly approaches to morality; the conflict surfaces when the mystic theorizes about evil. Having accepted grief and the dissolution of his body as aspects of a vital flow into "the wilds of the universe," Bly must logically confront experiences of grief and death, perhaps unnecessary grief and premature death, much less palatable to those who suffer them. The mystic usually returns to the world of men. The perception of dominant and perhaps inherent evil there can blunt his mystic acceptance, or it can become the basis for more strenuous efforts toward transcendence, a denial of the essential reality of certain aspects of the world in favor of higher realities. Allen Ginsberg, for instance, plays more or less seriously with the latter response when he chants, in "Wichita Vórtex Sutra": "I here declare the end of the War / Ancient days' Illusion."[24] But because Bly's mysticism remains untranscendental ("The two worlds are both in this world" (*Light,* 43)) neither traditional response is really possible. The social fact of pointless death forces a deeper examination of the mystic idea of death as a spiritual good, but Bly is unwilling to deny either view of death.

What he attempts to do instead, besides suggesting how the primitive sense of union has been lost, how death has been corrupted, is to create a prophetic vision of process toward a new world in which paradoxes resolve themselves. But the approach of this world is itself paradoxical, a terrible movement toward communal death which, like the individual death of *Silence,* is also the approach of spiritual birth. As the tension between inner and outer worlds grows more extreme Bly suggests that the center will not hold; however, the approaching apocalypse is also described as evolution. The final section of *Light* is called "A Body Not Yet Born." Like the rest of the book it contains images of despairing death, but if the dark night of the soul has become a universal darkness, it also carries implications of universal illumination. In "When the Dumb Speak," Bly describes

> . . . a joyful night in which we lose
> Everything, and drift
> Like a radish
> Rising and falling, and the ocean
> At last throws us into the ocean.
>   (*Light,* 62)

One ocean flows from the waters of inner experience described throughout much of *Silence,* but the other spreads through time as well as space. "When the Dumb Speak" ends with "images" which evoke traditional Christian visions of the world ending in apocalypse.

> Images of the body shaken in the grave,
> And the grave filled with seawater;
> Fires in the sea
>   . . .
> The house fallen,
> The gold sticks broken.

But "Evolution from the Fish," as its title indicates, describes what is to come not as a Christian end but as an evolutionary change which parallels earlier changes. Here the loss of "everything," which is a loss of self on the negative way, becomes a participation in the physical development of life from the beginning. "The grandson of fishes" is described

> . . . moving toward his own life
> Like fur, walking. And when the frost comes, he is
> Fur, mammoth fur, growing longer
>   . . .
> He moves toward the animal, the animal with furry head!

As the poem moves into our time the furry-headed one becomes specific, individual, "this long man with the student girl," but in the end he is embarking on another voyage, in darkness, through sleep.

> Serpents rise from the ocean floor with spiral motions,
> A man goes inside a jewel, and sleeps. Do

Not hold my hands down! Let me raise them!
A fire is passing up through the soles of my feet!

                                                    (*Light,* 59)

iii

Eschatological imaginings seem a natural aspect of contemporary mystical poetry. Sometimes, as in the case of Roethke, visionary
writings culminate simply in description of union, immersion in the flow,
but more often mystical poetry turns prophetic, like Bly's. Bly is also typical, or at least not unusual, in his semi-anthropomorphic imagery of new
divinity come to herald the apocalypse. Like transcendent mysticism, the
mysticism of immersion finally creates its own deities, though it tends logically to discover them (immersed) in the depths of the unconscious rather
than in the far reaches of heaven. A premonitory poem in *Light,* "Romans
Angry about the Inner World," which describes the world as "A jagged
stone / Flying toward them out of the darkness" (*Light,* 10), anticipates
the final articulation of Bly's evolutionary expectations. The poem describes "executives" watching Roman executioners torture "a woman /
Who has seen our mother / in the other world." Specifically the lines refer
to the mystical cult of Magna Mater, eventually suppressed by the
Romans. But the anachronistic presence of the executives implies a comparison between Rome and neo-imperial America, a comparison that goes
beyond ordinary politics. Later, in poetry readings and finally in the essay
"I Came Out of the Mother Naked," Bly elaborated the theory that the
Mother-goddesses smothered by one empire are finally returning to haunt
the consciousness of the other. His myth of cultural and spiritual development largely derives from the psychological and historical explorations of
the Jungian Erich Neumann and of the Swiss Bachofen, who wrote
Mother Right in 1861; it also owes something to *The White Goddess,*
which helped shape Plath's image of the Mother, both inspiring and
terrifying.

Like Plath, Bly describes the Mothers as archetypal forces operating in
the collective unconscious. Within us they engage in a progressively intensifying rebellion against patriarchial consciousness that will finally end
in a transformation of the culture which will be both destructive and
liberating, apocalyptic and evolutionary. Unlike Eliot's apocalypse, which
can lead only to heaven, Bly's may lead to some new illumination on this
earth, mother consciousness and father consciousness united. But first the
return of the repressed must be marked by violence. In "A Windy Decem-

ber Night," Bly sees a connection between "the feminine" and the night; the poem ends

> Some of us will die,
> others will lengthen out years on islands,
> but this night blows against hubcaps.
> Men will die for this night.
> (*Jumping,* unpaginated)

Critics tend to be cynical but indulgent about such prophetic visions. Belief is hardly the point; if Bly's convictions provided some sort of vital base for poetry (like Yeats's apocalyptic vision, or Eliot's, for that matter) why not allow him his eccentricity? In *The Sense of an Ending,* Frank Kermode's examination of traditional and early modern apocalyptic writing, he argues the conventional critical line. The idea of apocalypse, with its attendant myths, is a useful metaphor for poetic commentary on the changes of cultures; however, both poet and reader must sustain "clerical skepticism" about the ordering fiction.[25] The problem with such critical condescension is that it seems hard to imagine how a poet like Bly or Merwin, once having felt such skepticism, could go on writing poetry at all. Evidence suggests, anyway, that Bly sees clearly, though his hope for evolution may be in vain. Skepticism about the destruction at least of this culture seems now to involve deliberate blindness to the probabilities. Predictions of general nuclear or environmental destruction are less fashionable than they were in the late sixties, but they continue to flow with some regularity out of scientific think tanks as well as the mouths of poets. Without indulging in any unhealthy certainty about the imminence of doom, or about the reality of an end already begun, we can still give apocalyptic poetry the benefit of the doubt.

In part the contemporary American sense of apocalypse resulted from our war in Vietnam, as Lowell's resulted from World War II. The two genuinely contemporary (i.e., still alive) American poets in this study, Bly and W. S. Merwin, both published their most apocalyptic collections in 1967, treating Vietnam not only as rehearsal for apocalypse but as a metaphor for a more general movement toward dark ends and changes in being. The sense of cultural decay they felt is widespread. Again it is instructive to consider for a moment the prophetic voice of Ted Hughes, who corroborates Bly as well as Plath, providing a link between them not only in his theorizing about the Mother but in his anticipation of apocalypse.

Now it seems clear that when Hughes and Plath searched for "a completely new Holy Ground, a new divinity," the White Goddess they discovered was the same ominous archetypal force Bly was beginning to describe as the Great Mother. The apocalypse Hughes anticipates also reflects Bly's, though he projects a different response to it, one which, by negation, emphasizes Bly's basic optimism. He has even less in common than Bly with the traditional Christian apocalyptic writers. He seldom images an End, a single climactic event; rather the end is a long slow wearing away, "no calamitous change / But a malingering of now."[26] The attendant pressures take not physical but psychological forms: guilt, despair, and the desperate hope for changes once feared, changes better described in Darwinian than Christian terms. Often uncomfortable or appalled in the face of social actualities or possibilities, Hughes, like Bly and Merwin, attempts to renew ancient connections with the now alien world of nature and animals. So in Hughes as in Bly the eschatological imagination is diluted by the imagination of transition, the mystical dream of union with the animal flow of existence. But in the types of animal identification imagined by the two poets there emerges a basic difference. Bly's vision (like Merwin's) is often animated by the hope for evolution to a higher being; Hughes tends more to construct a calculus of survival, regarding terminal cultural stress as a condition which forces regression, devolution back to a state both more primitive and more spiritually pure.

Bly also imagines the return of ancient and violent states of being, but his hope for a new integration between male and female psychic forces is stronger than his sense of impending conflict. Hughes tends to be the poet of that conflict, celebrating the savagery of the Goddess. Even in the (comparatively) compassionate *Crow,* Hughes offers no hope for anything but survival. As Bly's evolutionary hero, containing all the past, moves into the luminous archetypes of the future, Hughes's survivor tends to return to the evolutionary past within and around him. Often he turns beast, either spiritually or physically, but Hughes's beasts, unlike Merwin's, have little to do with angels. As in Bly, Hughes's Goddess has returned to preside over the apocalypse. But while Bly's End may lead to a new dispensation, Hughes's continues indefinitely, as confused monsters feed and procreate in the afterglow of humanity. In "Notes for a Little Play," in which "the flame fills all space," something like human life obstinately continues in a weirdly elegant hymn to brute survival:

> . . . two strange items remaining in the flames —
> Two survivors, moving in the flames blindly.

Mutations — at home in the nuclear glare.

Horrors — hairy and slobbery, glossy and raw . . .

They fasten together. They seem to be eating each other.

They do not know what else to do.

They have begun to dance a strange dance.[27]

Despite the similarities in general vision, Bly's evolutionary prophecies are seldom so grim as Hughes's. His most extended poem about the destruction that attends the return of the Mothers emphasizes the terrors of continuing apocalypse, but it also imagines the resolution of agony, the end of the strange dance. "The Teeth Mother Naked at Last" was written about Vietnam at the height of the war. A prosy poem, deliberately propagandistic, its impact depends more on the force of its psychopolitical insights than the depth of its images. "Teeth Mother" contemplates a variety of deaths, but none are "the death we love." Here Bly enacts the same confrontation that Williams felt at the end of *Paterson IV,* or that Lowell struggled with in "Quaker Graveyard." For Bly, the evil of war defeats the mystical perspective, in this poem at least. Mystical acceptance is specifically parodied as an inadequate response, an evasion of the human and political reality of suffering. Understanding negates acceptance. Vietnam is presented as the desperate end of the "masculine" rage for order, the force that creates American prosperity but denies the inner world, nature, the dark flow of humanity toward the death which completes life. The desire for death as the fulfillment of life, repressed and corrupted, becomes a desire for death as grotesque destruction, the conventional death wish.

These lies mean that the country wants to die.
. . .
It's a desire to take death inside,
to feel it burning inside, pushing out velvety hairs,
like a clothes brush in the intestines —

(*Sleepers,* 21)

To this there appears no adequate response, no praise of death in the face of a diseased lust for death, no mystical acceptance. Bly the political moralist presents, ironically undercut, the plea of the contemplative dreamer, who sees the corporeal flow of existence in terms that recall *Silence.*

Tell me about the particles of Babylonian thought that still pass
    through the earthworm every day.
Don't tell me about "the frightening laborers who do not read books."
                                         (Sleepers, 26)

But Bly the visionary does suggest a way of understanding the horrors of
Vietnam. The violence against human and vegetable nature there can be
seen as a grim aspect of the apocalyptic evolutionary change described
in more positive images in the final pages of *Light*. One voice in "Teeth
Mother," looking for solace, suggests of the murders of "the Marine bat-
talion," "This happens when the seasons change / this happens when the
leaves begin to drop from the trees too early." Bly undercuts the suggestion
of solace, but the comparison remains. Vietnam, in some ways the death
of American dreams, is not an end but a transition, in which the Teeth
Mother necessarily appears as an aspect of change, a balance to the
"ecstatic" forces mentioned at the close of the poem.

The balance and the sense of cycles evolving provide no cure to present
agony. Bly knows it is the false transcendence of agony, with its attendant
repression, which distorts human consciousness in the first place. But the
vision of evolution enables Bly to sustain his paradoxical suspension of
despair and mystic hope, his sense of death as life. Perhaps that paradox
will always defy resolution, but in his latest poetry Bly continues to offer
hope for evolution into a state of consciousness in which despair can be
replaced by that grief which attends the natural movement of life, which
is not inconsistent with joy.

iv

Perhaps fortunately, the Teeth Mother only appears in the
title and the last lines of Bly's poem. The Mothers may be real psychic
forces; the contemporary importance of the archetype is corroborated not
only by Hughes's and Plath's dream visions (or Rich's), but by such
eccentric works of scholarship as *The White Goddess* or Elizabeth Davis's
The First Sex. But a theory of spiritual development too bluntly stated by
a mystical poet tends to flatten the poetry, as Eliot's more traditional beliefs
do in "East Coker." If a collection like *Light* is occasionally weakened by
an excess of mystery, obscurity, *Sleepers* shows at times the problem that
Bly knows too clearly and simply what he wants to say, has come too
quickly from contemplating Jung or Neumann to his poem. Jung's theories
about sexual characteristics especially may seem rather programmatic and

limited in our time. Bly's more recent poetry tends to stress integration, not opposition, between male and female. In a prose poem from the 1977 collection *This Body Is Made of Camphor and Gopherwood,* he specifically denies the sexist emphasis on sexual opposition: "What is asked of us? To stop sacrificing one energy for another. They are not different energies anyway, not 'male' or 'female,' but whirls of different speeds as they revolve. We must learn to worship both, and give up the idea of one god" (*Camphor,* 32). What replaces the sense of sexual tension here is the vision — like Roethke's or Lowell's — of loss of self into the whirlwind circle of natural energy. It seems both physical — Bly uses the term "force field" — and spiritual: "not a halo, but a background of flames."

Bly's most convincing Mother poetry derives not from theory but from the unconscious. Before he had read Neumann, or Jung, he had dreamed his own connections between women and liberating death: "Like those before, we move to the death we love / With pale women in Maryland" (*Silence,* 33). The image precedes the theory; if theory precedes image, either in the creative consciousness of the poet or in the receptive consciousness of the reader, this poetry of the deep psyche can suffer. Naturally Jung offers the greatest temptation here, for critic as well as poet. Jung can be invoked to explain everything: the origin of Bly's deep images is the collective unconscious, the conflict between the inner and outer worlds is a conflict between anima and persona, and Bly's constant water imagery implies a predictable symbolic pattern. Water, Jung writes in "Archetypes of the Collective Unconscious," is "no figure of speech, but a living symbol of the dark psyche," the realm "where I experience the other in myself." Even Bly's paradoxical discovery of vitality in death can be explained in terms of Jung's almost mystical contention, in "Psychological Aspects of the Mother Archetype," that "nothing can exist without its opposite; the two were one in the beginning and will be one again in the end. Consciousness can only exist through continual recognition of the unconscious, just as everything that lives must pass through many deaths."[28] Surely this is spiritually true and relevant, but it is not just a romantic attachment to mystery for its own sake that makes us feel that Bly's perceptions and paradoxes are not fully clarified by such ideas. Even Jung, in writing about the archetypes, warns that theoretical descriptions cannot capture them because they are manifestations of processes in the collective unconscious, inevitably distorted from the moment they come into the rational mind.

The general suspicion that Bly's poetry is not the type of poetry to be long sustained by abstract theories is reinforced by the problems in the title poem of *Sleepers Joining Hands,* a somewhat overtheoretical psychic saga about the struggle toward psychological and spiritual individuation and integration. As Michael Atkinson points out in "Robert Bly's *Sleepers Joining Hands:* Shadow and Self," "without the Jungian frame, and a fair amount of time to apply it, most readers will find some real problems of coherence"; he compares these to the problems that arise from "Eliot's classical eclecticism."[29]

Extraordinarily beautiful passages appear in "Sleepers," but they usually occur when Bly treats the Jungian scheme of development whimsically (the night-sea journey takes place "in the cooking pot") or when he allows his image-making imagination to drift beyond Jung into less predictable realms, as in the Whitmanesque *"An Extra Joyful Chorus for Those Who Have Read This Far."* This chorus is a poem of ecstatic meditation which touches the Jungian archetypes only occasionally, and with a dramatic immediacy not derived from any theory; it begins

> In the marshes the mysterious mother calls to her moor-bound chicks.
>
> I love the Mother
> I am an enemy of the Mother, give me my sword.
> I leap into her mouth full of seaweed.
>
> *(Sleepers,* 66)

The first line, its elegance in contrast with the plain bluntness of the others, seems a quote from Whitman, though perhaps not from "The Sleepers," the inspiration for Bly's title and some of his mystic leaps. Actually its imagery recalls the "fierce old mother" of "Out of the Cradle." Its combination of alliteration and long slow beats also recalls some of the aural pleasures of Whitman, as in *Sleepers* Bly begins to refute the critical commonplace that he has no ear.[30] The last lines, though, leave Whitman for Jung. They refer to the Jungian understanding of the mythic dragon fight as a symbol of the process of individuation, consciousness violently and lovingly separating from primal unconscious. But the passage embodies a deeper ambivalence, more spiritual than psychological. The passages of fierce energy in this poem come from Bly's primary interest in not psychic but mystical integration. Union with the Shadow leads not just to maturity but to that identification with the universe celebrated in the *"Extra Joyful Chorus."* But the full mystical union with all levels of being depends on negation of that self so painfully developed throughout most of the poem:

I am the crocodile unrolling and slashing through the mudded water,
I am the baboon crying out as her baby falls from the tree,
I am the light that makes the flax blossom at midnight!
I am an angel breaking into three parts over the Ural Mountains!
I am no one at all.

(Sleepers, 67)

Perhaps even the prior acceptance of the inner self, which allows this more general ecstatic union, is not best described in Jungian terminology about the Shadow. In "Sleepers" the Shadow gives way to a more mysterious being, marked by a light inseparable from darkness. He first appears in "Six Winter Privacy Poems," the beautifully simple series of poems of isolated meditation that begins the collection "Sleepers" ends. In the fifth poem, Bly discovers "someone" inside the music of Bach "who is not well described by the names / of Jesus, or Jehovah, or the Lord of Hosts!" In the final poem, it seems to be the same someone who comes closer:

When I woke, new snow had fallen.
I am alone, yet someone else is with me,
drinking coffee, looking out at the snow.

(Sleepers, 4)

This being, combination of self, archetype, and deity, is the one who finally replaces the Shadow in Bly's transformed Jungianism. Bly finds him, also, in the ecstatic visions of Kabir, finds him where other translators find only the usual Hindu deities. Bly, who knows no Hindi, used the translations of Rabindranath Tagore as a basis for his own more vivid and energetic versions.[31] His changes usually involve heightening Tagore's rather flat English and imagery, but in one area Bly's alterations suggest a different view of spiritual experience than Tagore's or probably Kabir's. The being that Tagore calls "the Lord," "the Supreme Brahma," often simply "He," only once "the Comrade," Bly consistently names "the Guest," "the friend," and, more explicitly "the Secret One inside us."[32] The deity has been absorbed by the psyche.

Ultimately in "Sleepers" the drama of mystical union overshadows the struggle for psychic wholeness. The Shadow expands to include all that is repressed or denied in nature as well as in self. Like Hughes's devil, it becomes nature, Bly's divine ground now discovered internally. In "Wallace Stevens and Dr. Jekyll" (the Shadow, of course, is Hyde) Bly connects the repressed Shadow with "the darkness under the earth," and adds that it thrives in matriarchies.[33] So the Shadow, now linked to the Mothers, is absorbed into Bly's black constellation of images of the holy, and the Sleeper's union with it means immersion in the flow of divinity: "I am divine" (*Sleepers*, 64). Water metaphors still dominate; to accept divinity you must "lose yourself in the curved energy" as fish "lose themselves in the river." But holiness is not just a flow, now, but a specific being. Bly describes him as "the King," who promises "I shall give you more pain than wounds at sea" (*Sleepers*, 65). Here meditative love of grief begins to sound much like the Christian ideal of purifying suffering, and Bly begins to sound like the older Roethke, flirting with the Judaeo-Christian vision of an anthropomorphic god.

Bly's interest in Kabir seems a return to another ancient tradition, whether he calls Kabir's divinity "the Guest" or not. But his use of the traditional religious hoard of words and symbols is, like his use of Jung, innovative, in the service of his own new visions. A revolutionary conservative, he revives the old idea of the Mother Goddesses to describe current psychic changes, using the distant past in aid of the near future. So he emphasizes the Kabir who opposes preoccupation with the afterlife, and who warns "lest silly people start talking again about the body and the soul" (*Kabir*, 4). Of course without such talk there can be no mysticism of transcendence. Emphasizing Kabir's belief in immanence, the divine in the self and the self in the world, Bly explains Kabir partly by opposing his mysticism to "a contrasting road" used by "some of the European saints of the Middle Ages . . . Eliot in his religious life consciously followed it." This of course is the *via negativa:* "On this path the link between the ego and the body is emphasized, and the ego is then dispersed through humiliation of the body" (*Kabir*, 64).

Bly correctly defines Kabir as a mystic who includes rather than rejects the world, and correctly dissociates Kabir from Eliot's negative way (despite the very traditional puritanism about the body's pleasures Kabir exhibits in some poems Bly does not translate). But the *via negativa* involves more than "humiliation of the body." The paradoxical negation of the intellect, which Eliot perceived as more important than the taming of the body, is evident in Bly's Kabir — "On this path there is no asking and no not asking" (*Kabir*, 31) — as well as in Bly himself. Bly remains the poet of the body, but often the body is immersed in darkness which suggests the medieval way toward loss of self. As usual, Bly's relation to his own mystical tradition, as well as Eastern traditions, is complex, ambivalent, and constantly changing. The climactic "I am no one at all" of "Sleepers" announces the same immersion in the physical world celebrated in *Light*. But now that immersion depends on the self-effacement of the *via negativa,* which Bly associates with transcendence. Like Lowell's, Bly's poetry frequently derives energy from unresolved tension between different visions of the world, the will toward mystical immersion balanced by the ancient and powerful rhetoric of transcendence, the inclusive way of the Mother in tension with the upward struggle of the Father. But perhaps the most basic ambivalence on Bly's mystical path involves a tension between the use of any such categories and his sporadic commitment to a deliberately simpler poetry, which discovers its ideas primarily in things. The Mother, the Shadow, the Friend, the King — all the anthropomorphic abstractions give way, in Bly's last several volumes of poetry, to the things of this world described in an increasingly plain style as mystical experience becomes almost indistinguishable from ordinary life. Even its frequent eruptions of surrealism are oriented more toward the inner life of objects than the development of psychological theories.

V

"What I have / to say I have not said" (*Tree,* 56). After *Sleepers,* and a pamphlet called *Old Man Rubbing His Eyes,* Bly moved away from open-form stanzaic poetry into the territory of the prose poem. Perhaps the unevenness of *Old Man* and some of *Sleepers* suggested the necessity of such a retreat from a certain type of stylistic tension. But Bly was probably more intent on the purification of his vision than on the poetry as such. What was needed was a return from increasingly self-conscious abstraction to the experience of the body, the vital base of Bly's poetry. As a terminal note to *Camphor* puts it, "Through the way the prose poem absorbs detail, it helps to heal the wound of abstraction" (*Camphor,* 61). So the prose poems seldom touch on Bly's scenarios for apocalypse, or the rise of the Mothers, though *Camphor* too often relaxes into the old, somewhat habitual, prophetic mode: "a new age comes close through the dark, an elephant's trunk waves in the darkness, so much is passing away" (*Camphor,* 53).

Though not dominated by prose poems, *This Tree* completes Bly's great circle back to the surreal simplicities of *Silence in the Snowy Fields.* Characteristically its poems begin with plain style observation ("Someone has left a light on at the boathouse" (*Tree,* 53)) and rapidly leap to cosmic or mystical pronouncements, still simply phrased ("Its path is a boatful of the dead, trying to return to life"). Bly seems to be reacting against

the ornate heaviness of *Sleepers,* or the occasionally baroque portentious-
ness of *Camphor; This Tree* contains poems written during the same period
when those collections were published. But he allows his lines little resonance, restricts himself, like the late Lowell, to a prosaic bluntness. Often
the result is poems so reticent about the inner life of the poet (Bly himself
worries that "sometimes they seem to me too impersonal" (*Tree,* 11)) that
their mystical assumptions about union with the inner life of objects can
seem more announced than enacted.

To the unenlightened reader (a category in which Bly would probably
dump most academic critics) such announcement can often seem mannered, or merely habitual. Bly's editors accurately claim that he is "one
of the country's most accomplished and widely read poets" (*Tree,* back
cover) — with Plath he is probably the only poet in this study widely read
by non-university audiences. But he presents constant problems to the
sympathetic critic, and considerable ammunition to the hostile one. After
the great but flawed *Sleepers* and the beautiful but minor *Morning Glory,*
his poetry has not always kept pace with his vision. Perhaps he has come
into a time of believing, with the late Eliot, that ultimately "the poetry does
not matter" as much as the search.

But when Bly does manage to get his full voice into his lines, he shows
himself still the mystic master. The problem of evaluation suddenly
becomes minor in those late poems, from *Sleepers* through the prose poems
to *This Tree,* in which Bly does what he has always done best: vividly
dramatize, not merely claim, the intersection of the two worlds in ordinary
experience, by allowing images of immersion to expand to reveal the open
spaces of revelation in physical being, combining the highest spiritual and
psychological abstraction with the greatest density of perception. Many of
his prose poems in *Glory* that describe the Pacific coast have the traditional
resonance of epiphany, as vision expands toward the visionary. In the fog
in "Sunday Morning at Tomales Bay," shore boulders become sea lions
which "roll seaward" like reverse waves, startling a feeding heron into
ascent. "And the Great Blue Heron flies away thin as a grassblade in the
fog" (*Glory,* 46). The perceptual movement from liquid immersion
through increasingly more mobile and elevated beings implies a developing
spiritual expansion, almost transcendent, almost into the nothingness of
infinity. For all his devotion to the body, Bly continues to be drawn to the
far edge of being. The poems collected in *Sleepers Joining Hands,* which
still represent his most ambitious and perhaps most sustained achievement,

are like the final poems of *Light,* poems of transition, examinations of boundaries. Beyond the boundary is not exactly transcendent otherness, but the other side of this-ness, "the other side of the light" (*Light,* 50). This is the territory of "Shack Poem," the ecstatic meditation which tries to draw the reader beyond ordinary vision and beyond ordinary reason.

The poem begins with a direct and simple negation — "I don't even know . . ." — to open a description of a flow which joins earth, air, fish, and water.

> 1
> I don't even know these roads I walk on,
> I see the backs of white birds.
> Whales rush by, their teeth ivory.
> (*Sleepers,* 8)

Bly's leaps grow longer as he approaches various boundaries, but flashes of logic still mark his trail. Birds and swift whales, those amibiguous mammals, suggest the range and flow of physical being; their whiteness (of whales' teeth and perhaps skin, like Moby Dick) both links them and elevates them. Here it suggests not purity but the blank; white is the color which is the absence of color, the color of the other world glimpsed in this world. So the sacred albatross is white, and the most otherworldly herons are the Great Blue (of "Tomales Bay") and the archetypal Great White. The next stanza uses this shore bird to mark yet another boundary.

> 2
> Far out at the edge of the heron's wing,
> where the air is disturbed by the last feather,
> there is the Kingdom. . . . [Bly's ellipses, here and later]

This is the edge between body and otherness, not in another world, but just out of reach. "The kingdom," not static, is a place of peaceful turbulence, constantly flowing.

As usual Bly's strongest visionary voice begins simply, with plain assertion which leads to descriptive leaping; then mythic extravagance in the third stanza will again be balanced by the plain (and finally semicomic) style of the fourth.

> 3
> Hurrying to brush between the Two Fish,
> the wild woman flies on . . .
> blue glass stones a path on earth mark her going.

4
I sit down and fold my legs . . .
The half dark in the room is delicious.
How marvelous to be a thought entirely surrounded by brains!

The totemic "Two Fish" are loosely prepared for by the earlier boundary
animals, especially the whales, but anti-Jungian critics may judge that the
wild woman comes, rather artificially, out of a book. If so it could be a
book of fairy tales, where as the archetypes are revealed women and fish
are often linked, and anima figures leave magic trails for questing heroes.
After the climactic appearance of the Great Mother figure, the rush of
rhetoric subsides as the speaker returns to ordinary consciousness, and even
to a small joke that plays on the fascination with physical/spiritual boundaries and the desire for near transcendence dramatized by the poem.

As most of this wandering meditation indicates, Bly's interest in the
point of intersection between density and nothingness links not only with
his preoccupation with death, but with his will to discover the blank space
of revelation within being. In *This Tree,* "An Empty Place" is a typical
poem of negative vision which argues "There is a joy in emptiness" and
uses the homely metaphor of an empty corncob to describe the vitality of
the emptiness in existence. In *Glory,* vision in emptiness often becomes the
similarly paradoxical vision of the invisible: "Whoever wants to see the
invisible has to penetrate more deeply into the visible" (*Glory,* xiii). The
best of Bly's prose poems defeat the separation between worlds that Kabir
frequently attacks, as Bly manages to find in the visible not just signs of
the invisible but something beyond metaphor, as in the heron poems. An
embodiment of the invisible, as the physical object fleetingly partakes of
the other world, creates a direct sensuous apprehension not of thought but
of a reality both psychic and spiritual. The real strength of *Sleepers* appears
not in the title poem but in such lyrics as "Water under the Earth," which
does not explain but embodies a combination of sensual and mystic
sensation.

It is a willow that knows of water under the earth,
I am a father who dips as he passes over underground rivers,
Who can feel his children through all distance and time!

(*Sleepers,* 7)

Here metaphorical language presented as literal creates the impression of
spiritual union — with natural waters, with the evolutionary future —
viscerally experienced.

Ideally such unity of perception fosters unity of being. The fatal human separation — Bly's original sin — lies not between self and world, not exactly between self and archetypes, but between psychic self and body. Mystical union becomes primarily a return to that wholeness which the body already knows, a return through the "bare" territory of revelation, perhaps through death, which may obliterate the mind but only returns the body to the materials of its origins, as the title poem of *Camphor* rather too breathlessly explains.

> Friend, this body is made of camphor and gopherwood. So for two days I gathered ecstasies from my own body, I rose up and down, surrounded only by bare wood and bare air, and some gray cloud, and what was in me came so close to me, and I lived and died!
> Now it is morning. . . .
>
> *(Camphor, 47)*

This form of the negative way, negation of the mind not the body, leads to a perception, like Stevens's, of matter as spiritual and physical energy, energy in constant passage between body and world. "My friend, this body is made of energy compacted and whirling. It is the wind that carries the henhouse down the road dancing" *(Camphor, 51)*. The whirling energy can specifically form whirlpools, like Lowell's, at moments heavy with revelation. "My eyes feel wild, as if a new body were rising, with tremendous swirls in its flow; its whirlpools move with their face upward, as those whirls in the Missouri that draw in green cottonwoods from collapsed earth banks" *(Camphor, 31)*.

The problem with such hieratic writing is not its irrationalism, but the contrary: its will to explain so bluntly that all will see. Fortunately, the overstated visionary testimonials of *Camphor* were corrected not only by the early, simple style restored in *This Tree,* but by the more developed simplicities of *The Man in the Black Coat Turns.* In general, *Coat* not only substitutes complexity of observation for overheated metaphor, it also turns in a direction sympathetic readers have found lacking in most of Bly's poetry. The rhapsody of self in *Camphor* is replaced, or at least balanced, by poetry about other people, loved ones, father and son and lover. Less solipsistic, the poems of *Coat* tend to be less visionary, more a record of life in the daily world. The book shows some mystical concern still; Bly assures us that "the advocate of darkness and night is not lost," but that persona is balanced by the voice of an ordinary man.

Even after Bly has put aside the role of theorist of the apocalypse, his deep images continue to resonate with the expectation of rebirth. This is rebirth into the real knowledge of the body that is, as W. S. Merwin will also suggest, not only beyond our present condition but in some ways beyond humanity entirely. Meditation becomes prophetic, a way to foresee this alien knowing. Finally the aim of meditation is not integration or knowledge of the self but something larger and less definable, something badly oversimplified by Jungian definition. Before he wrote "Sleepers," Bly articulated a different attitude toward human personality: "The West misunderstands 'meditation' or sitting because, being obsessed with unity and 'identity,' it assumes that the purpose of meditation is to achieve unity. On the contrary, the major value of sitting, particularly at the start, is to let the sitter experience the real chaos of the brain."[34] This chaos, which inevitably finds its way into the poetry, reflects and partakes of "the wilds of the universe." Bly can see it with an ecstasy usually undiluted by the terrible disorder of the flow of energy. For Bly, ecstasy is the prime result of mystical union, even if union carries terrible pressures and maddening visions. Bly's mystical negations are from the start qualified by his unquenchably affirmative instincts. For the most consistent poetry of negation, bleak by instinct, we must finally turn to the poetry of W. S. Merwin, whose myth of apocalypse contains no Mother to show either teeth or compassion. He dreams the End from a position that Robert Lowell long ago suggested was the only destination for the mystic: somewhere outside the human range of feeling, somewhere nearly lost in the field of otherness.

NOTES

1. Robert Bly, "Wallace Stevens and Dr. Jekyll," in *American Poets in 1976,* ed. William Heyen (Indianapolis: Bobbs-Merrill, 1976), p. 10.

2. Bly, "Wallace Stevens," p. 15.

3. Bly, "Wallace Stevens," pp. 9, 10.

4. Robert Bly, *Silence in the Snowy Fields* (Middletown, Conn.: Wesleyan Univ. Press, 1962), p. 16. Other Bly collections cited include *The Light around the Body* (New York: Harper & Row, 1967), *Jumping Out of Bed* (Barre, Mass.: Barre Publishers, 1973), *Sleepers Joining Hands* (New York: Harper & Row, 1973), *The Morning Glory* (Harper, 1975), *This Body Is Made of Camphor and Gopherwood* (Harper, 1977), *This Tree Will Be Here for a Thousand Years* (Harper, 1979). Titles are subsequently identified in the text by their initial word.

5. Robert Bly, "Looking for Dragon Smoke," originally in *Naked Poetry,* ed. Stephen Berg and Robert Mezey (Indianapolis: Bobbs-Merrill, 1969), p. 163.

6. From a revised version of "Dragon Smoke," in *Leaping Poetry,* ed. Robert Bly (Boston: Beacon, 1975), p. 4.

7. Bly, "Wallace Stevens," p. 12.

8. "The Metaphysical Poets," in *Selected Prose of T. S. Eliot,* ed. Frank Kermode (London: Faber & Faber, 1975), p. 63.

9. Robert Bly, *News of the Universe* (San Francisco: Sierra Club, 1980), p. 80.

10. For some critics, Bly the theoretician and liberator of other poets completely eclipses Bly the poet. In *Four Poets and the Emotive Imagination* (Baton Rouge: Louisiana State Univ. Press, 1976), George Lensing and Ronald Moran provide an admiring description of Bly's theories. So it comes as a surprise that they are able to say of the poetry, "Most of Bly's poems are whimsical and minor; they have no pretensions of being anything else. Frequently his political verse manages to go little beyond bald propaganda" (p. 85). And yet they describe him as "a vital phenomenon in American poetry since mid-century."

11. Robert Hass, "James Wright," in *Ironwood 10* (1977), 85.

12. Patricia Goedicke, "The Leaper Leaping," in *Of Solitude and Silence,* ed. Richard Jones and Kate Daniels (Boston: Beacon Press, 1981), p. 113.

13. Howard Nelson, "Robert Bly and the Ants," in *Of Solitude,* p. 175.

14. Robert Pinsky, *The Situation of Poetry* (Princeton: Princeton Univ. Press, 1976), pp. 8, 81. Such statements reveal some bias, including the regional bias that plays a more central role in American critical judgments than is usually recognized. And Pinsky still trails fragments of the old Wintersian flags, and ends his manifesto by praising other members of the Stanford mafia. Still, he moderates the old master's excesses, for instance praising Williams, whom Yvor Winters scorned in terms now used to abuse poets like Bly: "He is not even an anti-intellectual poet in any intelligible sense of the term, for he did not know what the intellect is. He was a foolish and ignorant man, but at moments a fine stylist" (*William Carlos Williams,* ed. Charles Tomlinson [Hammondsworth, Middlesex: Penguin, 1972], p. 383).

15. Pinsky, *Situation of Poetry,* p. 152.

16. Bly, *News,* p. 8.

17. Bly, *News,* p. 209.

18. J. Hillis Miller, *Poets of Reality* (Cambridge: Harvard Univ. Press, 1965), p. 291.

19. Charles Altieri, *Enlarging the Temple* (Lewisburg, Pa.: Bucknell Univ. Press), p. 92. After this parenthetical complaint, Altieri goes on to talk very interestingly about Bly's use of death, and to compare it with Whitman's.

20. See the revealing interview with Ekbert Faas, Bly's most skillful interviewer, in Robert Bly, *Talking All Morning* (Ann Arbor: Univ. of Michigan Press, 1980), p. 250.

21. Bly, *Leaping,* p. 4.

22. Charles Molesworth, *The Fierce Embrace* (Columbia: Univ. of Missouri Press, 1979), p. 119. Actually, Molesworth turns out to be one of the strongest defenders of Bly's antiwar poetry, which he considers "Blakean" (p. 125).

184 Mythologies of Nothing

23. Lensing and Moran, *Four Poets,* p. 80. Their judgments about most of Bly's poetry seem to me reductive. It may not be exactly Blakean, but it is neither shrill nor simply whimsical.

24. Allen Ginsberg, *Planet News* (San Francisco: City Lights, 1970), p. 110.

25. Frank Kermode, *The Sense of an Ending* (New York: Oxford Univ. Press, 1967), p. 109.

26. Ted Hughes, *Lupercal* (London: Faber & Faber, 1960), p. 15.

27. Ted Hughes, *Crow* (London: Faber & Faber, 1970), p. 74.

28. C. G. Jung, *The Basic Writings,* ed. Violet Staub de Lazlo (New York: Random House, 1959), pp. 300, 347.

29. Michael Atkinson, "Robert Bly's *Sleepers Joining Hands:* Shadow and Self," *Iowa Review,* 7 (Fall 1976), 145.

30. Frequently, like Williams, Bly is too intent on the image to think much about sound, but his poetry shows, throughout, flashes of aural beauty; one striking example is the delicate almost anapestic beat of the last lines of "A Journey with Women" (*Light,* 56). "We are still falling like a room / Full of moonlight through the air...." Even here, some resolutely prosaic (puritan?) instinct in Bly insists on that rhythmically dead "still."

31. *One Hundred Poems of Kabir,* trans. Rabindranath Tagore (London: Macmillan, 1962).

32. Robert Bly, *The Kabir Book,* "versions by Robert Bly" (Boston: Beacon, 1977), p. 29. Hereafter, *Kabir.*

33. Bly, "Wallace Stevens," p. 4.

34. Bly, *Leaping,* p. 65.

6

W. S. Merwin and the Nothing That Is

Of the immortal in "Blue" Merwin writes, "There is no pity in him. Where would he have learned it?"[1] Colder than any of his contemporaries, Merwin himself seems to aspire to such supernatural neutrality. Even more than the frequently glacial Wallace Stevens he has actually achieved Stevens's "mind of winter," not simply in order to behold the mystic dream of the Nothing beyond man's knowing, but to describe human emptiness and cultural death with the chill accuracy it deserves. Among the poets of negative mysticism, Merwin is the purest, more constantly preoccupied with the subject of revelation than Plath or Bly, but more starkly negative about the conditions of such revelation. At the end of the *via negativa* repeatedly dramatized in his poetry, there is often nothing but negation; nothing comes to the mind turned to nothingness. When he does imagine some genuine revelation it often depends on doom. More even than Bly or Hughes, Merwin explores the apocalyptic dimension of mystical awareness, confronting the End that excites them with an inhuman calm, studious avoidance of fear or exultation.

His earliest collections of poems involve a variety of subjects treated in an impressive variety of styles. But his most characteristic and powerful work began in *The Moving Target* (1963), the volume in which he discovered an oracular voice that would resound throughout an unusually productive decade. His collections of that period seem almost obsessive, as single-minded in tone as in apocalyptic vision. Richard Howard is not simply having rhetorical fun when he describes the poems in *Target* as "the fewmets of what Yeats rightly called a dying animal."[2] Merwin the stylist is busy refining one style to the point of monotony, a style which focuses with grim frequency on the subject for which it was perfectly devised: the continuing apocalypse that fails to bring revelation. But even in *The Lice* the poet of Nothing will not completely renounce a dim hope for the revelation that will afford us not only understanding but a sense of connection, union, perhaps by taking us somehow beyond the hopeless spiritual limitations of the human condition. Like Eliot, he tends to define humanity as deficiency, but unlike Eliot he imagines the cure for that deficiency not in movement upwards toward angels but downwards toward beasts and animal unknowing.

Perhaps simply because periodic change seems a poetic necessity for Merwin, perhaps because of the darkness of his perspective, he was unable to sustain it indefinitely. By the time (1973) of *Writings to an Unfinished Accompaniment,* his voice had begun to seem mannered, as he pushed black prophecy and stylistic spareness beyond repetition to exhaustion in many poems, sometimes almost parodying his own restraint. For Merwin this was less a sign of poetic failure than a mark of transition. As Cary Nelson points out in his analysis of Merwin's "deconstructive" approach to his own poetic forms, each of his "stylistic metamorphoses has followed from a self-conscious craft that turned into self-parody and even revulsion."[3] What follows *Writings* is an alteration of vision for once deeper than the change in verbal style; in Merwin now, emptiness can give way to something approaching lushness. In several sections of *The Compass Flower* (1977), Merwin turns away from the expectation of apocalypse, modifying his spare visionary style to illuminate the things of this world. Among his dream visions are now dreams of simple realism, stocked with such mundane things as supermarkets, a love affair, St. Vincent's Hospital, and landscapes and animals plainly rendered. But traces of Merwin's oracular voice remain; even his (comparative) acceptance of the world is characterized by the vocabulary of negation. His richly romantic sequence "Kore" is marked by words like "nothing," "not," "without," "no one," "nowhere," and of course "unknowing." Merwin's essential voice, developing through all his changes, depends on such negative terms; they will continue, to link new visions with old.

As his similarities with Bly and Plath indicate, the development of his apocalyptic and oracular vision was not unusual as America changed in the early sixties. Harold Bloom remarks in his essay on the new transcendentalism that Merwin is from certain perspectives "the indubitably representative poet of my generation."[4] With the increasingly surrealist style that was becoming common in American poetry, there came an unusually

literal sense of the mystical role of the poet, far more widespread than
when Stevens wrote about his "theory of poetry . . . become mystical theology." For many contemporary poets vatic surrealism was simply a novel
style to play with; for Merwin that style released a new way of apprehend-
ing the world. He sounds much like Stevens when he writes prose about
that apprehension, about the nature of poetic utterance. One of his conspicuous problems is to distinguish poetry from theology. Introducing
the aphorisms of Antonio Porchia, which he doubtless chose to translate
because of a sense of deep affinity with the aphorist, he writes: "the entries
and the work as a whole assume and evoke the existence of an absolute,
of the knowledge of it which is truth, and of the immense desirability of
such knowledge. . . . Porchia's utterances are obviously, in this sense, a
spiritual, quite as much as a literary, testament. . . . It is their ground
of personal revelations and its logic, in the sentence, that marks their kinship, not with theology but with poetry."[5] Predictably this description
works for Merwin's poetry too, though in both Merwin and Porchia the
nature of the absolute remains hidden behind various veils, the most common of which is death.

Perhaps Porchia's aphorisms provide the most telling way into Merwin's
poetry of negative vision. In the context of this study of paradoxical mysticism and the *via negativa,* they tend to have a familiar ring, as in Porchia's
typically hesitant affirmation, "He who has seen everything empty itself is
close to knowing what everything is filled with."[6] The mystic way down
is the way up, and emptiness is the condition of fullness. But initially Merwin seems almost exclusively preoccupied with the way down, emptiness.
His poem "A Scale in May," published in *The Lice* in 1967, the year of
his translation of *Voices,* consists of a series of aphoristic statements reminiscent of Porchia. One of the most strangely compelling reads:

> Of all the beasts to man alone death brings justice
> But I desire
> To kneel in a doorway empty except for the song.
>   (*Lice,* 50)

The sense of an absolute here is almost eclipsed by the sense of its
mystery, but the outline of a meaning is clear. "Justice" means not simply
retribution — though clearly only man can deserve death, and the mankind Merwin describes in *Lice* deserves nothing better. Justice also has
something to do with an ultimate revelation, "the song" that as always in
Merwin comes, or may come, only from emptiness; man cannot deserve

this knowledge, which lies beyond his patterns of knowing, but he cannot help desiring it, hoping for some final compromise between justice and desire. Constantly Merwin suggests that some revelation may accompany the end man clearly does deserve: the End. "Death" in *Target* and especially in *Lice* usually means death for everyone, and often premonitions of that destruction blot out vision.

> The bird of the end with its
> Colorless feet
> Has walked on windows
>
>   . . .
>
> In the mirrors the star called Nothing
>
> Cuts us off.
>
>   (*Target,* 63)

However Merwin confronts the End not only with absolute belief in its imminence ("I am sure now," he writes in "Glimpse of the Ice" (*Lice,* 46)) but with equanimity and even quiet eagerness. For if death darkens our collective vision it may bring its own incredible illumination "so that we may know why."

> some alien blessing
> is on its way to us
> some prayer ignored for centuries
> is about to be granted to the prayerless
> in this place.
>
>   (*Carrier,* 75)

Of course an "alien blessing" may be experienced as a curse; Merwin's interest in what happens to the prayerless as often derives from an ambivalent desire for retributive justice as for undeserved revelation. The reasons for the desire, and for his sudden preoccupation with ends, can be found not only in the poet's eccentric soul but — to admit a connection between poetry and politics evident in Merwin as well as Bly — in the collapsing world. One external factor that doubtless helped to change Merwin's sense of the world while his poetic style was changing was an incident in the American protest movement with which he became deeply involved in 1962, after the publication of *Drunk* and before the radically different *Target.* In San Francisco, anti-bomb demonstrators attempted to sail the trimaran *Everyman,* itself a moving target, into the Atomic Energy Commission nuclear test area near Christmas Island in the Pacific; naturally the boat was stopped just outside the harbor, and the test boomed on. Merwin's account of the attempt and the related trial and demonstrations filled an entire (Christmas) issue of *The Nation*. It is a report written more in anger than in sorrow, and lightened by very little hope. Though Merwin's sympathy for the protestors is clear, his sense of the futility of their mission in the face of official American stupidity and self-destructiveness is dominant. And his grim vision of the future is evident, though he remains the comparatively objective reporter, letting others voice his prophecy. He quotes a cynical but perfectly logical onlooker: "Maybe that's why the human race isn't justified in looking forward to a long and happy future. They've temporized with everything. It's too late for an act of conscience, any act of conscience, to be effective any longer." Then he paraphrases a somewhat more dramatic (or poetic) rendition of the same idea, the rather traditional old black woman's scenario projecting the ocean's response to the bomb. "Going to rise up. Going to blow up and destroy the whole beautiful earth God gave them, and God is going to let them do it because they don't care for each other at all any more."[7]

This sounds like an abstract formulation of the dominant idea behind *The Lice,* which Merwin would publish five years later, a collection which focuses on the End even more mercilessly than *Target*. The apocalyptic poetry he wrote in the middle sixties frequently shows the same political awareness Merwin brought to his report of the *Everyman* demonstrations. The decayed empire that seems to welcome its own collapse in "Unfinished Book of Kings" has distinctly American characteristics, conspicuous at the last.

> v . . . the lips of the last prophets had fallen from the last trees

> vi They had fallen without sound they had not stayed in spite of the assurances proceeding from the mouths of the presidents in the money pinned thick as tobacco fish over the eyes of the saints

> vii And in spite of the little votes burning at the altars.

> (*Lice,* 13)

In this land of no possible "assurances," no human contact, the End comes because men have failed to "care for each other at all," and the violence of that failure is usually the violence of war. In "The Gods," which describes "the other world" already come as a lone survivor waits "Till night wells up through the earth" (*Lice,* 30), the only evidence of human life beyond his dying voice is "the fighting in the valley" which has been constant for "centuries." "The gods are what has failed to become of us."

ii

Like many Americans Merwin had of course considered the possibility of cultural destruction before the *Everyman* protest, but his few early treatments of the topic seem more to subject it to ultimate play than to consider it seriously. "Birds Waking" goes so far as to say "let it be now" (*Green,* 71), but only in the context of an elaborate conceit. And "One-Eye" (*Drunk,* 34), despite the symbolic suggestiveness of the descending giant thumb which threatens the unsuspecting country of the blind, is located in an old legend kept comparatively remote from poet and readers. Though effective, these poems simply lack the visceral significance characteristic even of the least of the later apocalyptic poems in collections like *Carrier,* where Merwin repetitiously but convincingly creates a burned-out landscape that seems almost physically present. The difference is not only a change in Merwin's sense of political reality, but an altered conception of mythic reality, one which deepens the final significance of his stylistic changes. Merwin begins as a conventionally mythic poet but ends an oracular one; though the two tend to use similar materials the distance between them is immense. Like Plath or Bly discovering the Mother archetype, Merwin developed a mythology powerful enough to support a mystical apprehension of the world. Not a Mother myth, in which the final experience is contact with the deity, but like Bly's it is a myth of evolution into new being, far less removed from other species of earth than our condition now, and in proportion distant from our present lonely human selves.

Like Merwin's sudden interest in apocalypse, this development in the poet's mythology has cultural as well as personal roots. Many American poets and critics in the fifties, influenced partly through Eliot by the preoccupation with classical tales that still dominates some British poetry, grew fascinated by myth, but myth considered at a distance, folktales suited to the construction of metaphor. Except the Christian one, myths were simply ancient stories, with their own "universal" truth, of course, but that truth was usually abstract, metaphorical, something to be worked up out of *The Golden Bough* rather than one's own deep visions. And if the mythic or magical materials failed to fit the poet's metaphor, they could simply be changed; so Eliot "quite arbitrarily" invented fake Tarot

cards "to suit my own convenience" in *The Waste Land*.[8] Few poets
would do so today, partly because of the emphasis on a new visceral
honesty that developed in the poetry of the sixties. But critics continue
to regard mythic utterance with a certain protective cynicism that avoids
embarrassing questions of belief. Harvey Gross, for instance, in a 1970
article follows Frank Kermode in insisting that Merwin's sense of an imminent ending is a "metaphor," even a "sustaining fiction."[9]

Merwin did start with elaborate metaphors. When W. H. Auden, in his
introduction to *A Mask for Janus* (1952), explains that Merwin's mythic
poetry succeeds because it is *not* "a mere elegant manifestation of the
imaginative work of the dead without any live relation to the present of
the writer or his reader" (*Janus,* viii), we can only admire the precision
with which he describes Merwin's problem, while disagreeing with his
evaluation. Two decades later *Janus* seems, in part because of its self-
conscious and often archaic elegance, a collection of beautiful imitations,
visions of past myths not vivified by any real sense of a present consciousness, and therefore unsuccessful even as metaphor, or as evocation
of the past. There is no face behind the mask of the title; as in some of
Plath's early excursions into other people's myths, the mystery at the heart
of myth is too easily subdued by excesses of technical "control."

Merwin's elegant technique is less self-conscious, more assured, in
The Dancing Bears, but myths, as in "East of the Sun and West of the
Moon," are still deliberately exploited as metaphors. Merwin is explicit:
"All magic is but metaphor" (*Bears,* 50). His poetry of mythic and mystical exploration becomes progressively more convincing, in visceral human
terms, as he begins to feel his way into animal consciousness, or at least
into the mysterious realm between human and natural which is the
source of much genuine myth. As he moves deeper into the animal world,
he prospects for new myths rather than revising old ones. Generally the
beast poems make *Green with Beasts* wholly more successful than *Bears,*
though the collection also contains several fine poems of human interaction
with the inanimate world. "The Mountain" is a speculation on the origins
of myth and mysticism which remains suggestive rather than prescriptive,
which does not explain myth away but retains the mystery of confrontation
with an alien strangeness. But in the same volume "The Annunciation"
provides a typical contrast, failing even as it enunciates the mystical concerns that will animate much of Merwin's finest later poetry. Though
stylistically direct and beautiful in some particulars, the poem seems
forced, in part because Merwin again exploits a traditional myth for its

metaphorical possibilities. Even the old abstractor Eliot conveys, in *Four Quartets,* a more convincing sense of Christian mythology, doubtless because for him the myth is really believable.

And real belief is finally the point. For Merwin too, as for many of his contemporaries, notably Bly and Plath, the ultimate stage in the poetic use of myth is genuine acceptance of mystery, the discovery of a mythic vein so deeply felt that it lies beyond abstracting metaphor — because it lies beneath the type of reasoning on which metaphor depends. Merwin the oracular surrealist will develop a mythic consciousness which has much in common with the ancient mythic imagination, especially its instinctive animism and its conviction that unknowable cosmic unities exist at the root of mystery, but he will achieve this by creating a new arcane symbolism touching on the old but not derived from it. By 1970, in the prose collection *The Miner's Pale Children,* Merwin had evolved visions — like "Blue" and the apocalyptic "The Dark Sower" — characterized by a new sense of mystery balanced by a stylistic clarity not always evident in his late poetry. Like acts of magic, many of these visions compel belief as they resist explication; without apology they are based on the conviction that the miraculous is the ground of existence.

Viewed retrospectively, the emergence of surrealism in Merwin's style, which accompanied his developing mystical concerns and his fascination with the apocalypse, seems a logical extension of stylistic and thematic tendencies already evident in *Green* and even *Janus.* Inevitably a poet whose early stylistic experimentation suggests a basic discontent with the available linguistic forms, perhaps a discontent with language itself, would ultimately choose a style marked by a reaching beyond language, and refine that style until it became progressively more terse, the poems on the page surrounded by more and more of the empty white space of possibility, as negation becomes style as well as substance. But the surrealism that Merwin developed in *Target,* made his own in *Lice,* and exercised sometimes to the point of repetition in *Carrier* and *Writings to an Unfinished Accompaniment,* was not simply the exfoliation of his own concerns. The years of writing the poems in *Target* and *Lice* were also years when Merwin translated extensively, especially continental and Latin American poetry in which magic is commonplace, from the crude fairy-tale magic of medieval Spanish ballads to the sophisticated transformational magic of Lorca or Neruda.

At least in the twentieth century the strength of American poetry seems to depend on periodic infusions of vitality from other literatures — French and Oriental at the beginning of the century, Spanish and Oriental in the late fifties and early sixties. The genesis of new American movements is aided by foreign seeds, and the influence is not merely stylistic; a transmitted style carries with it a vision of the world, and now the Spanish even more than the Oriental influence seems to encourage in our poets an implicitly mystical vision. About influence, of course, we can never be sure in any individual instance. Merwin probably owes more to Wallace Stevens than to Lorca the celebrant of mystical death, or to the plain style surrealist Pablo Neruda. He has said, "I have felt impelled to keep translation and my own writing more and more sharply separate" (*Translations*, viii). The separation is not readily apparent, though this proves nothing about influence. A sensitive poet translator must instinctively or consciously choose poetry that reflects tendencies in his own work. Clearly Merwin was a master of aphoristic poetry before he translated Porchia's *Voices*. But he was not a surrealist master before he translated Neruda (in 1959) or Follain (first in 1960). Their effect on him shows in his mastery of a language that is now too common in American poetry, though not too well described. Surrealism is the language of transformations; it has too often been called the language of distortion by those with a bias toward traditional realism or impressionism. Ideally its transformations work a direct magic on ordinary perception, suggesting hidden patterns and mystic unities in the visible world, the visionary attitude built into the style.

Both the primitive folk poetry that Merwin often translates and modern surrealist poetry, especially Spanish, are dominated by preoccupation with death. More often than not death becomes an animated abstraction in the center of the poem's field of vision, or it provides a context which defines the view. Often it is curiously beautiful. Merwin translates a Juan Ramon Jimenez poem about "the resplendent and blessed dream, / the bud of death flowering," where death is described as "the water / that flows from the infinite / into your white hand" (*Translations*, 78). Imagery of dark water, or here "dead water," or water under the earth probably occurs in the death poetry of any culture; it appears as much in Spanish poetry as in recent American surrealist poetry by Roethke, Bly, and others. In Merwin as usual the death-water is connected somehow with sleep, the moon (or its tides), and woman; so it is in the Jimenez poem. The pattern of images occurs in Merwin's "Sailor Ashore," in which the grounded sailor still feels the flow of ocean underfoot.

> ... the waters
> Under the earth. Nowhere to run from them.
> It is their tides you feel heaving under you,
> Sucking you down, when you close your eyes with women.
>
> (*Drunk*, 7)

Merwin's style is not particularly surreal here, but even later, when it is, his tone goes against the tradition. When Roethke or Bly writes about death it becomes desirable, in fact lovable, not because it leads to afterlife but because it creates a corporeal union with the flow of time and matter into eternity. Despite his preoccupation with dark water (especially in *Lice*), and his intimation of the revelation possible in death, Merwin is less drawn to the sense of death. He may describe earthly existence as "a sickness" (*Lice*, 74), and call the living "us the unfinished" (*Lice*, 4); in "For the Anniversary of My Death" he calls life "a strange garment," and implies reverence for death, "bowing not knowing to what" (*Lice*, 58). But his respect for death seldom turns enthusiastic; unlike Jimenez (or Bly, or Plath) he will never visualize it flowering. What death is for Merwin is dramatized by a very different image from the same Jimenez poem, a picture of death as "the black / mouth of the first nothing." Here is the blank heart of Merwin's fascination: death considered not as a way to union but as the entrance to Nothing, which for him is more obsessively present than any of the things which it is not.

iii

Like Jean Follain, whose poetry he translated in *Transparence of the World,* Merwin often regards nothingness, like death, with a neutral vision which may logically be appropriate to it. Admiringly, he argues that "the creation of this 'impersonal,' receptive, but essentially unchanging gaze often occupies, in Follain's work, the place of the first person."[10] Unlike the passionate first person implied by the poems of Bly or Plath, the nearly neutral self dramatized by Merwin also seems sufficiently free of personality to be totally "receptive." But when the object of his gaze is the Nothing that may contain revelation, the internal neutrality often coalesces into a self, usually marked by quiet joy. This emotional progression is captured in Merwin's Borghesian story "The Permanent Collection," in which he describes an ornate museum, the monument to a tragic winter love, full of empty picture frames and statueless pedestals. Naturally most visitors to the museum become irritated or bored, but there are "those

who emerge from time to time in silence, with their faces shining"
(*Miner's,* 198). The effect here is somewhat derivative, but the idea is
essential: in nothing there is implied a basic something, something indescribable. Merwin often suggests that it is available only to those able
to efface themselves enough to be genuinely receptive to what is alien,
nothing to their human understanding. He probably has the last lines of
Stevens's "Snow Man" by heart.

> For the listener, who listens in the snow,
> And, nothing himself, beholds
> Nothing that is not there and the nothing that is.[11]

Merwin writes many such invocations to internal transparency; in "The
Well" he describes "immortal" water, silent but "with all its songs inside
it":

> It is a city to which many travellers
> come with clear minds
> having left everything even
> heaven
> to sit in the dark praying as one silence
> for the resurrection.
>
> (*Carrier,* 37)

St. Theresa speaks of the Prayer of Silence in describing the *via negativa;*
while she emptied her mind to accommodate God, Merwin seeks to internalize the secrets hidden in water, or animals, or things: "oh objects come
and talk with us while you can" (*Carrier,* 107). Without such contact the
observing self may remain nothing, since identity seems to depend on
what is most radically not the self. Evan Watkins finds in *Carrier* "a recognition that at the very point of personal identity itself there is an otherness which presses continually upon us."[12]

Paradoxically, that intimate otherness can be more remote and evasive
than Watkins suggests. Psychic emptiness permits mystic openness, but it
may also remain psychic emptiness. In a brief evocative piece on "the
negative aesthetic," Sandra McPherson rather tentatively says of one
Merwin poem "my first thought was that he took the easy way out by trying to make a dead end into something profound."[13] Over a decade earlier,
before Merwin's full development as a surrealist, M. L. Rosenthal, also
tentatively, proposed the possibility of "some inhibition of psychic energy
in Merwin's imaginative make-up."[14] Clearly some of Merwin's poetry is
weakened by failures of energy, to such an extent that it is not simply cool

or subtle, but passive, almost motionless. But behind some of the critical complaints about Merwin's limitations whispers the ancient critical impulse to reward affirmation, to deny the potential richness of negation.[15] Not only is Merwin's negative approach appropriate to the state of things now; as L. Edwin Folsom clearly establishes in comparing Whitman and Merwin, the cosmic and imperial optimism of the later "open road" Whitman now seems politically and ecologically ridiculous; only "an anti-song of the self" is imaginable.[16] But also Merwin creates a poetics grounded in negation; like the traditional mystic "he seeks to find out what is on the other side of despair . . . to uncover a kind of secular absolute," as Charles Altieri explains. "The model is mystical — the *via negativa* — and not the affirmative intensity of visionary poets like Blake and Yeats . . . no American except Eliot (and he with a doctrine to support him) has risked as much emptiness as Merwin in the pursuit of plenitude."[17]

Such a tactic is dangerous for the poet. The emptiness which kills a poem is sometimes difficult to distinguish, in any concrete way, from the emptiness which opens the poet to the world, the Nothing which conceals plenitude. In fact there appears a deeper paradox: the two types of emptiness may not be mutually exclusive. The very consciousness of the deadening sort of spiritual emptiness may — as in the traditional dark night of the soul — create the desperate energy necessary for the leap into a state of absolute receptivity to otherness. Surely this is consistent with Merwin's frequent suggestions that the apocalyptic culmination of our culture and spiritual decadence provides the ground for some ultimate revelation. Now as in other times of high mystic energy (like the fourteenth century), a growing sense of cultural desperation prompts us at least to ask the basic questions, in ways that Merwin plays on in the prose piece "Make This Simple Test," which begins by posing questions about the unimaginable adulteration of our food by chemicals and ends, "Guess at the taste of water. Guess what the rivers see as they die. Guess why the babies are burning. Guess why you were ever born" (*Miner's*, 19).

On the other hand, while spiritual desperation may involve a desire for revelation, it may also block revelation, and this becomes part of Merwin's obsessive theme. More often than not, he writes of the failure of vision, silence in heaven, a silence rendered more frustrating by the felt imminence of revelation. Despite the vocabulary he shares with Bly and the other poets of immanent spiritual realities, Merwin is a poet of spiritual distance, separation, divorce. The contrast shows conspicuously in two poems which use the biblical Noah story to explore the one common theme of communication between men and spiritually sensitive animals. In *Genesis* Noah sends birds over the flood to find land. Bly's "Where We Must Look for Help" celebrates the (apocryphal) crow, who "shall find new mud to walk upon."[18] The title and the generally triumphant tone of the human speaker in the poem suggest that the crow's discovery will eventually become man's. But Merwin's "Noah's Raven" is spoken by the raven, who unlike Bly's or Gary Snyder's or James Dickey's holy beasts rejects the task of bringing "the unknown" to men, and refuses to return to Noah.

> Why should I have returned?
> My knowledge would not fit into theirs.
> I found untouched the desert of the unknown,
> Big enough for my feet. It is my home.
> It is always beyond them.
>
> *(Target,* 10)

The knowledge of beasts and angels will not fit ours, according to Merwin, for many reasons. Perhaps the most easily explained is the traditional one explored by Stevens, our dependence on categorical knowing, on words and naming, which by extension includes our tendency to use beasts symbolically, even as Merwin does in "Noah's Raven." As early as "White Goat, White Ram" he indicates awareness of the problem:

> ... Mark this; for though they assume
> Now the awkward postures of illustrations
> For all our parables, yet the mystery they stand in
> Is still as far from what they signify
> As from the mystery we stand in.
>
> *(Green,* 21)

There exist "true names" for things — as Merwin translates Porchia, "All things pronounce names"[19] — but our words block the names even as they reach toward them. In "An End in Spring" Merwin writes of the deities "that are not there," "The centuries are named for them the names / Do not come down to us//On the way to them the words / Die" *(Lice,* 7).

But if nothing of the truth will come to us then it is with Nothing that we must deal, hoping that "It is when I assent to nothing that I assent to all."[20] Extending the surrealist habit of concretizing abstractions like silence and death Merwin constantly reifies nothing, writing, for instance, of lakes "Into which nothing keeps dropping like a stone" *(Target,* 31), or affirming its negative physical presence by an opposed negation: "I will not

bow in the middle of the room / To the statue of nothing" (*Target*, 55).
So when a negating poem like "February" ends *"I know nothing / learn
of me"* (*Carrier*, 51) we are prepared to accept the mystical paradox.
Spiritual knowledge begins with an intimate awareness of nothing.

Nowhere is this clearer than in "The Saint of the Uplands," an early
example of Merwin's negative style which clearly articulates the theological
ambitions implicit in the style itself. Paradoxically affirmative negation
forms the poem's spiritual as well as rhetorical stance, as Merwin seems to
dramatize Heidegger's contention that "only because Nothing is revealed
in the very basis of our Da-sein is it possible for the utter strangeness of
what is to dawn on us."[21] The being of the poem's speaker, the saint, is
defined almost entirely in negative terms, creating a strange glow.

> Their prayers still swarm on me like lost bees.
> I have no sweetness. I am dust
> Twice over.
> > In the high barrens
> The light loved us.
>
> Their faces were hard crusts like their farms
> And the eyes empty, where vision
> Might not come otherwise
> Than as water.
>
> They were born to stones; I gave them
> Nothing but what was theirs.
> I taught them to gather the dew of their nights
> Into mirrors. I hung them
> Between heavens.
>
> I took a single twig from the tree of my ignorance
> And divided the living streams under
> Their very houses. I showed them
> The same tree growing in their dooryards.
> You have ignorance of your own, I said.
> They have ignorance of their own.
>
> Over my feet they waste their few tears.
>
> I taught them nothing.
> Everywhere
> The eyes are returning under the stones. And over
> My dry bones they build their churches, like wells.
> > > (*Target*, 17)

Dead, with no sweetness, doubly dust, with nothing to give but ignorance, dry bones without a mouth, he speaks with prophetic authority. Merwin conveys this authority partly through a characteristic mastery of sound. The blunt declarative sentences achieve an aphoristic sureness, reinforced by the rhythm and the subtle internal rhyme of a line like "They were born to stones." Frequent repetition and subtle parallelisms create the impression of litany — "I gave them . . . I taught them . . . I hung them . . ." — but Merwin avoids straight liturgical repetition simply by varying the placement of the "I" in each line.

Sound only reinforces the positive resonance Merwin can discover/create in words suggestive of emptiness and sterility. Partly the paradoxical logic is rooted in normal logic: in a sense eyes must be "empty" before vision comes; the "water" that carries vision suggests tears, the grief that often gives way to new understanding. But Merwin also uses metaphor with great rhetorical cleverness to alter logic. Once "ignorance" is described, however arbitrarily, as a "tree," it seems logical enough that its "twig" should lead like a divining rod to water. As the poem develops its own private logic, water, streams, the dew, and tears are consistently associated with emptiness, ignorance, and nothingness. The conflation of negative terminology and the imagery of spiritual flow makes the final metaphor seem simply right, all paradox for a moment simply accepted: "over / my dry bones they build their churches, like wells." He has become the font of their visionary immersion. The "nothing" of "I taught them nothing" we also read positively. Strongly colored by the single word in the next line, which begins "every-," it translates into "everything."

Of course "nothing" may also be understood literally — the saint's talent consists simply of turning disciples back on their own undiscovered knowledge — but it must also be understood paradoxically, for he teaches them what he knows. A similar ambiguity complicates the stone imagery of the poem, since the stones are both indicators of sterility and the final locus of vision. Often Merwin, like the other oracular poets, suggests that one route to revelation leads through participation in the being of stones, which approach as close to spiritual nothing as existing substance can. In "Eyes of Summer" stones are connected with vision through still another paradox; they are "the witnesses" who "day after day are blinded / so that they will forget nothing." Here the implication that stones possess something distantly related to human consciousness is not simply figurative; in the flow of earthly matter "All the stones have been us / and will be again" (*Writings*, 4).

In attempting to give sight to his unenlightened disciples the saint of
the uplands teaches them "to gather the dew of their nights / Into mirrors," as Merwin employs one of the most common and deeply complex
of his visionary emblems. Suggestions of revelation constantly appear in
mirrors; the question constantly posed is whether "revelation" is merely
reflection, the imposition of human visions of order against which Stevens
wrote so many poems. Merwin suggests that something more is possible;
in "Lemuel's Blessing" the wolf prays to his savage god:

> But lead me at times beside the still waters;
> There when I crouch to drink let me catch a glimpse of your image
> Before it is obscured with my own.
>
> (*Target*, 8)

The mirror is a gap in ordinary vision, a vacuum which may be filled with
another reality if the watcher can open himself to it, knowing that the
spirit he seeks — though it can occupy his own shape in the mirror — is
always beyond him. The paradox is embodied in image when Lemuel
prays "Run with me like the horizon." Like the mirror image this line
uses one of the illusions of common experience to depict a spirit both
united with Lemuel and forever beyond his reach; the deity includes both
self and world, briefly joined in moments of vision. But such union is not
for men. When the mirror does open to the revelations of Nothing, the
effect is usually ominous, especially if the watcher is human: "In the
mirrors the star called Nothing / Cuts us off" (*Target*, 63).

At times these evocations of Nothing, in mirrors or elsewhere, seem
repetitious and even facile, but Merwin's successful evocations of evasive
fearful revelations are strangely convincing, though often deeply obscure.
His most developed treatment of the image of empty spaces in the world
into which vision may suddenly flare involves not mirrors but windows,
used in "Forgetting" to create a sense of revelation hidden somewhere in
an infinite regression. In this prose piece, seeking "the unnameable stillness
that unites" the various sense perceptions of "the kingdom of change,"
"we" seek something that "is ours," is within us, but that we cannot perceive. With unusual negative specificity Merwin locates the emptiness
that receives mystical truth at the heart of the experience of the various
senses, but truth remains as unattainable as it is immediate. Of "the unnameable stillness" Merwin writes:

> At the heart of change it lies unseeing, unhearing, unfeeling, unchang-
> ing, holding within itself the beginning and the end. It is ours. It

is our only possession. Yet we cannot take it into our hands, which
change, nor see it with our eyes, which change, nor hear it nor
taste it nor smell it. None of the senses can come to it. Except
backwards.

Any more than they can come to each other.

Yet they point the way.

(Miner's, 56)

There follows an extended metaphorical description of the attempt to follow this "way": "we" climb a ladder to look through a sealed window in
a wall, which reveals another watcher at another window, which reveals
the same scene again. "Somewhere on the other side of that a voice is
coming. We are the voice. But we are each of those others." And we are
also, it seems, the barrier which blocks the voice. As in the emblem of the
revelation which tries to come through our reflection in the mirror, the
final truth is somehow news of ourselves, blocked by ourselves. In the end
of "Forgetting" "we" practice the negative discipline of reducing all the
senses ("backwards") to "nothing," attempting a windowlike transparency of self which will allow the true voice of the central self and the
world to emerge. But that transparency cannot be sustained: "Then nothing has gone. The voice must have come. Because it has gone" (*Miner's*,
58). If this is affirmation it remains cruelly faint, stated in negative and
perhaps ironic terms, as Merwin's ambivalence persists. His mythical desire
for intimations of absolute reality is seldom supported by the faith that
traditionally sustains the mystic through the nothingness of the dark night:
"what I live for I can seldom believe in" (*Carrier*, 4). But the preoccupation with intimations and possibilities is constant. "An open doorway /
Speaks for me / Again (*Target*, 97).

If the doorway often seems more blank than open, the cause is not
simply the inadequacies of human naming and logic. Especially in Merwin's more apocalyptic writings it seems rather that the tantalizingly close
voice of revelation is inaudible because of some human failing analogous
to original sin. In *Miner's* Merwin creates several original sin legends, most
of which imply that man's present nature was shaped by some forgotten
wound, and that man free of this injury would no longer be man. In "The
Remembering Machines of Tomorrow" machines are developed to "recall
why the spirit of man walks with a limp," and to make men whole. But
when the cure actually seems imminent "men will begin to lose their
machines" (*Miner's*, 131). Although this limitation must apparently be
accepted as an essential part of man, acceptance is impossible, for the

destructiveness the wound implies will finally become apocalyptic. The elimination of animals has already begun, and Merwin appropriately suggests that original sin is simply man's evolved estrangement from the natural world, the separation from animals which will destroy us but which is still somehow the locus of final meaning.

> and on a Sunday that we were severed
> from the animals
> with a wound that never heals
> but is still the gate where the nameless
> cries out.
>
> (*Writings*, 22)

As in Stevens, meaning is sound, a cry, the voice of the world, incomprehensible unless a man can achieve that original union which preceded the rising of barriers between external and internal. To hear the voice of the world the mystic recipient must contain the voice of the world. The attempt to do this is mockingly described in Merwin's late prose piece "The Element," which involves a quest for essential contact with what surrounds us. Not surprisingly Merwin uses imagery of liquid immersion to describe the hope for contact.

> The young man had wondered why we did not hear our element, whatever it was, with our whole bodies [as he believes fish do]. . . . He built a boat shaped like a fish, with ribs laid like fish spines, and he lay in it listening to the current. If you could live that way, he decided, . . . you would begin to be able to recognize the sound of the element in which you were living, passing through you.
>
> (*Houses*, 54)

Like the sound that Stevens imagines, this one exists; what seems impossible is experiencing contact with it, especially by such absurd means. Not only does the young man fail to hear the sound, his progress only takes him to the point where he can no longer hear humans, his unknowing another dead end. Something similar happens to the somewhat more dignified protagonist of "The Chart," another who seeks "knowing for which he had given up fragments of his hearing." He charts animal hearing, searching for the "unborn overflowing" which will allow him that perfect union which is for Merwin the only true identity. What he wants to hear "would complete the fragmentary nature of his consciousness until it was whole at last — one tone both pure and entire floating in the silence of the egg, at the same pitch as the silence" (*Houses,* 71). The usual paradox is invoked. As unknowing is knowing, sound is silence.

No matter how richly they may describe revelation, Merwin's people continue to miss it. The separation yawns too wide; our distance from "the undivided" increases through psychic space and, especially, time. Humanity devolves, in the long fall from natural union. Even in his political writing, like the account of the *Everyman* episode, Merwin seems as disturbed by man's arrogant manipulation of nature as by the deadly conflict between man and man. And the anger of his antiwar poems, like Lowell's in "Quaker Graveyard," is offset by little general love for humanity. Even "The Asians Dying," in which the war is both local apocalypse and prophetic of a larger doom, tends to point more to poisoned land than dead men; so Lowell seems more concerned about whales, as real victims and apocalyptic symbols, than Warren Winslow dead at sea. Appropriately, because his early poetry is also full of oceans, Merwin too feels even greater anger over violations of the sea, whether atomic tests or the increasingly methodical extermination of whales (whose recorded songs carry all the mystic resonance that Merwin habitually invokes whenever he uses the word "song"). In "For a Coming Extinction" he takes a coolly savage satisfaction in the proposal that our driving whales to "the black garden" (*Lice,* 68) is only a logical antecedent of our own doom; man's end began when he became nature's enemy, cutting off a part of himself. "The Current" rather obscurely develops this idea, describing "a thin cold current" which flows through us even though we forget "that we are water"; "yes and black flukes wave to it / from the Lethe of the whales" (*Writings,* 24).

But if the sense of our participation in the flow of natural existence involves intimations of approaching extinction for which we — because we deny and alienate ourselves from that flow — are partly responsible, there also appear in the gathering dark Merwin's usual remote suggestions of revelation:

> but the eels keep trying to tell us
> writing over and over in the mud
> our heavenly names.
> 　　　　　(*Writings,* 24)

These lines from "The Current" suggest that in our emptiness animals may attempt messages, as plants seem to in "A Scale in May":

Now all my teachers are dead except silence
I am trying to read what the five poplars are writing
On the void.

(*Lice*, 50)

Later in "Scale" Merwin writes "If you find you no longer believe en-
large the temple." To the extent that hope exists in Merwin's poetry of
negation it is based on intimations of animal values, imagined in human
terms. If the animals of "Noah's Raven" and "Lemuel's Blessing" enjoy
a distance from man that allows a proportionate spiritual purity, the
speaker of "Words from a Totem Animal" blends human and imagined
non-human patterns of thought to investigate the faint possibility of approach to an alien god, "lord cold as the thoughts of birds" (*Carrier*, 19).
But the most human quality of the totem animal involves his pessimism
about revelation, again imagined as an essential sound sensed but never
heard:

I am never all of me
unto myself
and sometimes I go slowly
knowing that a sound one sound
is following me from world
to world
and that I die each time
before it reaches me.

Merwin remains the poet of failed mysticism in "Totem," but the poem
is distinguished by an animal faith in the eventual possibility of union,
needed for internal wholeness as well as spiritual fullness:

Maybe I will come
To where I am one
and find
I have been waiting there
as a new
Year finds the song of the nuthatch.

For now, though, the lord remains cold and silent.

All Merwin's gods are even more irreducibly alien than Plath's darkest
image of the Mother. Even if it does not ultimately locate god in the mind
of the visionary much contemporary unorthodox mysticism — like orthodox mystical wisdom — tends to suggest that cosmic spiritual unity, while
not dependent on individual vision, is somehow enriched by human per-

ception of it. But the divinities Merwin images are as indifferent to humanity as he seems to be when in "December Night" he writes something like a basic statement of his values: "I find a single prayer and it is not for men" (*Lice*, 43). In "The Widow" men seem simply irrelevant to the larger spiritual movement of the world. Here earth is defined not as man's great mother but as the only survivor of an ancient union with man that long ago ended in opposition which like our severance from the animals meant spiritual death for man.

> Not that heaven does not exist but
> That it exists without us
>
>   . . .
>
> Everything that does not need you is real
>
> The Widow does not
> Hear you and your cry is numberless.
>   (*Lice*, 34)

The poem ends not only in negative moral judgment but in existential denial of men: "numberless," we simply do not count; divorced from the vital ground of being man inhabits a waking dream, "invisible invisible invisible."

Predictably Merwin finds it almost impossible to sustain this degree of negation while continuing to develop as a poet, and especially in his collections since 1970 there appear flashes of light amid the rather repetitive excursions into the nothing that suggests but seldom conveys revelation. The last piece in *Miner's* is entitled "Dawn Comes to Its Mountain in the Brain," and though its final affirmation is rather flat, it is irreducibly definite: "the suns rises with its message: Sun" (*Miner's* 325). The reason for any affirmation at all, the reason Merwin can suggest — as he does in "The Moles" — that we may after all manage to regain contact with our "lost mothers" (*Miner's*, 119) is not immediately clear. However the way is suggested in "Being Born Again," which quite viscerally describes the travail of birth from a mysterious "new mother." The present intolerable sense of pressure will lead to "a delivery from a confinement. . . . And the pressure has come from some other existence of myself, unknown to me or at least unnoticed, that has grown, curled in itself, until it can no longer be contained and is now undergoing a change in its very cosmos" (*Miner's*, 46).

The sense of another existence enwombed in the present one and stirring toward emergence in some cosmic change is almost commonplace among

oracular poets. Though never so explicit as Bly, with his prophecy of the
return of Mother consciousness, Merwin hints at a cycle back to the time
before humans were severed from animals, a time when human existence
was and still will be richer than now, free of its existential "wound." In
several poems the hope for such evolution seems to counterbalance Merwin's bleak sense of the present state of man. But usually he makes it clear
that the evolved consciousness will no longer be human, that the flow to
union means the end of man.

> We are the echo of the future
>
> On the door it says what to do to survive
> But we were not born to survive
> Only to live.
>   ("The River of Bees," *Lice,* 33)

The eerie quality of "The Herds," set in an ice-age landscape of voyaging
animals which could as easily be prehistoric as postapocalyptic, is created
partly by the mystery of its speaker; what voice is this that uses our words
to "once more celebrate our distance from men" (*Lice,* 56)? "Among
stones," under an "ancient sun," a new world begins with a celebration of
man's finish.

   So if apocalypse bears revelation — and we must not forget that
"apocalypse" *means* "revelation" — the message is not for us, is nothing
to us. This is part of what "The Initiate" learns, in tears:

> he is singing Not a hair
> of our heads do we need to take with us
> into the day.
>   (*Writings,* 105)

Nothing of ourselves can go with us "into the light." The paradox implicit in "with us" is developed in more specifically mystical terms in
"The Lantern," a projection of human consciousness into the non-human
realm of cosmic union "A little way ahead."

> for in that world nothing can break
> so no one believes in the plural there
>
>   . . .
>
> so no one believes in us there.
>   (*Writings,* 77)

All there is one "held together by nothing" without severance or separation, and the union is "a god" who is both all different things and one

thing alone, both "an image of you" and "an image of no one / carrying a lantern." If something of man survives into this unity, perhaps a final reunion with a ground of unity that has always existed, nothing of man remains distinct in union. Unlike Bly, Merwin often suggests that there can be no psychological or emotional continuity between our being and being in the time of revelation. Usually he offers not hope but a vision.

In *Compass* the vision becomes comparatively mundane, and the hope reduced to a simpler human level. Like the aging Williams, the Lowell of *Dolphin,* the older Roethke (and conceivably even Plath if she could have aged in peace) Merwin in *Compass* uses mystic terms to describe sexual love, love of a human, not the Mother or the savage god. In "Kore" he seeks union not with lord or land but with the loved one, so the end of his quest is no longer unknown, though it passes through mystery.

> Already on the first hill with you beside me
> at the foot of the ruins I saw through the day
> and went on without pausing
> loving the unheld air
> as a wing might love it flying
> toward you unknowing
> knowing.
>
> (*Compass,* 50)

Merwin's love poetry seems at first too lush for his stark voice, especially when he allows himself the almost trite tropical imagery of a poem like "Islands." But its simple beauty grows with contemplation. It begins to seem appropriate that the poet, like Lowell, moving into his fifties and a less violent American period, should turn his reverence away from unknown divinities and toward the known human and mundane. Not that *Compass* renounces the visionary perspective entirely; it simply moves to discover the unknown in the known, emphasizing with less ambivalence about the human that the quest makes us what we are.

> What is unseen
> flows to what is unseen
> passing in part
> through what we partly see
> we stood up from all fours
> far back in the light
> to look.
>
> (*Compass,* 20)

This gentle sentiment would perhaps be more fully satisfying if we had not been so strikingly convinced by the dark apocalyptic preaching of *The Lice.* But perhaps the gentleness constitutes a sort of maturity. Merwin could not always be the poet of the black garden, any more than Lowell could endlessly rewrite "Quaker Graveyard." The poets who continue to develop their mystical vision into middle age tend not — except Ted Hughes — to be poets of the savage god. But in apocalyptic times Merwin's recent mellowness seems (unfortunately for us all) less impressive than his bold confrontations with nothingness. The pessimism of his early poetry offers small comfort, but comfort seems of small importance in the face of the inhuman clarity of his vision, which embodies otherness even as it describes it.

Something essential about the otherness fascinates, and though Merwin cannot long imagine union, he captures more distance than most. At his most visionary, seeing as far as Stevens does in "The Owl in the Sarcophagus," he captures a final mystery. When he does imagine anthropomorphic gods, posed as hallowed archetypes, they seem as indifferent to human concerns as they are mysterious to us, but from their indifference comes a blessing all the more positive because it depends on nothing human, need not be deserved or even acknowledged, a blessing not of man but of all life. For all his rage at human evil and frustration over what is not revealed, Merwin finds a conspicuous peace in the time of struggle with distant deities, like the immortal in "Blue."

> ... The dead drift past him in their gray boats but he never knew them.
>
> But there is no harm in him. Over his door, where no mortal eye could read anything, it is written, "We Are All Children of the Light."
>
> (*Miner's,* 123)

NOTES

1. W. S. Merwin, *The Miner's Pale Children* (New York: Atheneum, 1970), p. 123. Subsequent references to this and other Merwin collections will be identified in the text by the first word of the title. Other collections cited are *A Mask for Janus* (New Haven: Yale Univ. Press, 1952), *The Dancing Bears* (Yale, 1954), *Green with Beasts* (New York: Knopf, 1956), *The Drunk in the Furnace* (New York: Macmillan, 1960), *The Moving Target* (New York: Atheneum, 1963), *The Carrier of Ladders* (Atheneum, 1970), *Writings to an Unfinished*

Accompaniment (Atheneum, 1973), *The Compass Flower* (Atheneum, 1977), and *Houses and Travellers* (Atheneum, 1977).

2. Richard Howard, *Alone with America* (New York: Atheneum, 1969), p. 375. By "fewmets" Howard must mean the fragments of excrement of a hunted beast which lead trackers to the kill. So T. H. White uses the term (to refer to dragon droppings, which are few indeed) in *The Once and Future King.*

3. Cary Nelson, *Our Last First Poets* (Urbana: Univ. of Illinois Press, 1981), p. 186.

4. Harold Bloom, *Figures of Capable Imagination* (New York: Seabury Press, 1976), p. 124.

5. W. S. Merwin, "A Note on Antonio Porchia," in Antonio Porchia, *Voices,* trans. W. S. Merwin (Chicago: Big Table, 1969), p. 8.

6. Porchia, *Voices,* p. 10.

7. W. S. Merwin, "Act of Conscience," *The Nation,* Dec. 29, 1962, p. 477.

8. T. S. Eliot, "Notes on 'The Waste Land,'" *The Complete Poems and Plays 1909-1950* (New York: Harcourt, Brace, 1952), p. 51.

9. Harvey Gross, "The Writing on the Void: The Poetry of W. S. Merwin," *Iowa Review,* 1 (Summer 1970), 98.

10. W. S. Merwin, "Foreword," *Transparence of the World* (New York: Atheneum, 1969), p. vi.

11. Wallace Stevens, *The Palm at the End of the Mind* (New York: Knopf, 1971), p. 54.

12. Evan Watkins, "W. S. Merwin: A Critical Accompaniment," *Boundary 2,* 4 (Fall 1975), 193.

13. Sandra McPherson, "Saying No," *Iowa Review,* 4 (Summer 1973), 84.

14. M. L. Rosenthal, *The Modern Poets* (New York: Oxford Univ. Press, 1960), p. 262.

15. Cary Nelson writes, "Criticism often capitulates, in its final pages, by finding affirmation in the most bleak of modern works; it is part of the impulse to socialize the experience of reading literature. In criticism of American literature these affirmative conclusions also show that the critic wishes to push the culture's myths toward a positive fulfillment" (*Last First Poets,* p. 217).

16. L. Edwin Folsom, "Approaches and Removals: W. S. Merwin's Encounter with Whitman's America," *Shenandoah,* 39 (Spring 1978), 60.

17. Charles Altieri, *Enlarging the Temple* (Lewisburg, Pa.: Bucknell Univ. Press, 1979), p. 196. Nelson also mentions the influence of Eliot on Merwin, heavily stressing the similarity of specific lines (*Last First Poets,* p. 192).

18. Robert Bly, *Silence in the Snowy Fields* (Middletown, Conn.: Wesleyan Univ. Press, 1962), p. 29.

19. Porchia, *Voices,* p. 64. Merwin placed this aphorism last in the collection.

20. Porchia, *Voices,* p. 16.

21. Martin Heiddeger, *Existence and Being* (London: Vision Press, 1949), p. 378.

7

Journey to Love

Even the most earthly mysticism demands a concentration on otherness which creates isolation from other humans. In the end, the lonely visionary often turns back toward love. After the death-oriented *Paterson*, as he sensed "my own death" peacefully approaching, William Carlos Williams wrote not a final hymn to mystic union, but a love song to his wife.[1] Like Robert Lowell's late chronicles of sexual love, "Asphodel, That Greeny Flower" appropriates many of the habitual devices and attitudes of the poetry of negative mysticism. But it begins and ends with simple romantic apology and affirmation.

In the other poetry in *Journey to Love*, Williams occasionally celebrates "another world" (*Journey*, 123) in this world, but that realm, hardly the locus of visions, remains even more rooted in the commonplace than in his early epiphany poems. "Asphodel," too, has the plain tone of an account of ordinary human experience, though it describes a descent into hell, a dark night of the soul, and confrontation with death both spiritual and physical. The asphodel itself, mythic flower of Hades, is "colorless," "wooden," "odorless," always an emblem of death and negation. But this flower of nothing, in a reversal that echoes the paradoxes of mysticism, becomes the flower of all being. Specifically it becomes the flower of sexual vitality, as Williams again finds life in the confrontation with death. As in the frame of mysticism, death here varies through many meanings, once even suggesting atomic apocalypse. "The bomb / also / is a flower," and

> The end
> will come
> in its time.

(*Journey*, 165)

But the illumination that follows the dark night of "Asphodel" comes not from the presence of death, individual or collective, or from union with nature; its source is loving forgiveness for sexual betrayal, a grace of forgiveness which will restore sexual union. Williams seeks that state of grace which flows from literal marriage, not the figurative marriage with the Mother that he celebrated in "The Wanderer." But his images evoke the same timeless radiance:

> the light stood before us
> > waiting!
> > > I thought the world
> stood still.
> > At the altar
> > > so intent was I
> before my vows,
> > so moved by your presence.
> > > (*Journey,* 181)

This wedding (which Williams describes as "Medieval pageantry") sends "an odor" forward to the poet in Hades, a scent with the power to restore this devoted but unfaithful lover. Very early in the poem he specifies that this is "a moral odor, / that brings me / near to you" (*Journey,* 155). Morality is seldom the focus of any poetry of mysticism, immanent or transcendent, for the mystic tends to exist alone with the world, without human obligation or connection. His can be a state of almost complete separation from others of his species, and often, like Merwin, he revels in the distance. Like Williams's final reversal, Merwin's later conversion to erotic poetry suggests that the implicit conflict between the art of silence and the words of poetry had grown too extreme. As Williams finally claims in "Asphodel," "you do not get far / with silence" (*Journey,* 159).

This is not to say that the poetry of silence and nothing was self-defeating, or that the poetry of sexual love suddenly emerged from nowhere to become the dominant mode. Minor strains of love poetry had been there all along, but its gradual increase, in the careers of individual poets and in general, signals an inevitable transition. Like the transcendent mystic, the mystic of immanence must finally return to the sphere of quotidian experience, bearing his dark illuminations back to the ordinary world of men and women.

The most recent turn to the ordinary is reflected in the title of Robert Bly's 1981 collection *The Man in the Black Coat Turns.* This is a line from "Snowbanks North of the House," a poem about failure of human contact as well as the failure of revelation under "the unattached heavens."

> And the sea lifts and falls all night, the moon goes on
> through the unattached heavens alone.
> The toe of the shoe pivots
> in the dust . . .
> And the man in the black coat turns, and goes back down the hill.
> No one knows why he came, or why he turned away, and did not
> climb the hill.[2]

No one knows, but this man may be the messenger of otherness, repelled by the human emptiness described in the poem. If this is so, the ominous image and the curiously flat tone of the narrative may signify a deep ambivalence about otherness however defined. Enough visits from men in black coats, or equally deadly thin men with no coats, the poet may feel; let there be real people in these poems.

The whole collection extends the ambivalence caught by the eponymous image. It includes a few of the usual poems of visionary metaphor and mystical immersion. But it seems dominated by the poems of reality, in which actual individuals other than the poet appear, in which "nothing" means absence and "death" simply signifies the end of life. "The Grief of Men" describes two types of death, neither of them "the death we love." The first is the death of mystic isolation:

> Men have died on high slopes, as others watch.
> They look around, and do not see
> those they love most.
>
>   (*Black Coat,* 34)

Not only is the visionary search presented as potentially destructive, it is juxtaposed to the daily destructiveness of life, death redefined in the plainest style as death, unbearable and ordinary.

> The doctor stands
> by the bed, but Bertha
> dies, her breath ends, her knees quiver and are still.
>
> Her husband will not lie quiet.
> He throws himself against the wall.

Bly's most explicit hymn to the quotidian comes, appropriately, in the form of a prose poem of acceptance of the prose world, its plain style conspicuously opposed to the flourishes of *This Body Is Made of Camphor and Gopherwood.* "Eleven O'Clock at Night" begins as the autobiography of a Bly day — "So this is how my life is passing before the grave?" — and builds to a meditation not on death or the grave but on the plain things of domestic existence:

> There is no way to escape from these. Many times in poems I have escaped — from myself. I sit for hours and at last see a pinhole in the top of the pumpkin, and I slip out that pinhole, gone! . . .
> Now more and more I long for what I cannot escape from. The sun shines on the side of the house across the street. Eternity is near, but it is not *here.*
>
> (*Black Coat,* 18)

The effect of the negative rhetoric — "no way to escape," and later "for that there is no solution" — is to recall mystical escapes while denying them. Bly wills to find no solace in any mysticism, no matter how immanent. He accepts the plain world, in part because only the world contains "the woman I love," and "my children." But to accept his dying generations is to accept death without recourse to mystic transformations: "For the winter dark of late December there is no solution."

So death has become for Bly an end to be confronted in simple practical terms. One of *Black Coat*'s most precise reversals of Bly's customary imagery comes in "Mourning Pablo Neruda," where the usual dark water is no longer the flow to death in which the self is immersed. On the contrary water becomes the dead immersed within the self.

> **For the dead remain inside**
> us, as water
> remains
> inside granite —
> hardly at all —
> for their job is to
> go
> **away.**
> (*Black Coat,* 12)

To accept mystical death is a stage on life's way, but for the death of individuals loved from near or far there is no solution. People matter. A note at the end of *Black Coat* informs us that Bly "is at work now on a collection of love poems," and so he follows Williams and Merwin back to the world.

The shape of the cycle reveals a transparent logic. As it probably always has, the poetry of human love provides a moral and psychic balance to the poetry of either divine inspiration or negative mysticism. Through the decades examined by this study the mysticism of immersion has outweighed that which reaches up toward divinity, but it has retained traces of transcendent longings, evident in the use of traditional religious vocabulary to describe immanence. The ambivalence dramatized by "Sunday Morning" has persisted. That movement evident in the poetry of Stevens and Williams has continued, through the generations of Roethke and Bly, toward a complete acceptance of the physical world as the basis of spiritual value. But it could be argued that the final step in the descent from transcendent imaginings would involve acceptance of this world without insistence on its otherness, on its distance from the human.

In retrospect, the degree of ordinary negation of human connections that developed in this poetry of negative mysticism seems too extreme to have been sustained for long. What began as an insistence on the mystical basis of genuine perception in Stevens, Williams, and to a lesser extent Eliot, developed into a perceptibly darker preoccupation with literal union in Roethke and his followers. As the shore poem became dominant, somewhat gloomy image clusters — involving sinking to oneness, dark water, stones, and mythic women — occurred repeatedly. The darkness also appeared in the slight but pervasive emphasis on medieval ways of perceiving that persisted after Lowell, when most of these poets more or less consciously adopted some version of the *via negativa*, the logic of unknowing, as a mystical approach. But more pervasive, even in Lowell or Merwin, than that specific way of negation was a constant instinctive association between visionary union and death, whether imagined as actuality, metaphor, or something in between. Especially as the imagery surrounding vision turned increasingly violent in Lowell and Roethke, as the Teeth Mother emerged in Bly's poetry, and as blood sacrifice returned to triumph in Plath, the mystic affirmation within the negative vision began at times to seem faint, almost desperate.

The cutting edge of misanthropy in Lowell's celebration of the guilt of his dead relatives, Plath's romance with her own vengeful self-destruction, Bly's near-exclusion of other humans from his poems, and Merwin's frank shame about being human flowered in an ambivalent fascination with apocalypse. The end of mysticism had become not simply vision or union, but transformation into a new humanity. The will to change was based on desperation about the possibility of real union in our present spiritual state, but also on varieties of rage against present humanity, on a sort of glee over imminent destruction. As the sense of lost original union (Williams's "divorce") acquired an ecological dimension, it began to seem to a poet like Merwin that we had wounded the Mother so badly that restoration of real contact was no longer conceivable, that only destruction could right the balance. Such a visionary perspective was deep and genuine for the poets of immersion, but pushed to its logical extreme it implied a contradiction of the original premise of the mysticism of earth. Such extreme denial of the worth of present humanity and the possibilities of physical existence led logically to a philosophy of neo-transcendence, under the stress of absolute human pessimism (as in the early Robert Lowell) the only visible alternative to some variety of nihilism. Confronting this return to something like the old patterns, most of these poets came, individually or collectively, to the end of the negative road. (Especially if, like Merwin, they came to this pass during the seventies, their enthusiasm for the mystical perspective was probably further dampened by the multiple parodies of the visionary existence then spreading through the general culture. When amid increasing cultural desperation innumerable gurus emerged to start new religions, or to build old ones into financial or political empires, the ways of unknowing seemed to come dangerously close to the ways of ignorance.)

So poets that had joined in celebration of the Great Mother retreated somewhat, into celebrations of particular women, lovers and friends, often drawing the vocabulary of unknowing into songs of human love. As Williams shifted from the mothers and muses of *Paterson* to a celebration of his wife and marriage in "Asphodel," Lowell progressed from Mary to Lizzie and Caroline in the sixties. Roethke's posthumous *The Far Field* was, after "North American Sequence," divided between "Love Poems" and the frequently transcendent "Sequence, Sometimes Metaphysical." Plath died. Merwin turned to this world and a passionate romanticism in *Compass Flower*. And even Bly is now on the verge of publishing a volume of love poems. Never a dominant mode in American poetry, the poetry of sexual love seemed (especially if homosexual romantic poetry is included) to come into its own in the seventies.[3] The celebration of a different and more intimate sort of otherness had come to balance the mystical search for another world. Love of the human other became a corrective to mystical misanthropy.

But mystical poetry continues to fascinate, as do its supporting myths, whether Edenic or apocalyptic. Such poetry aims more overtly at what all poetry implicitly attempts: to see beyond the limits of human language and ordinary human experience, in Stevens's phrase to play "a tune beyond us, yet ourselves." With almost inhuman clarity, the strongest visionary poems embody the other world even as they describe it. Perhaps what draws us to that otherness is the shared perception implicit in Stevens's phrase: that it remains paradoxically closer to our own natures, something distant in ourselves that must always be confronted. The fundamental power of all mystical poetry depends less on the evocation of love or light than on this sense of something totally different, another life and another world embedded in the ordinary this-ness of self and earth. That intimately distant spiritual flow speaks constantly to humanity, whether in the brief flash of epiphany or in the timeless union of the classical mystical experience, orthodox or not. All this poetry makes a small answering sound. Its essential excitement involves the celebration of what is far away in us. The more the distance, the greater the power of union, and of the poems that attempt that union. Perhaps the highest poetry is that poetry always doomed to failure because it attempts the impossible: somehow to capture in language visions of the heart of nothing. But in the best romantic tradition, it fails triumphantly as it alters and heightens our vision of everything, of that reality which — as *Ordinary Evening* says it — is made of "things seen and unseen, created from nothingness."

NOTES

1. William Carlos Williams, "Asphodel, That Greeny Flower," in *Pictures from Brueghel and Other Poems* (New York: New Directions, 1962), p. 162. Subsequent references to the *Journey to Love* sections of this anthology will be identified in the text.

2. Robert Bly, *The Man in the Black Coat Turns* (New York: Dial, 1981), pp. 3-4. Subsequent references to *Black Coat* will be so identified in the text.

3. With the usual mixed results. A highly interesting negative commentary on the early "new erotic poetry" is provided by Marjorie Perloff's "The Corn-Porn Lyric: Poetry 1972-73," *Contemporary Literature*, 16 (Winter 1975), 84-125.

Index

A Note on the Author

Anthony Libby received his doctorate in English from Stanford University and is a member of the English Department of Ohio State University. He has written several scholarly articles on modern poetry.